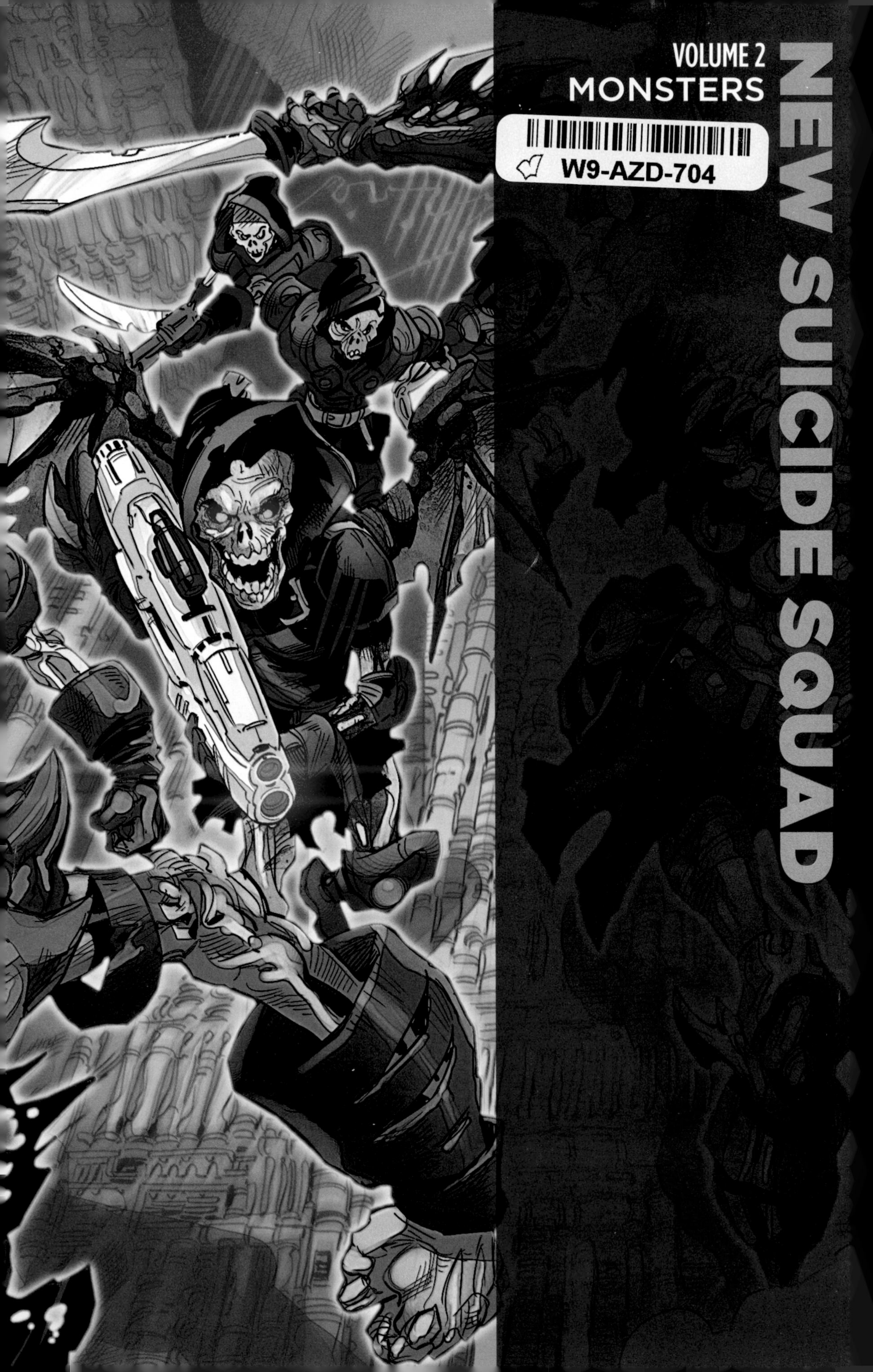
VOLUME 2
MONSTERS
NEW SUICIDE SQUAD

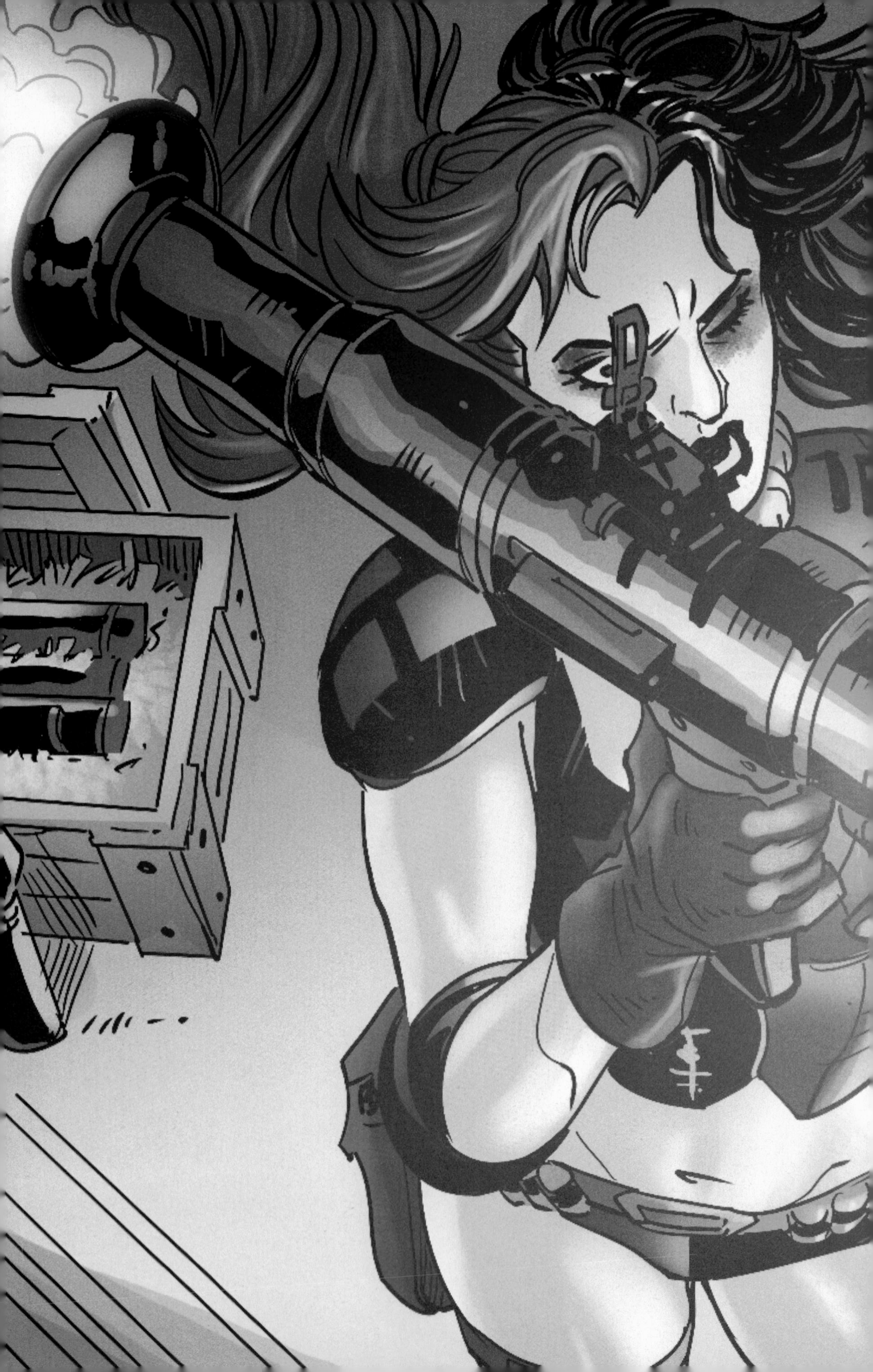

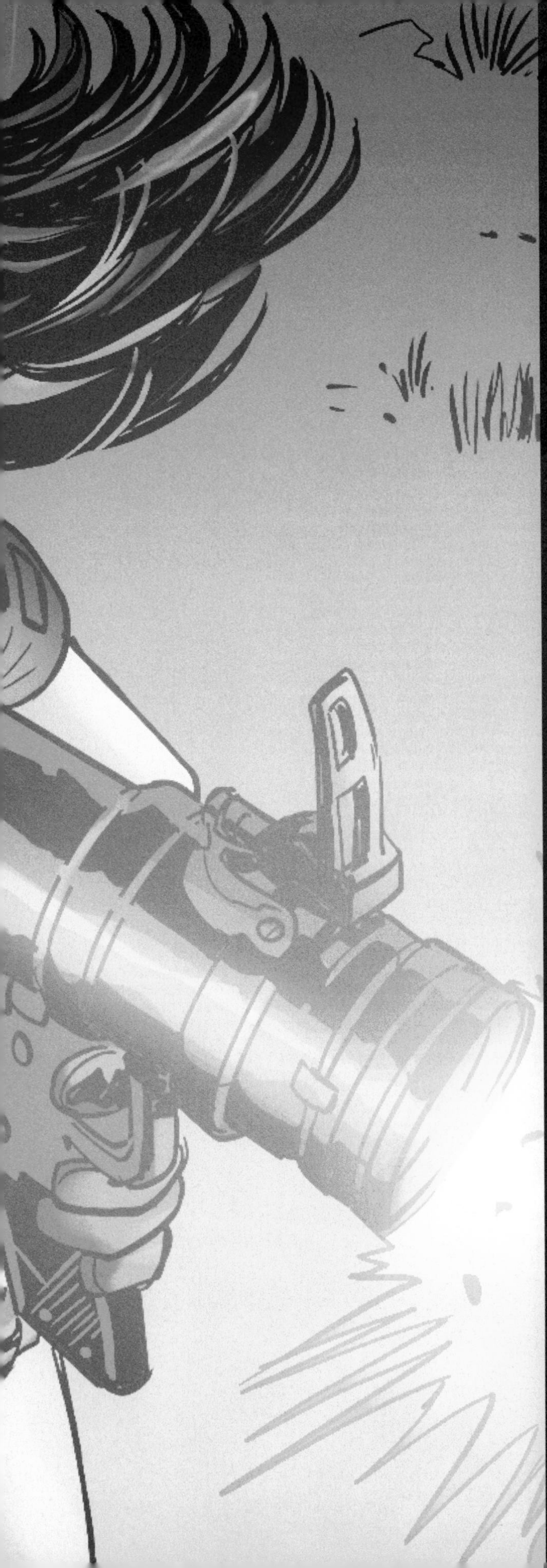

NEW SUICIDE SQUAD

VOLUME 2
MONSTERS

WRITTEN BY
SEAN RYAN

ART BY
PHILIPPE BRIONES

COLOR BY
BLOND

LETTERS BY
TOM NAPOLITANO
TRAVIS LANHAM

SERIES & COLLECTION COVER ART BY
JUAN FERREYRA

BRIAN CUNNINGHAM ANDY KHOURI Editors – Original Series
HARVEY RICHARDS Associate Editor – Original Series
AMEDEO TURTURRO Assistant Editor – Original Series
JEB WOODARD Group Editor – Collected Editions
STEVE COOK Design Director – Books
LIZ ERICKSON Editor – Collected Edition

BOB HARRAS Senior VP – Editor-in-Chief, DC Comics

DIANE NELSON President
DAN DIDIO and JIM LEE Co-Publishers
GEOFF JOHNS Chief Creative Officer
AMIT DESAI Senior VP – Marketing & Global Franchise Management
NAIRI GARDINER Senior VP – Finance
SAM ADES VP – Digital Marketing
BOBBIE CHASE VP – Talent Development
MARK CHIARELLO Senior VP – Art, Design & Collected Editions
JOHN CUNNINGHAM VP – Content Strategy
ANNE DEPIES VP – Strategy Planning & Reporting
DON FALLETTI VP – Manufacturing Operations
LAWRENCE GANEM VP – Editorial Administration & Talent Relations
ALISON GILL Senior VP – Manufacturing & Operations
HANK KANALZ Senior VP – Editorial Strategy & Administration
JAY KOGAN VP – Legal Affairs
DEREK MADDALENA Senior VP – Sales & Business Development
JACK MAHAN VP – Business Affairs
DAN MIRON VP – Sales Planning & Trade Development
NICK NAPOLITANO VP – Manufacturing Administration
CAROL ROEDER VP – Marketing
EDDIE SCANNELL VP – Mass Account & Digital Sales
COURTNEY SIMMONS Senior VP – Publicity & Communications
JIM (SKI) SOKOLOWSKI VP – Comic Book Specialty & Newsstand Sales
SANDY YI Senior VP – Global Franchise Management

NEW SUICIDE SQUAD VOLUME 2: MONSTERS

Published by DC Comics. Compilation Copyright © 2016 DC Comics. All Rights Reserved.

Originally published in single magazine form as NEW SUICIDE SQUAD 9-12, NEW SUICIDE SQUAD ANNUAL 1, and online as
DC SNEAK PEEK: NEW SUICIDE SQUAD 1 © 2015 DC Comics. All Rights Reserved. All characters, their distinctive likenesses and related
elements featured in this publication are trademarks of DC Comics. The stories, characters and incidents featured in this publication are
entirely fictional. DC Comics does not read or accept unsolicited ideas, stories or artwork.

DC Comics, 2900 West Alameda Avenue, Burbank, CA 91505
Printed by RR Donnelley, Owensville, MO, USA. 12/30/15. First Printing.
ISBN: 978-1-4012-6152-8

Library of Congress Cataloging-in-Publication Data is available.

PEFC Certified

Printed on paper from
sustainably managed
forests and controlled
sources

PEFC/29-31-75   www.pefc.org

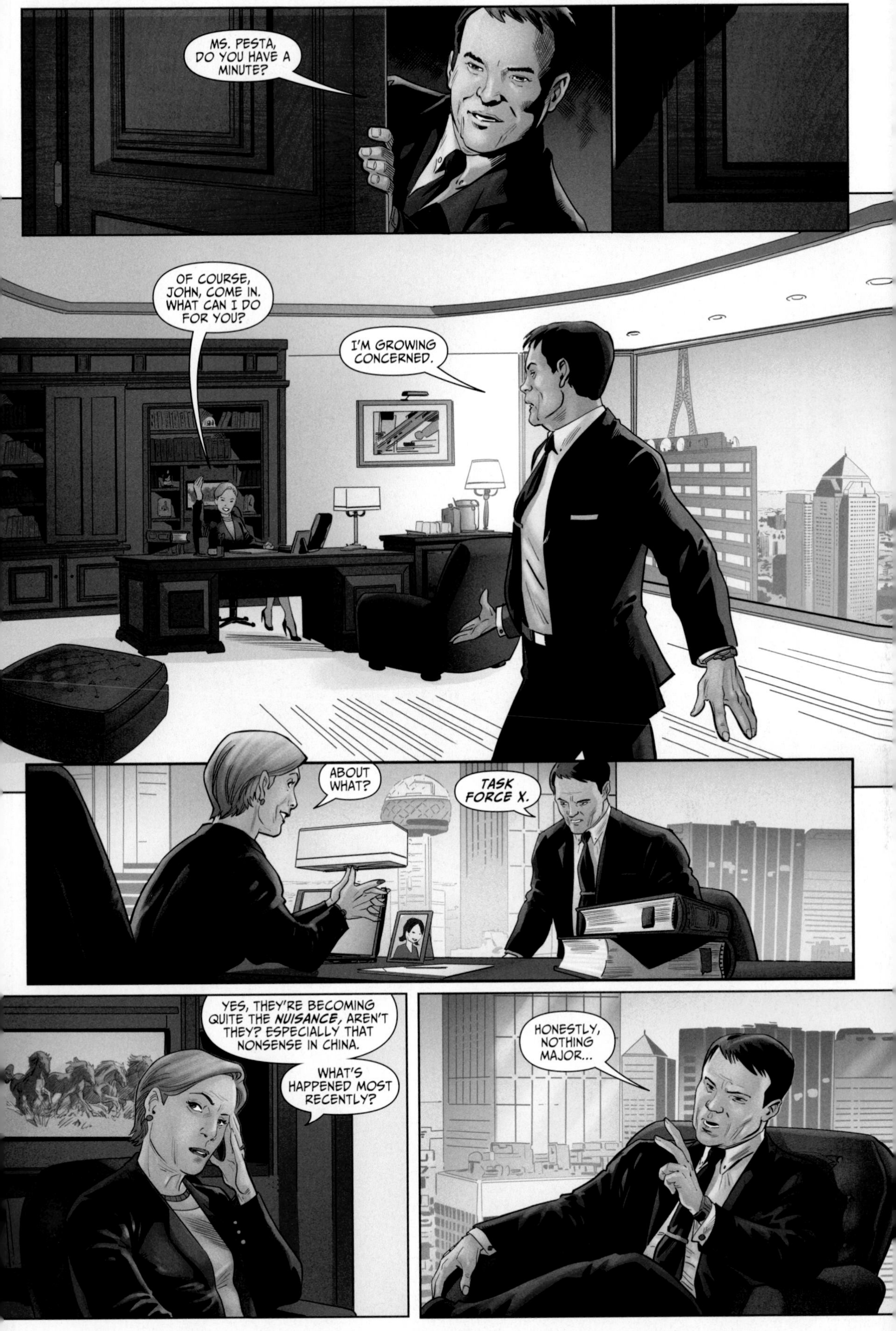
MS. PESTA, DO YOU HAVE A MINUTE?
OF COURSE, JOHN, COME IN. WHAT CAN I DO FOR YOU?
I'M GROWING CONCERNED.
ABOUT WHAT?
TASK FORCE X.
YES, THEY'RE BECOMING QUITE THE NUISANCE, AREN'T THEY? ESPECIALLY THAT NONSENSE IN CHINA.
WHAT'S HAPPENED MOST RECENTLY?
HONESTLY, NOTHING MAJOR...

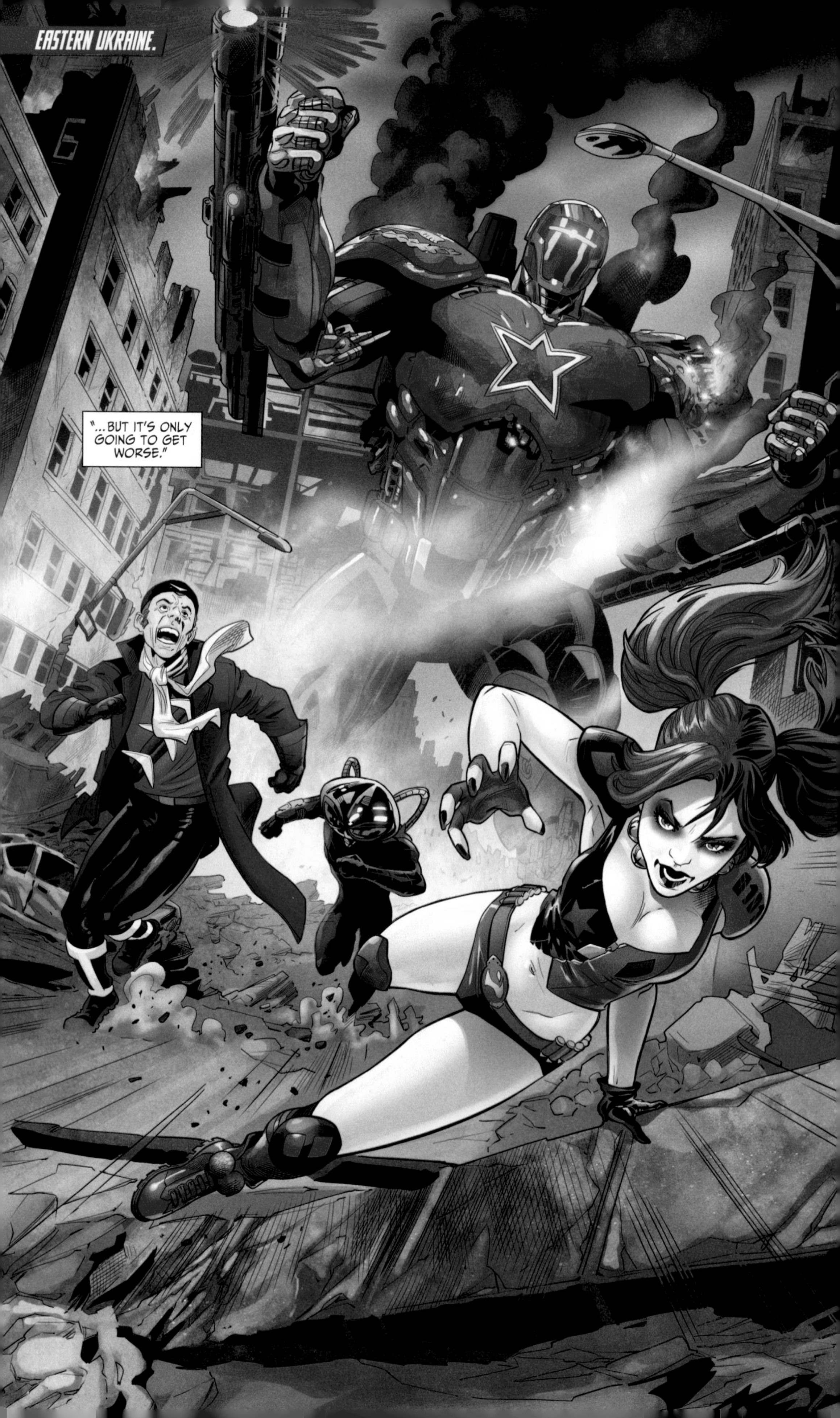
EASTERN UKRAINE.
"...BUT IT'S ONLY GOING TO GET WORSE."

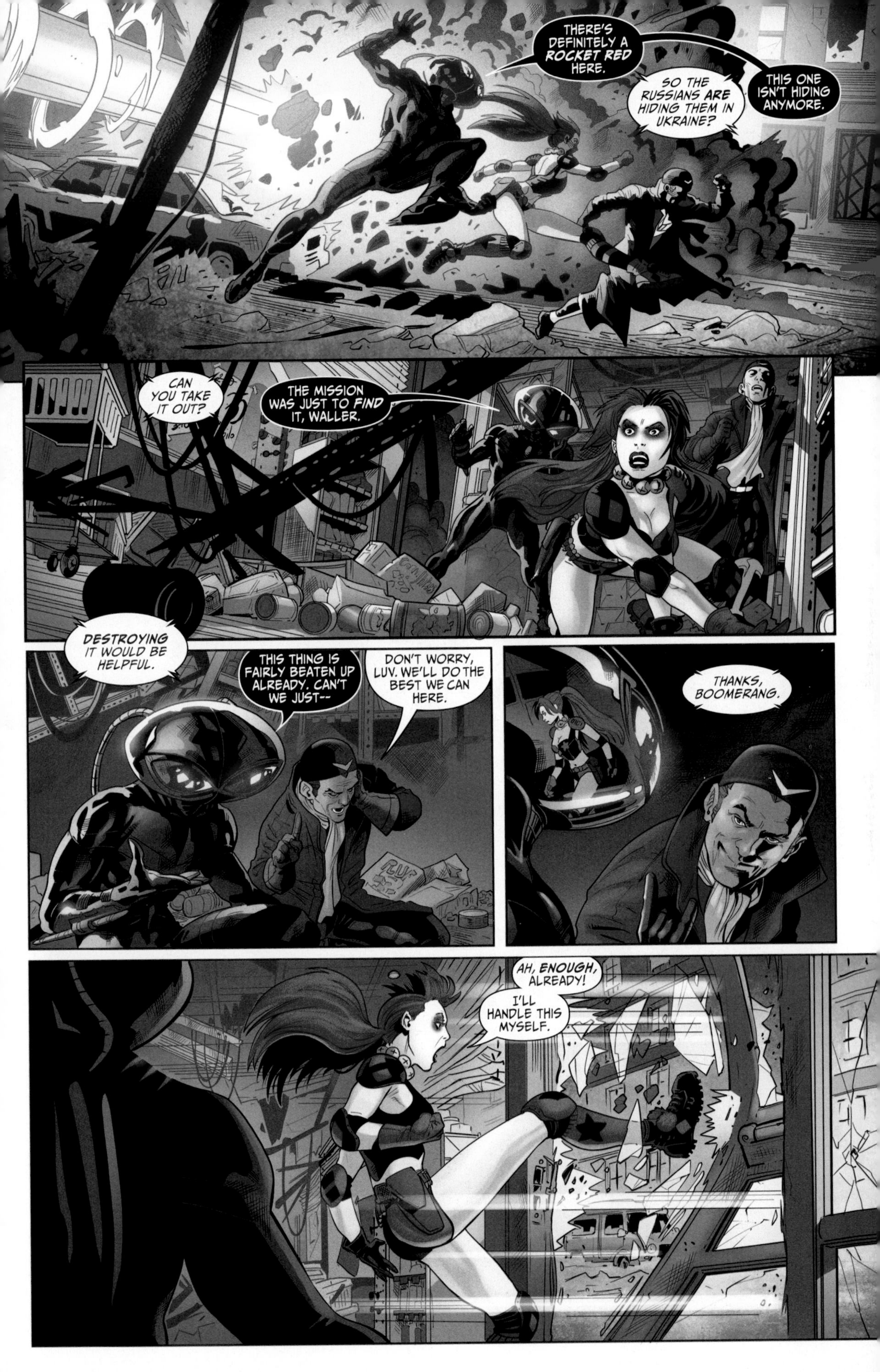
THERE'S DEFINITELY A ROCKET RED HERE.
SO THE RUSSIANS ARE HIDING THEM IN UKRAINE?
THIS ONE ISN'T HIDING ANYMORE.
CAN YOU TAKE IT OUT?
THE MISSION WAS JUST TO FIND IT, WALLER.
DESTROYING IT WOULD BE HELPFUL.
THIS THING IS FAIRLY BEATEN UP ALREADY. CAN'T WE JUST--
DON'T WORRY, LUV. WE'LL DO THE BEST WE CAN HERE.
THANKS, BOOMERANG.
AH, ENOUGH, ALREADY!
I'LL HANDLE THIS MYSELF.

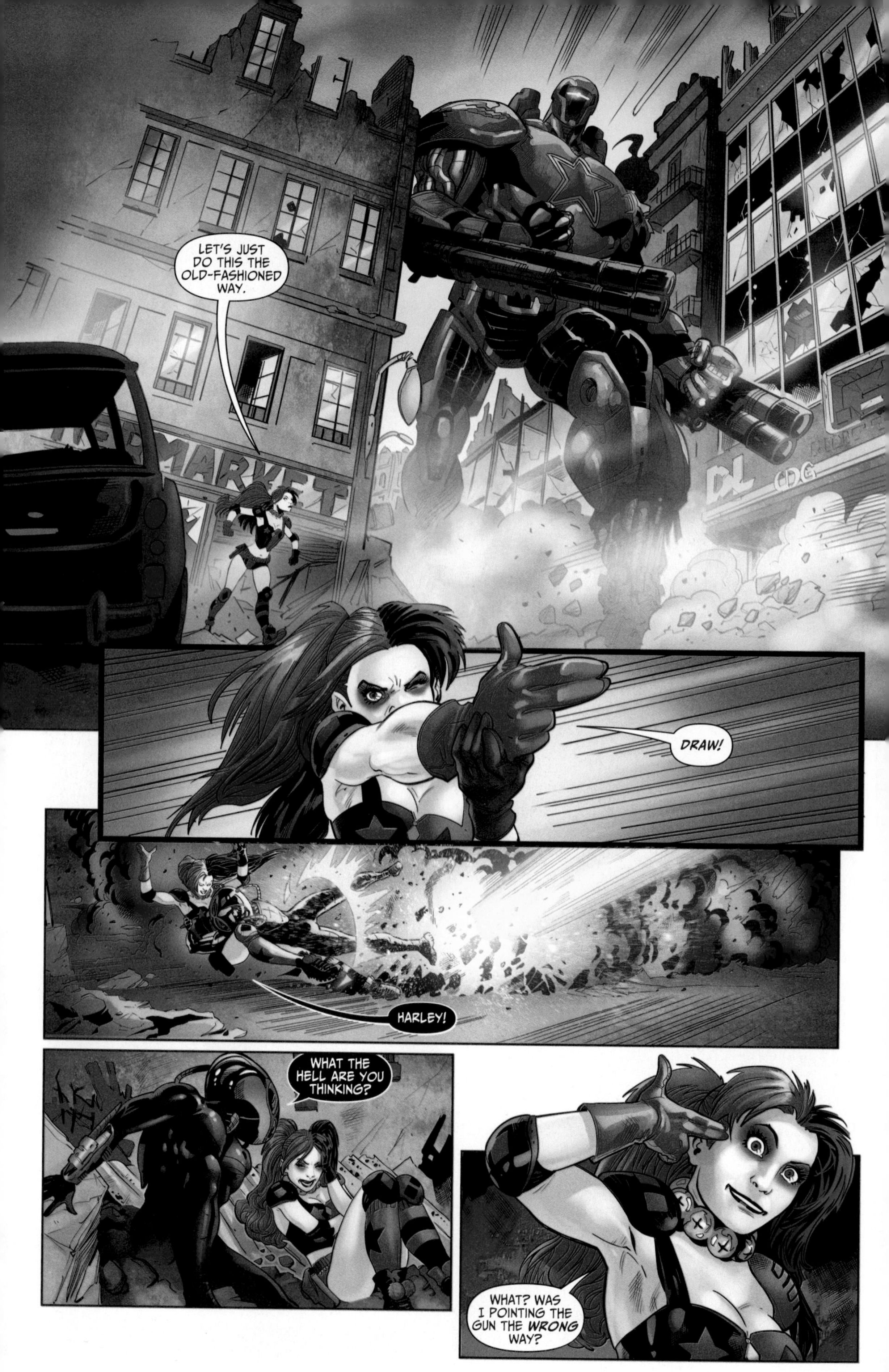
LET'S JUST DO THIS THE OLD-FASHIONED WAY.
MARKET
DRAW!
HARLEY!
WHAT THE HELL ARE YOU THINKING?
WHAT? WAS I POINTING THE GUN THE WRONG WAY?

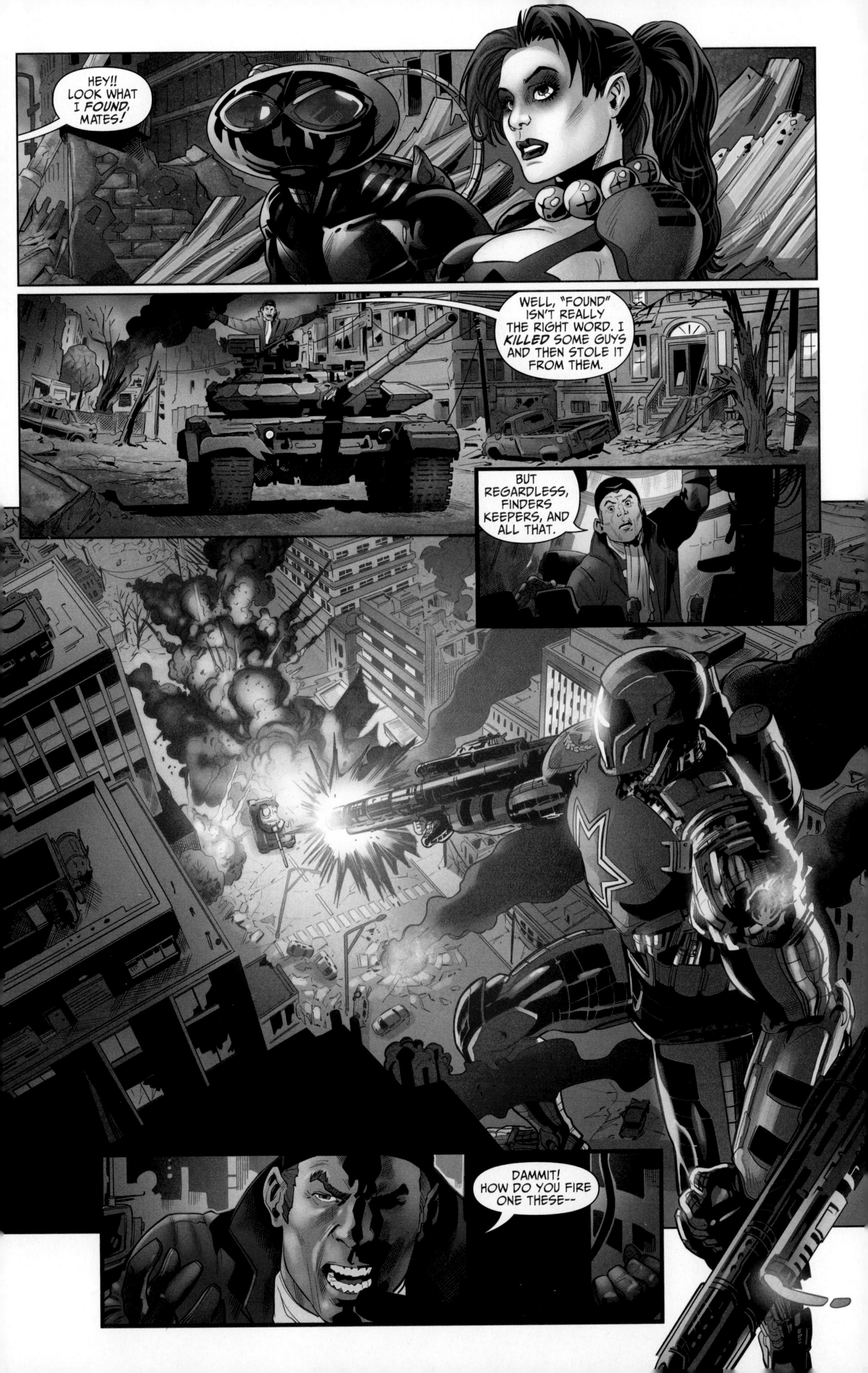
HEY!! LOOK WHAT I FOUND, MATES!
WELL, "FOUND" ISN'T REALLY THE RIGHT WORD. I KILLED SOME GUYS AND THEN STOLE IT FROM THEM.
BUT REGARDLESS, FINDERS KEEPERS, AND ALL THAT.
DAMMIT! HOW DO YOU FIRE ONE THESE--

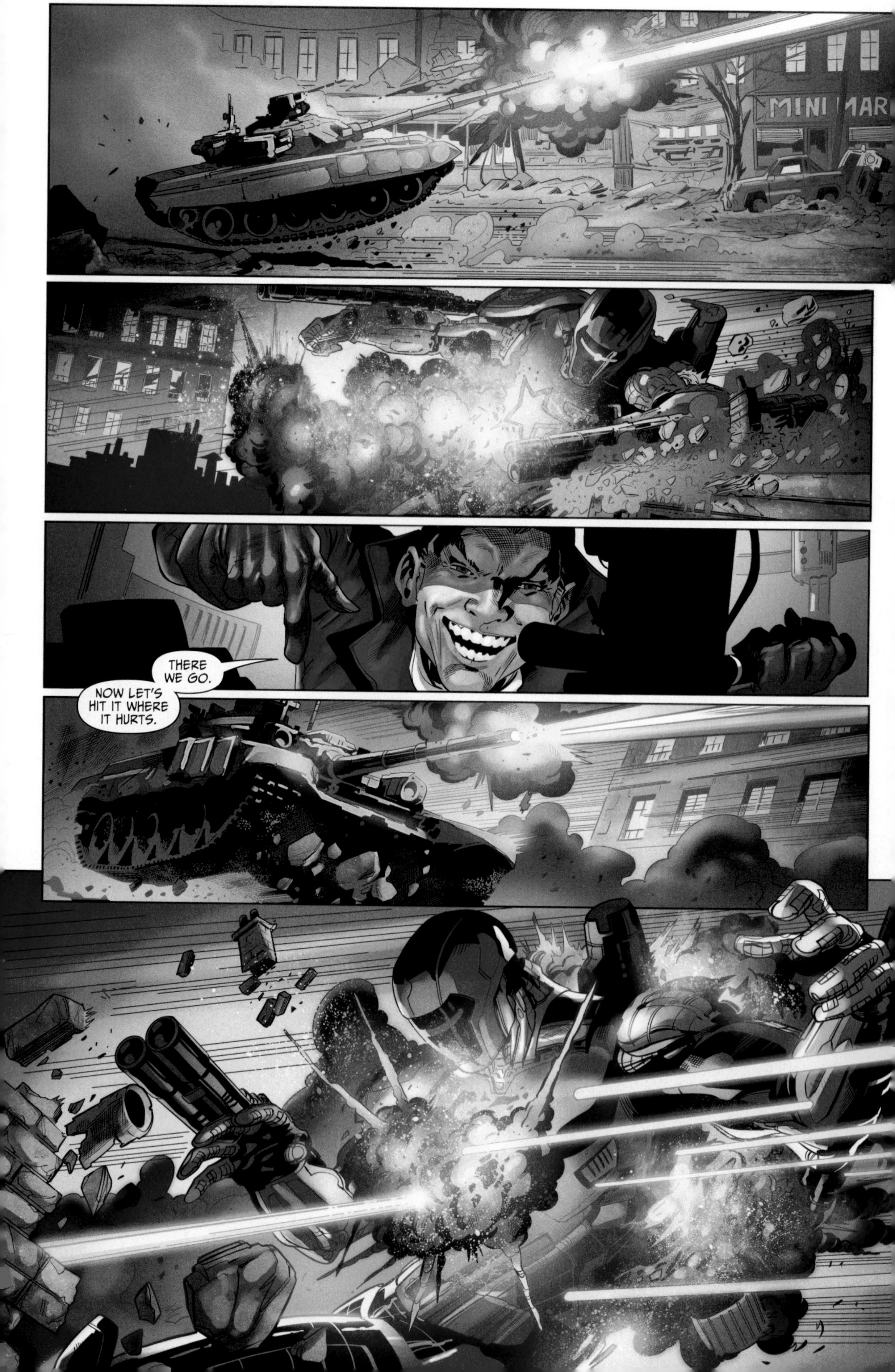
MINI MAR
THERE WE GO.
NOW LET'S HIT IT WHERE IT HURTS.

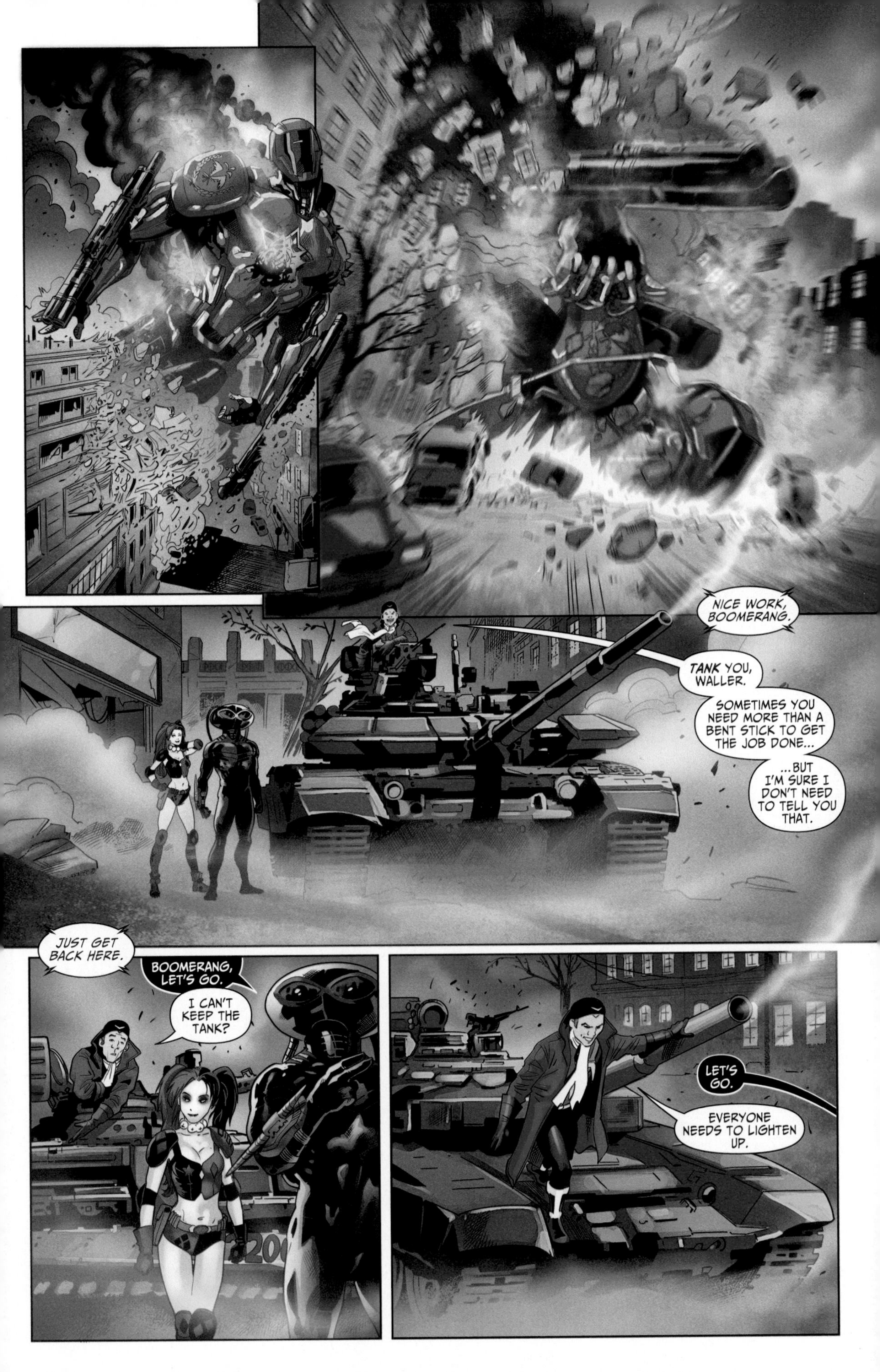
NICE WORK, BOOMERANG.
TANK YOU, WALLER.
SOMETIMES YOU NEED MORE THAN A BENT STICK TO GET THE JOB DONE...
...BUT I'M SURE I DON'T NEED TO TELL YOU THAT.
JUST GET BACK HERE.
BOOMERANG, LET'S GO.
I CAN'T KEEP THE TANK?
LET'S GO.
EVERYONE NEEDS TO LIGHTEN UP.

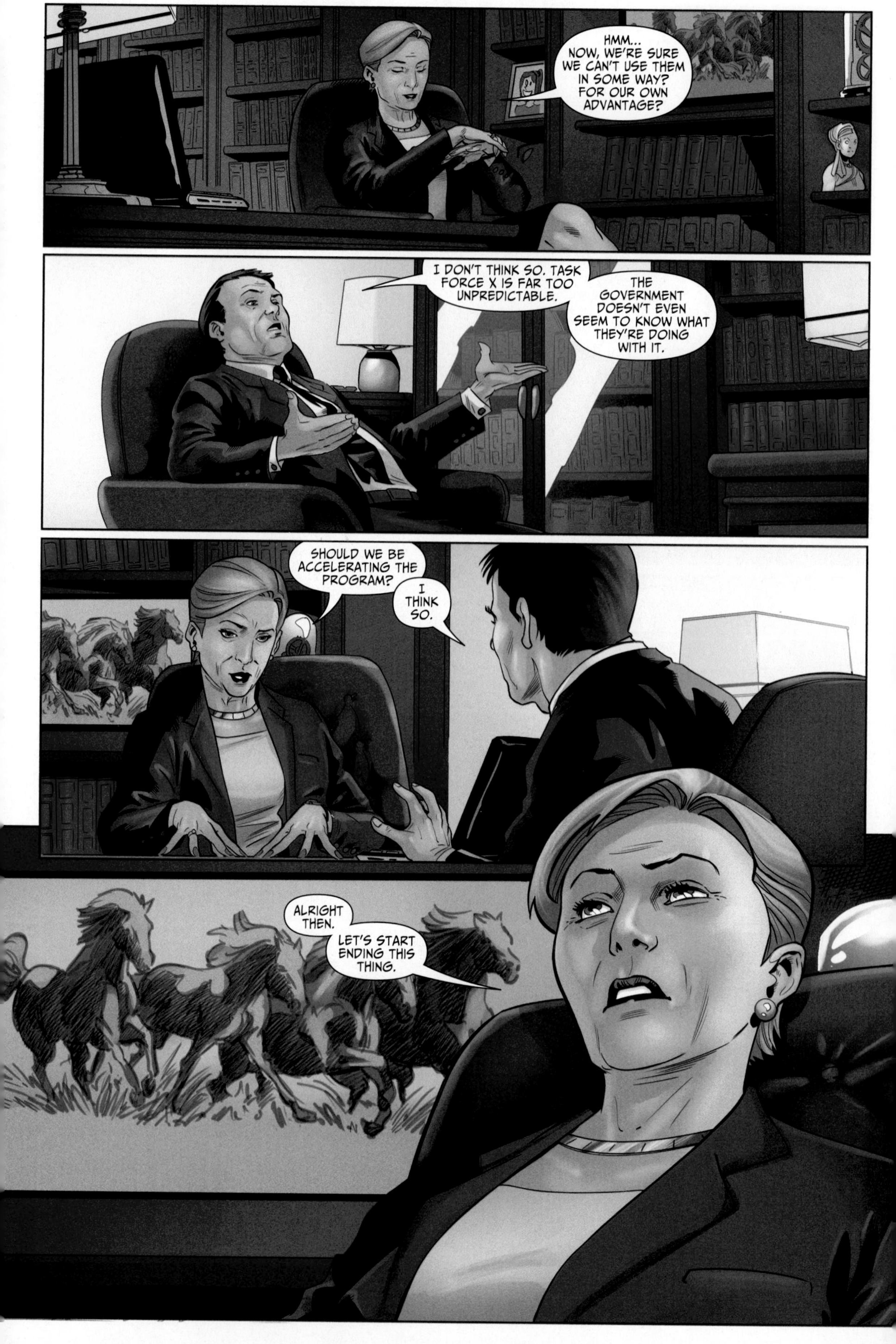
HMM... NOW, WE'RE SURE WE CAN'T USE THEM IN SOME WAY? FOR OUR OWN ADVANTAGE?
I DON'T THINK SO. TASK FORCE X IS FAR TOO UNPREDICTABLE.
THE GOVERNMENT DOESN'T EVEN SEEM TO KNOW WHAT THEY'RE DOING WITH IT.
SHOULD WE BE ACCELERATING THE PROGRAM?
I THINK SO.
ALRIGHT THEN.
LET'S START ENDING THIS THING.

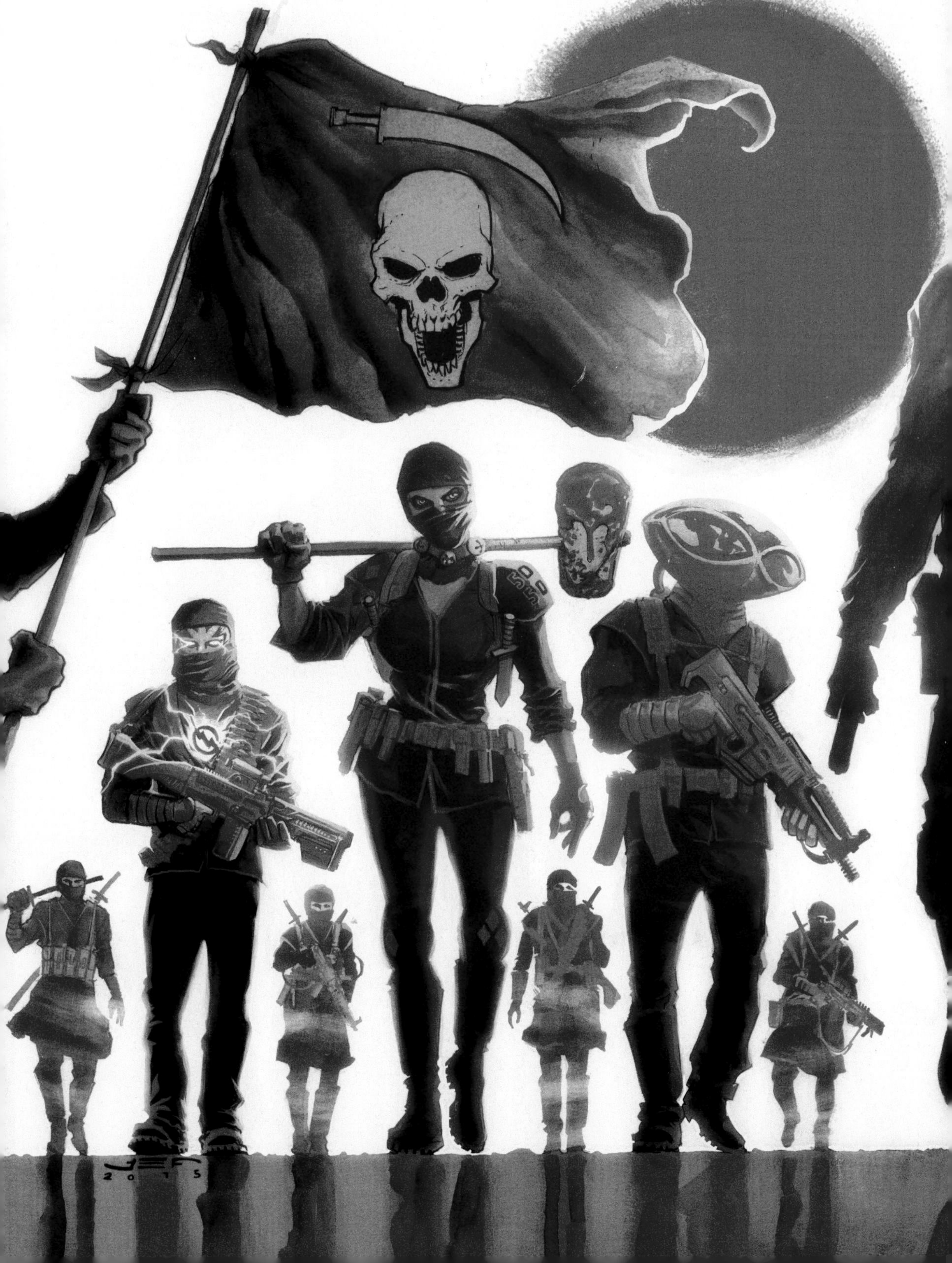

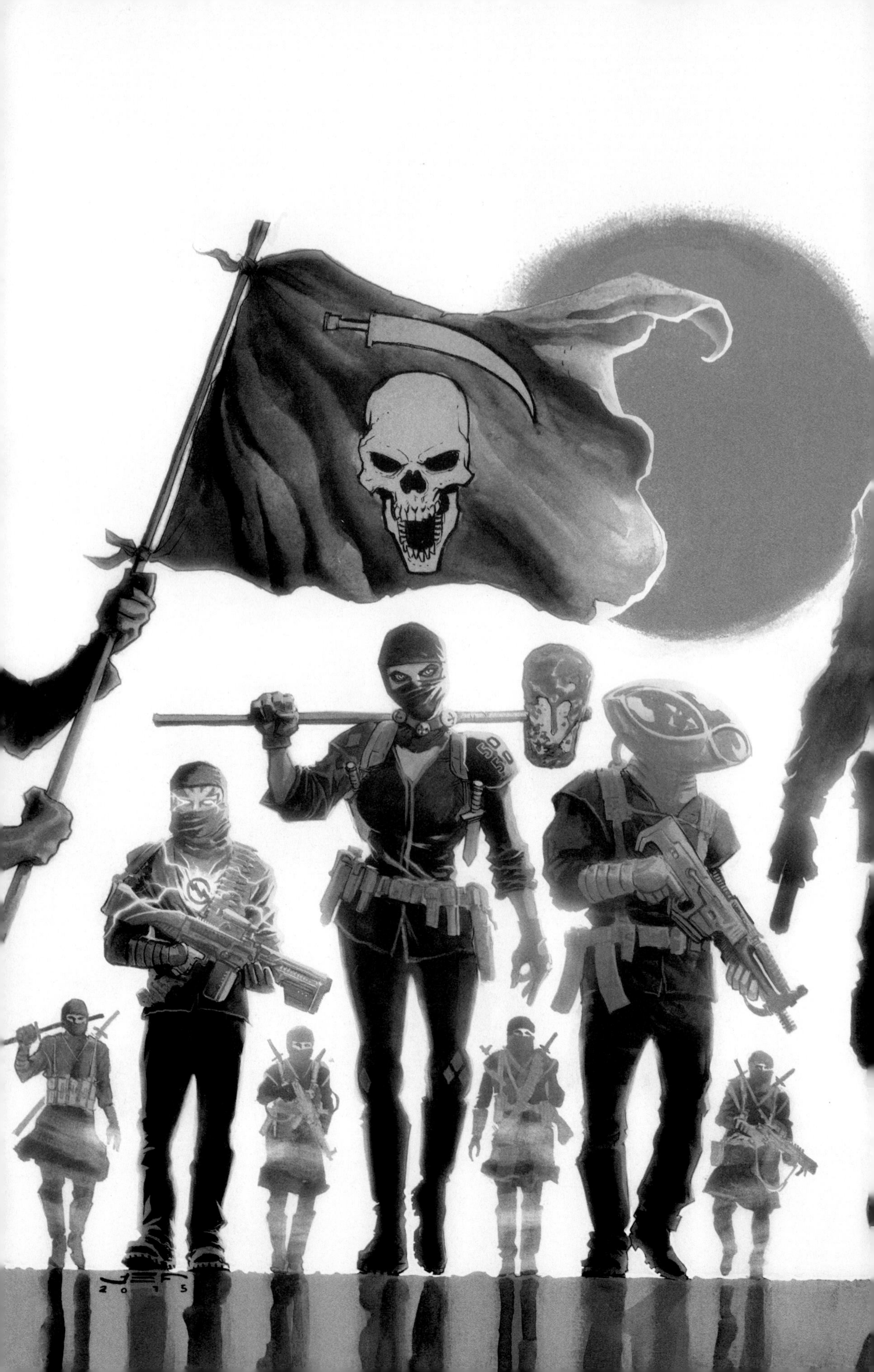

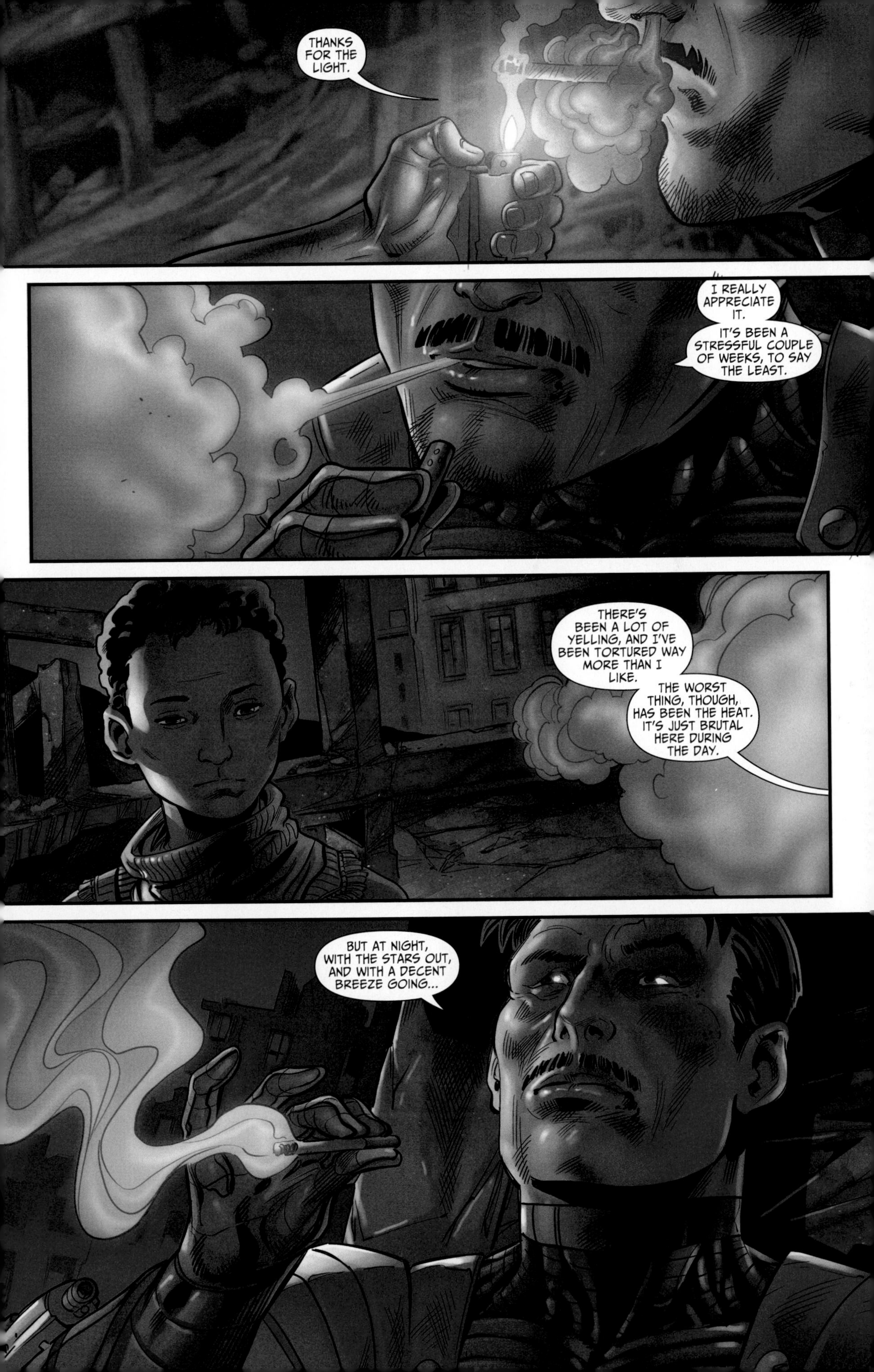
THANKS FOR THE LIGHT.
I REALLY APPRECIATE IT.
IT'S BEEN A STRESSFUL COUPLE OF WEEKS, TO SAY THE LEAST.
THERE'S BEEN A LOT OF YELLING, AND I'VE BEEN TORTURED WAY MORE THAN I LIKE.
THE WORST THING, THOUGH, HAS BEEN THE HEAT. IT'S JUST BRUTAL HERE DURING THE DAY.
BUT AT NIGHT, WITH THE STARS OUT, AND WITH A DECENT BREEZE GOING...

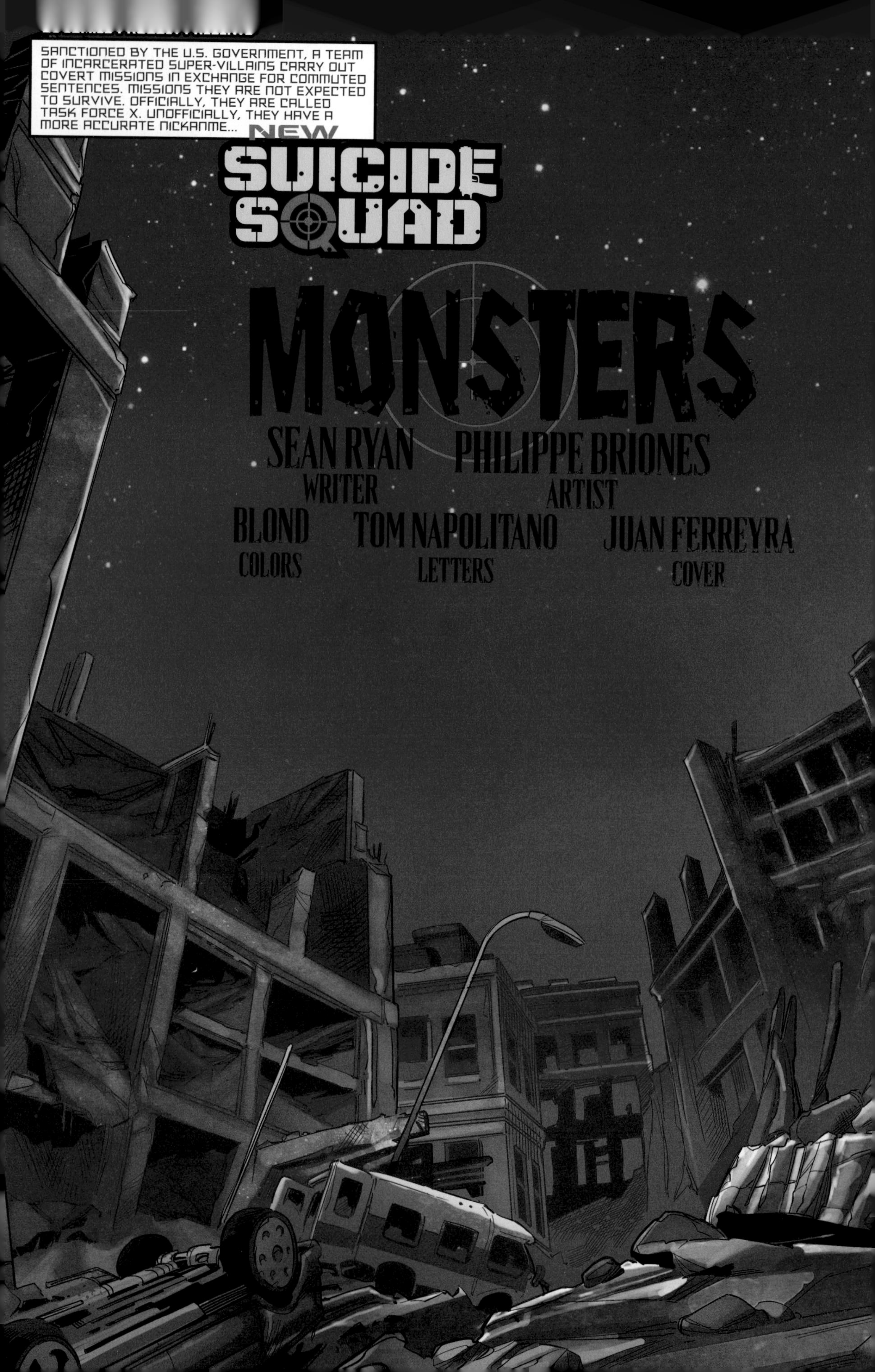
SANCTIONED BY THE U.S. GOVERNMENT, A TEAM OF INCARCERATED SUPER-VILLAINS CARRY OUT COVERT MISSIONS IN EXCHANGE FOR COMMUTED SENTENCES. MISSIONS THEY ARE NOT EXPECTED TO SURVIVE. OFFICIALLY, THEY ARE CALLED TASK FORCE X. UNOFFICIALLY, THEY HAVE A MORE ACCURATE NICKANME...
NEW SUICIDE SQUAD
MONSTERS
SEAN RYAN WRITER
PHILIPPE BRIONES ARTIST
BLOND COLORS
TOM NAPOLITANO LETTERS
JUAN FERREYRA COVER

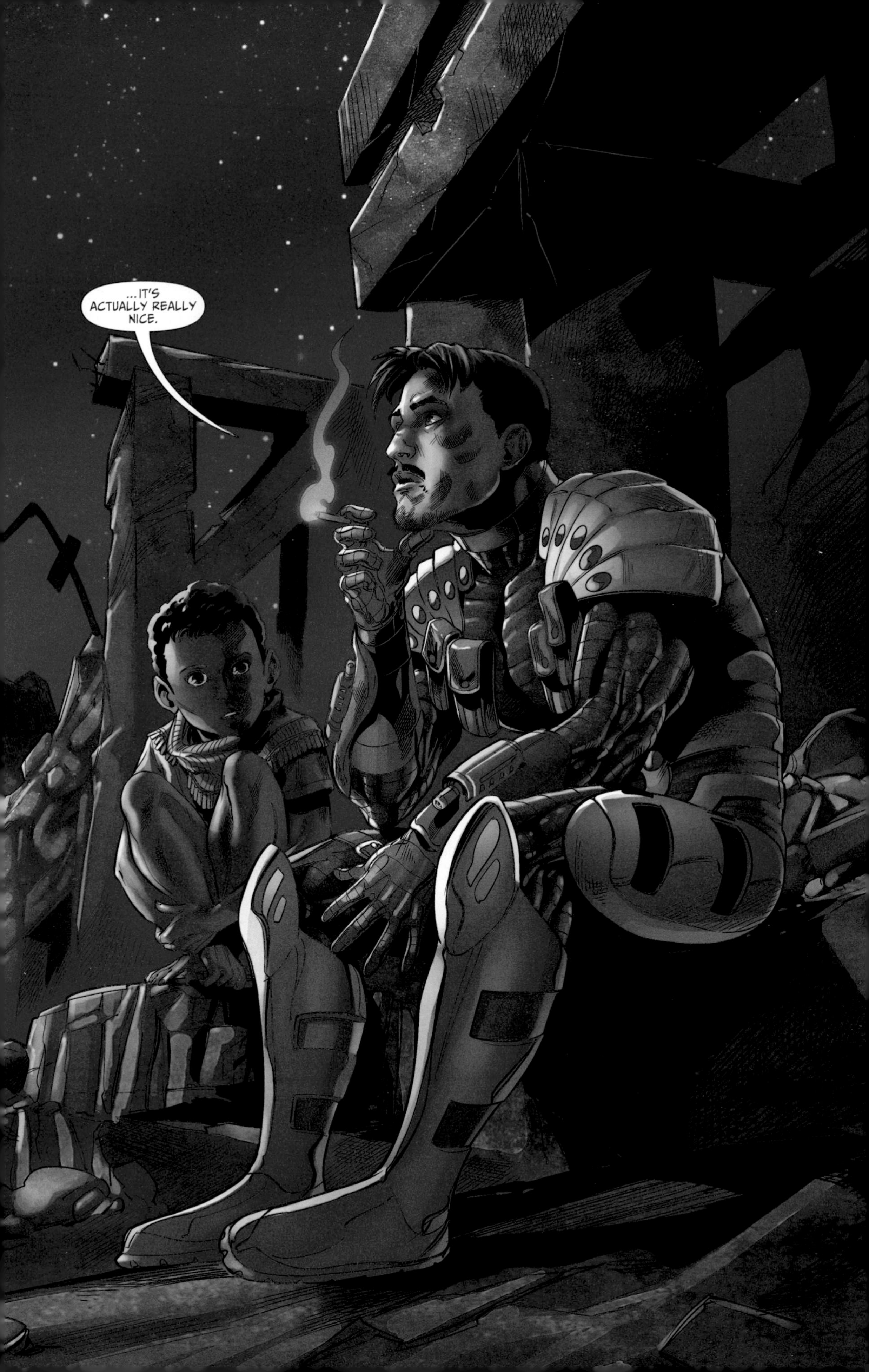
...IT'S ACTUALLY REALLY NICE.

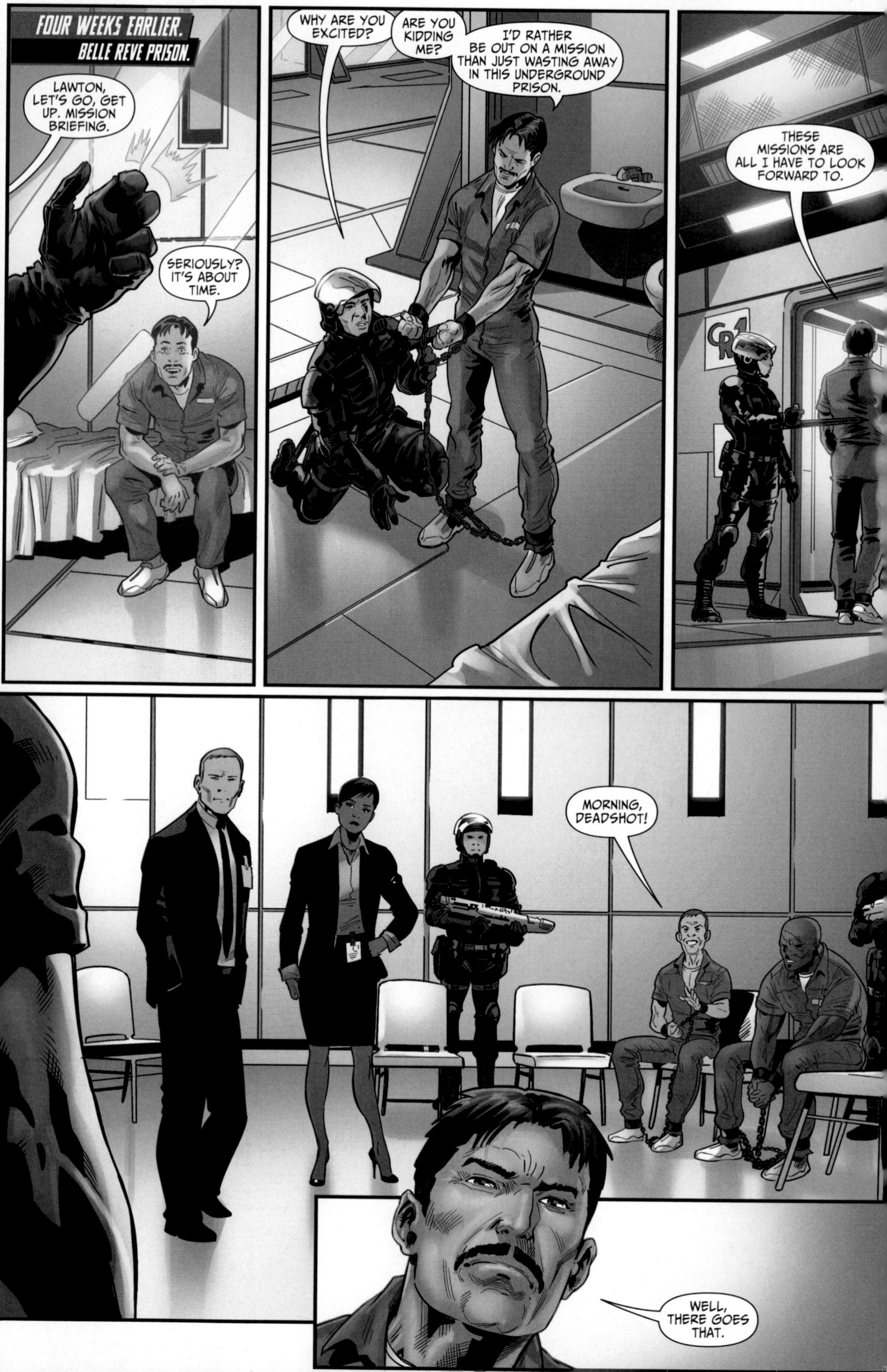
FOUR WEEKS EARLIER.
BELLE REVE PRISON.
LAWTON, LET'S GO, GET UP. MISSION BRIEFING.
SERIOUSLY? IT'S ABOUT TIME.
WHY ARE YOU EXCITED?
ARE YOU KIDDING ME?
I'D RATHER BE OUT ON A MISSION THAN JUST WASTING AWAY IN THIS UNDERGROUND PRISON.
THESE MISSIONS ARE ALL I HAVE TO LOOK FORWARD TO.
CR1
MORNING, DEADSHOT!
WELL, THERE GOES THAT.

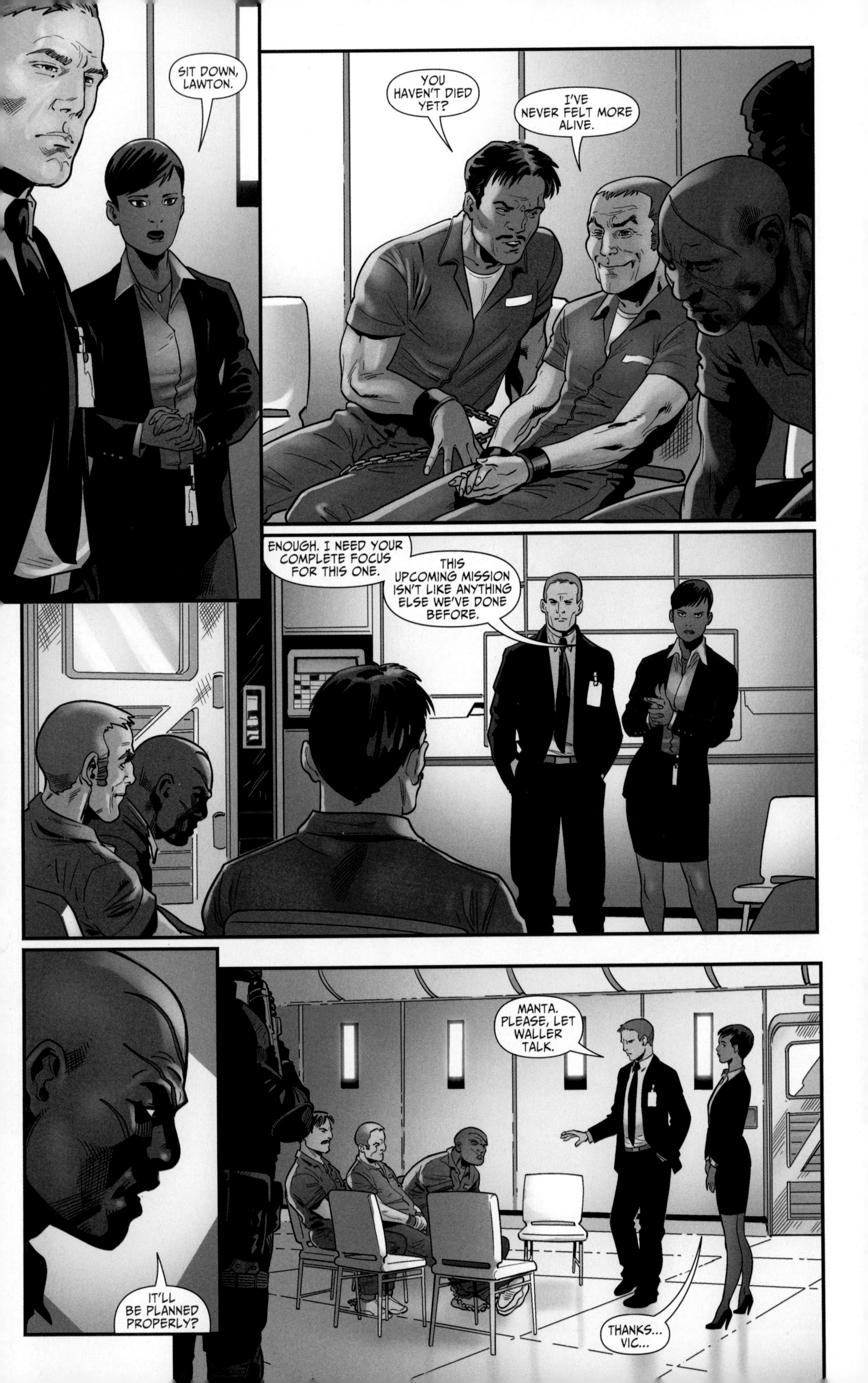
SIT DOWN, LAWTON.
YOU HAVEN'T DIED YET?
I'VE NEVER FELT MORE ALIVE.
ENOUGH. I NEED YOUR COMPLETE FOCUS FOR THIS ONE.
THIS UPCOMING MISSION ISN'T LIKE ANYTHING ELSE WE'VE DONE BEFORE.
IT'LL BE PLANNED PROPERLY?
MANTA. PLEASE, LET WALLER TALK.
THANKS... VIC...

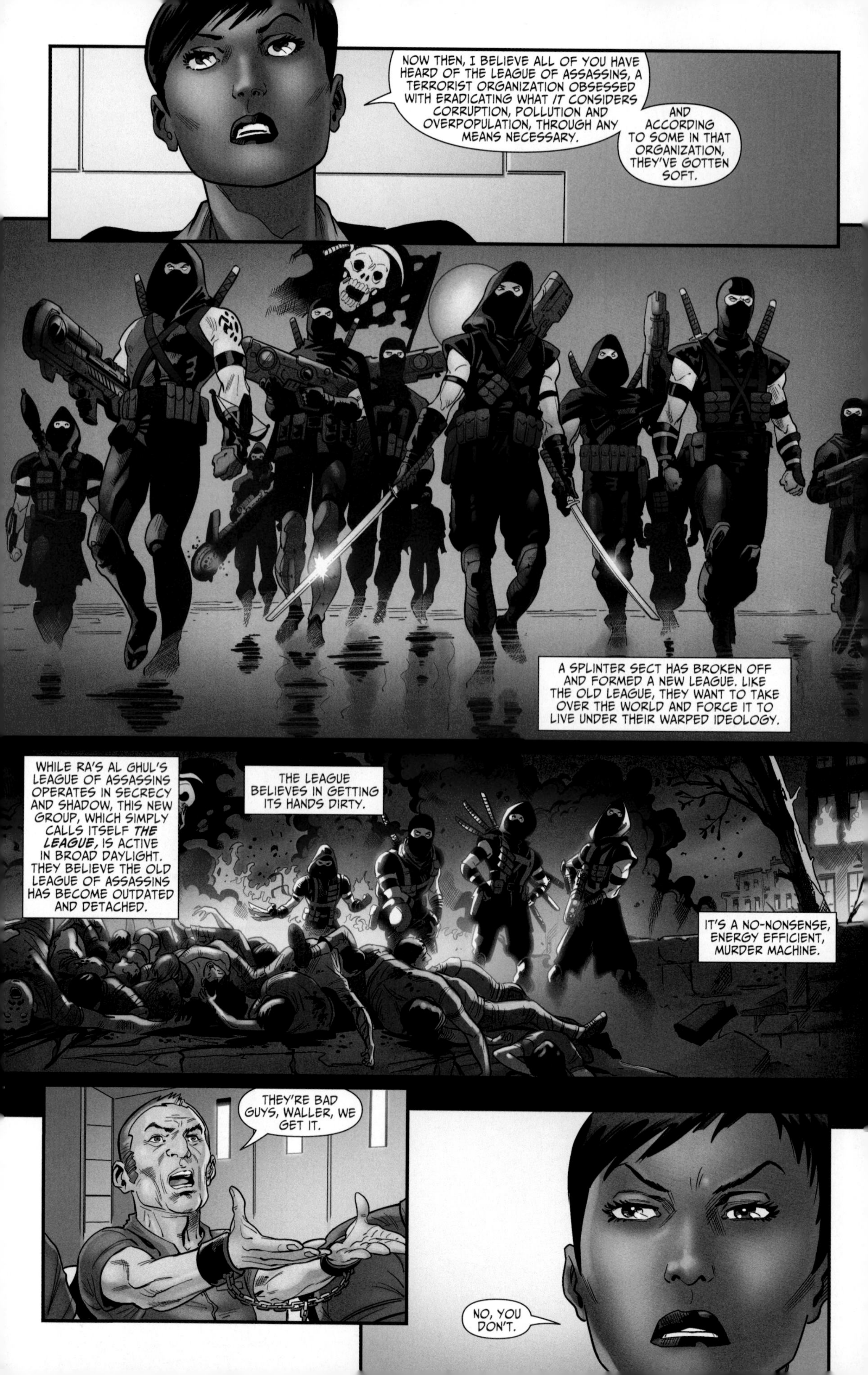
NOW THEN, I BELIEVE ALL OF YOU HAVE HEARD OF THE LEAGUE OF ASSASSINS, A TERRORIST ORGANIZATION OBSESSED WITH ERADICATING WHAT *IT* CONSIDERS CORRUPTION, POLLUTION AND OVERPOPULATION, THROUGH ANY MEANS NECESSARY.
AND ACCORDING TO SOME IN THAT ORGANIZATION, THEY'VE GOTTEN SOFT.
A SPLINTER SECT HAS BROKEN OFF AND FORMED A NEW LEAGUE. LIKE THE OLD LEAGUE, THEY WANT TO TAKE OVER THE WORLD AND FORCE IT TO LIVE UNDER THEIR WARPED IDEOLOGY.
WHILE RA'S AL GHUL'S LEAGUE OF ASSASSINS OPERATES IN SECRECY AND SHADOW, THIS NEW GROUP, WHICH SIMPLY CALLS ITSELF ***THE LEAGUE,*** IS ACTIVE IN BROAD DAYLIGHT. THEY BELIEVE THE OLD LEAGUE OF ASSASSINS HAS BECOME OUTDATED AND DETACHED.
THE LEAGUE BELIEVES IN GETTING ITS HANDS DIRTY.
IT'S A NO-NONSENSE, ENERGY EFFICIENT, MURDER MACHINE.
THEY'RE BAD GUYS, WALLER, WE GET IT.
NO, YOU DON'T.

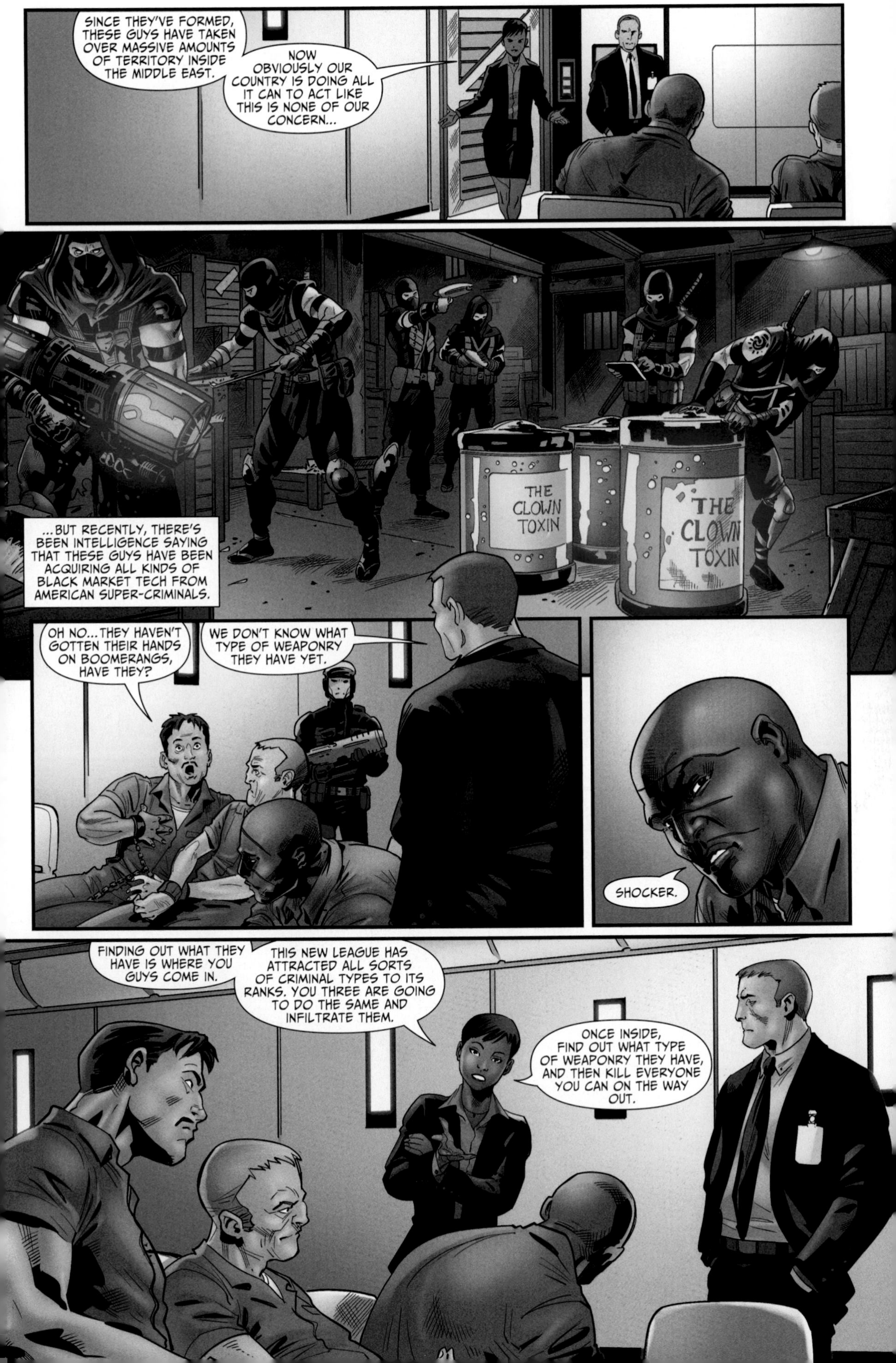
SINCE THEY'VE FORMED, THESE GUYS HAVE TAKEN OVER MASSIVE AMOUNTS OF TERRITORY INSIDE THE MIDDLE EAST.
NOW OBVIOUSLY OUR COUNTRY IS DOING ALL IT CAN TO ACT LIKE THIS IS NONE OF OUR CONCERN...
THE CLOWN TOXIN
THE CLOWN TOXIN
...BUT RECENTLY, THERE'S BEEN INTELLIGENCE SAYING THAT THESE GUYS HAVE BEEN ACQUIRING ALL KINDS OF BLACK MARKET TECH FROM AMERICAN SUPER-CRIMINALS.
OH NO...THEY HAVEN'T GOTTEN THEIR HANDS ON BOOMERANGS, HAVE THEY?
WE DON'T KNOW WHAT TYPE OF WEAPONRY THEY HAVE YET.
SHOCKER.
FINDING OUT WHAT THEY HAVE IS WHERE YOU GUYS COME IN.
THIS NEW LEAGUE HAS ATTRACTED ALL SORTS OF CRIMINAL TYPES TO ITS RANKS. YOU THREE ARE GOING TO DO THE SAME AND INFILTRATE THEM.
ONCE INSIDE, FIND OUT WHAT TYPE OF WEAPONRY THEY HAVE, AND THEN KILL EVERYONE YOU CAN ON THE WAY OUT.

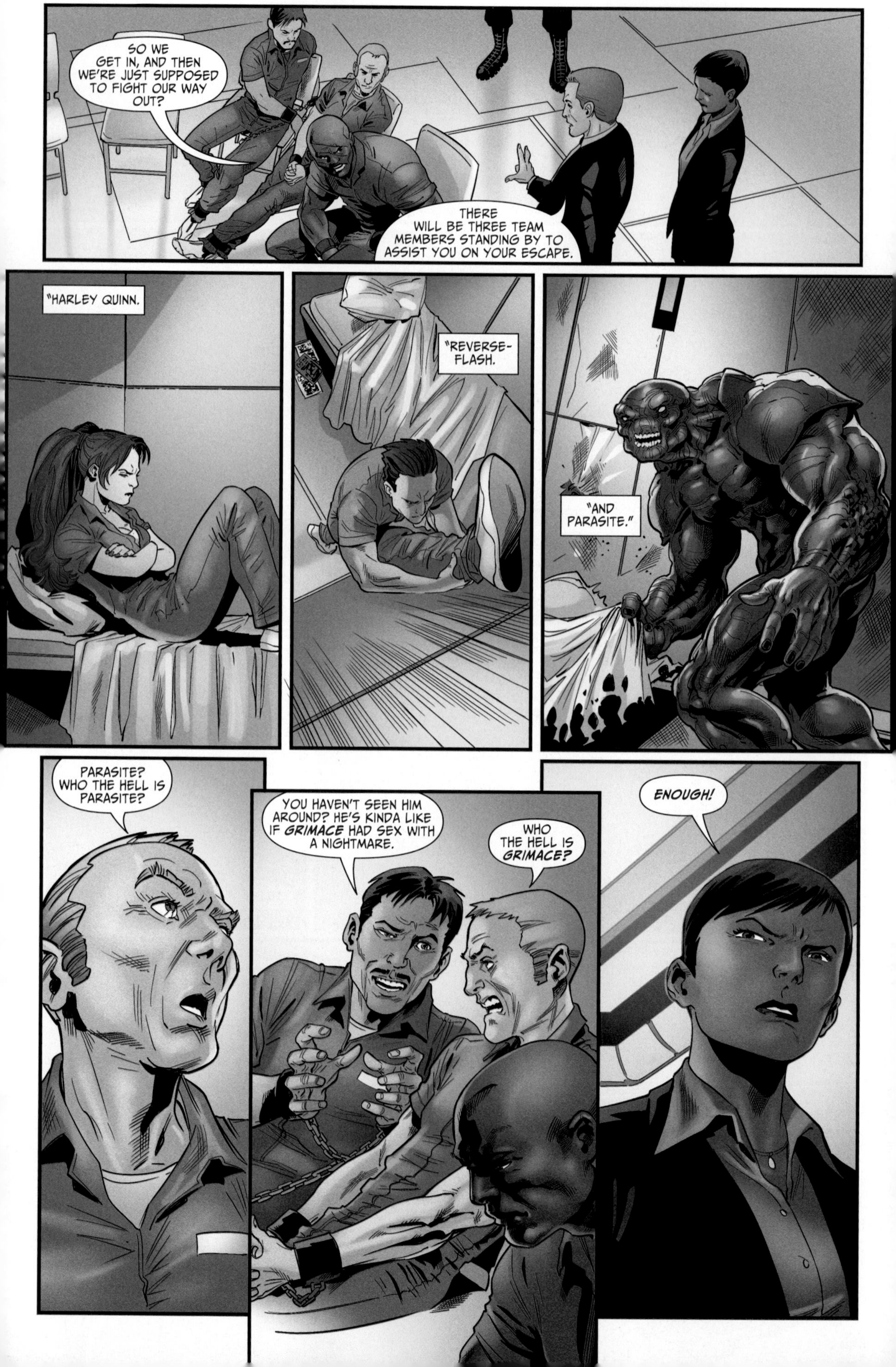

SO WE GET IN, AND THEN WE'RE JUST SUPPOSED TO FIGHT OUR WAY OUT?
THERE WILL BE THREE TEAM MEMBERS STANDING BY TO ASSIST YOU ON YOUR ESCAPE.
"HARLEY QUINN.
"REVERSE-FLASH.
"AND PARASITE."
PARASITE? WHO THE HELL IS PARASITE?
YOU HAVEN'T SEEN HIM AROUND? HE'S KINDA LIKE IF GRIMACE HAD SEX WITH A NIGHTMARE.
WHO THE HELL IS GRIMACE?
ENOUGH!

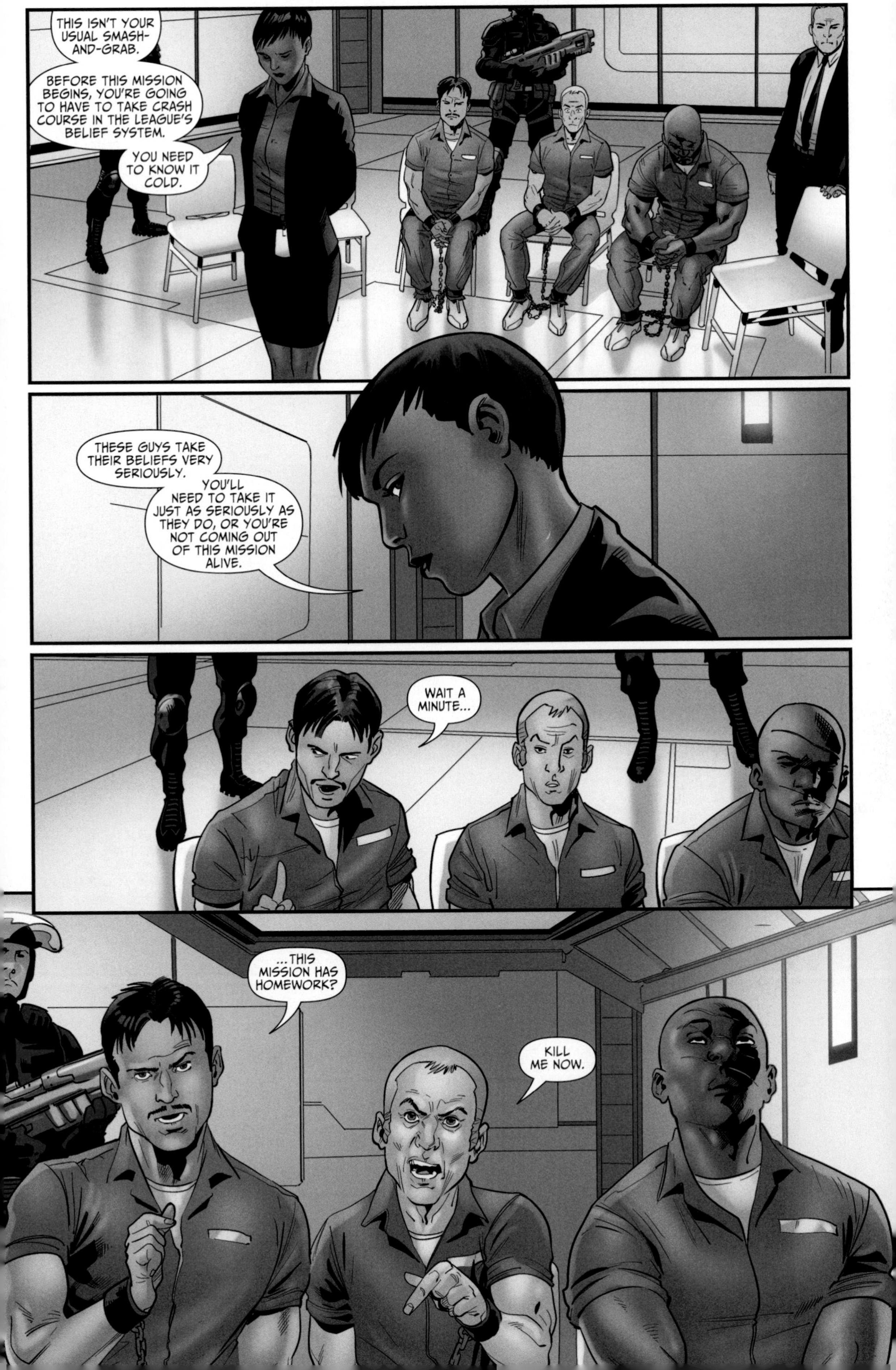
THIS ISN'T YOUR USUAL SMASH-AND-GRAB.
BEFORE THIS MISSION BEGINS, YOU'RE GOING TO HAVE TO TAKE CRASH COURSE IN THE LEAGUE'S BELIEF SYSTEM.
YOU NEED TO KNOW IT COLD.
THESE GUYS TAKE THEIR BELIEFS VERY SERIOUSLY.
YOU'LL NEED TO TAKE IT JUST AS SERIOUSLY AS THEY DO, OR YOU'RE NOT COMING OUT OF THIS MISSION ALIVE.
WAIT A MINUTE...
...THIS MISSION HAS HOMEWORK?
KILL ME NOW.

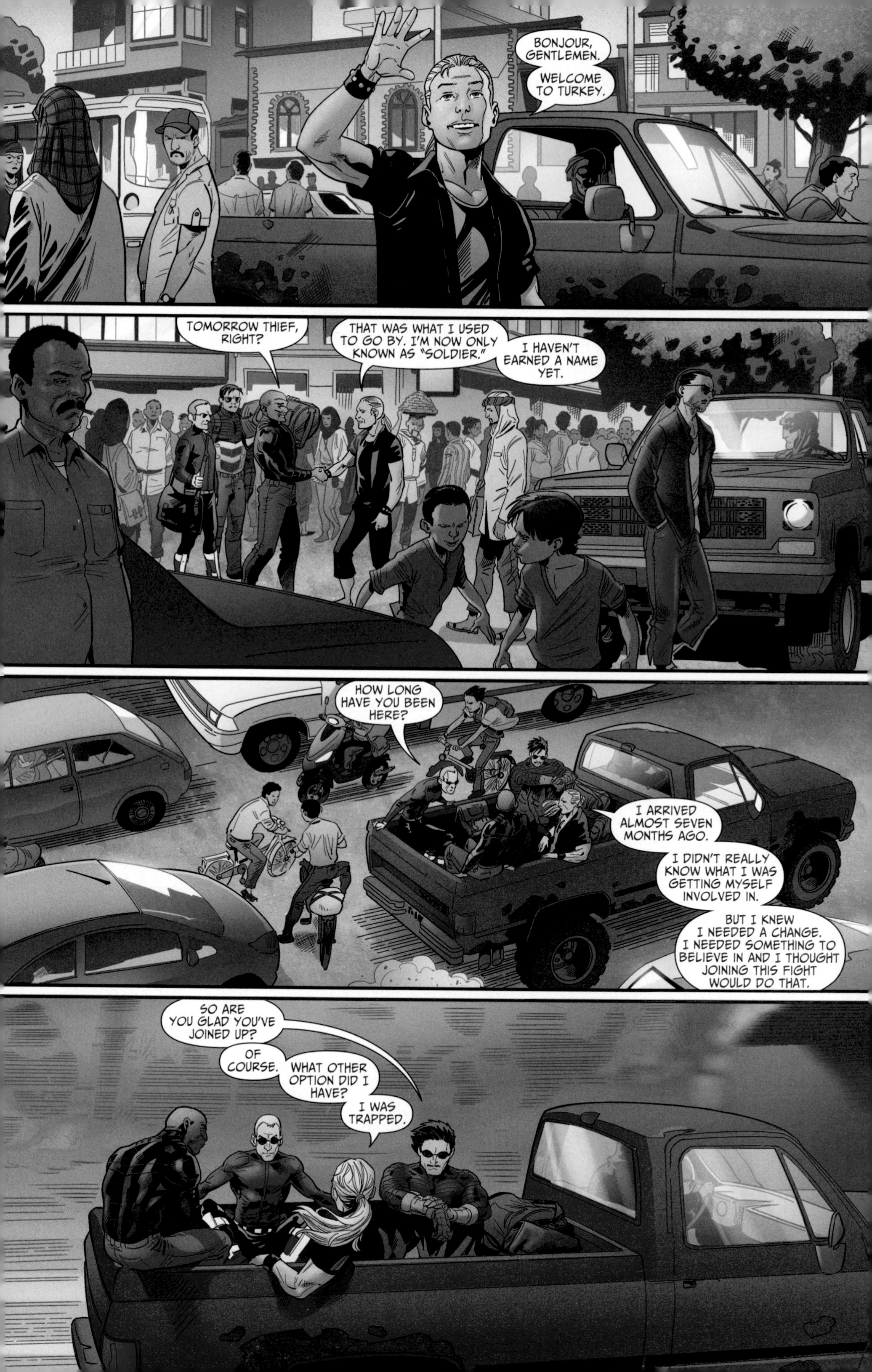
BONJOUR, GENTLEMEN.
WELCOME TO TURKEY.
TOMORROW THIEF, RIGHT?
THAT WAS WHAT I USED TO GO BY. I'M NOW ONLY KNOWN AS "SOLDIER."
I HAVEN'T EARNED A NAME YET.
HOW LONG HAVE YOU BEEN HERE?
I ARRIVED ALMOST SEVEN MONTHS AGO.
I DIDN'T REALLY KNOW WHAT I WAS GETTING MYSELF INVOLVED IN.
BUT I KNEW I NEEDED A CHANGE. I NEEDED SOMETHING TO BELIEVE IN AND I THOUGHT JOINING THIS FIGHT WOULD DO THAT.
SO ARE YOU GLAD YOU'VE JOINED UP?
OF COURSE.
WHAT OTHER OPTION DID I HAVE?
I WAS TRAPPED.

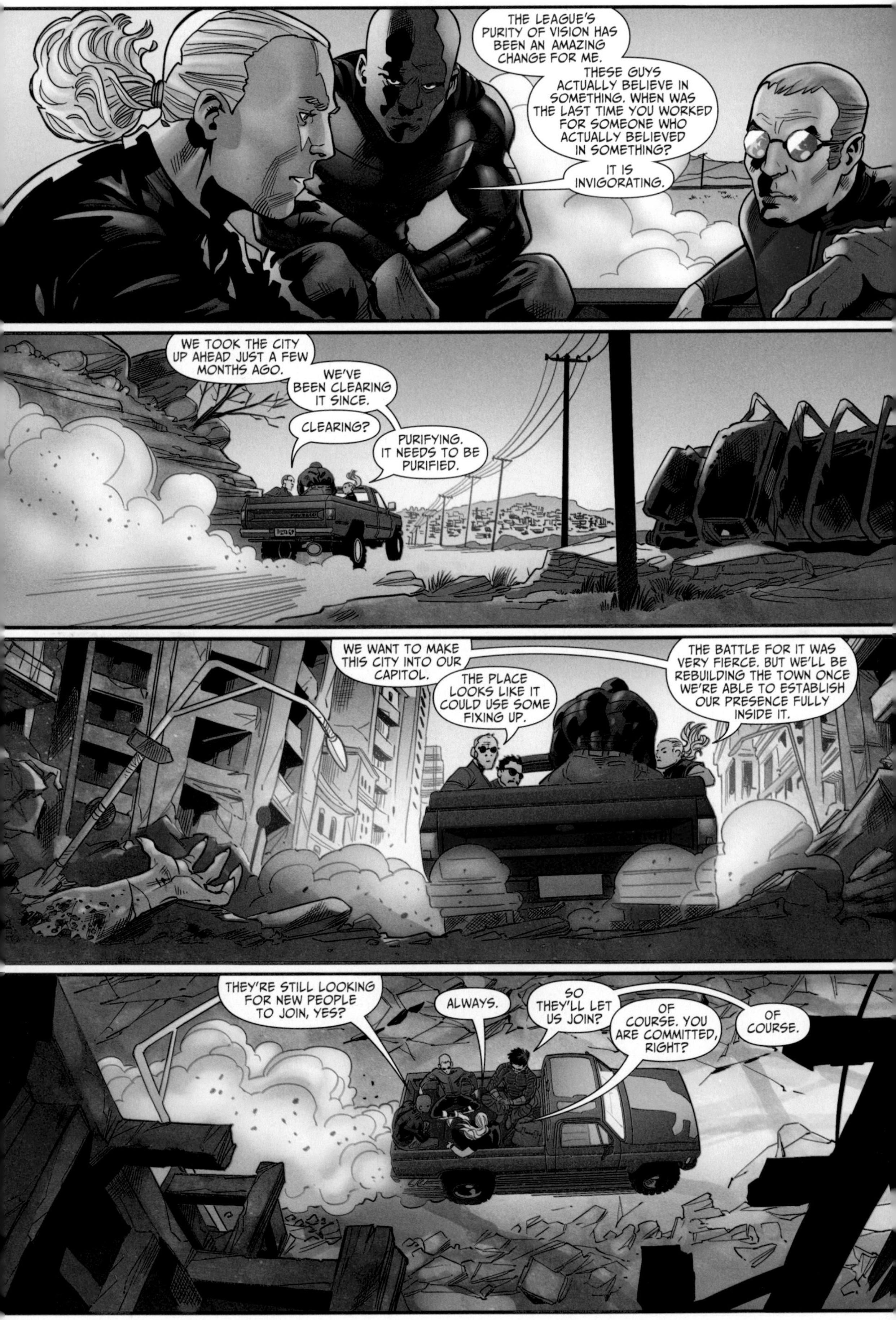

THE LEAGUE'S PURITY OF VISION HAS BEEN AN AMAZING CHANGE FOR ME.
THESE GUYS ACTUALLY BELIEVE IN SOMETHING. WHEN WAS THE LAST TIME YOU WORKED FOR SOMEONE WHO ACTUALLY BELIEVED IN SOMETHING?
IT IS INVIGORATING.
WE TOOK THE CITY UP AHEAD JUST A FEW MONTHS AGO.
WE'VE BEEN CLEARING IT SINCE.
CLEARING?
PURIFYING. IT NEEDS TO BE PURIFIED.
WE WANT TO MAKE THIS CITY INTO OUR CAPITOL.
THE PLACE LOOKS LIKE IT COULD USE SOME FIXING UP.
THE BATTLE FOR IT WAS VERY FIERCE. BUT WE'LL BE REBUILDING THE TOWN ONCE WE'RE ABLE TO ESTABLISH OUR PRESENCE FULLY INSIDE IT.
THEY'RE STILL LOOKING FOR NEW PEOPLE TO JOIN, YES?
ALWAYS.
SO THEY'LL LET US JOIN?
OF COURSE. YOU ARE COMMITTED, RIGHT?
OF COURSE.

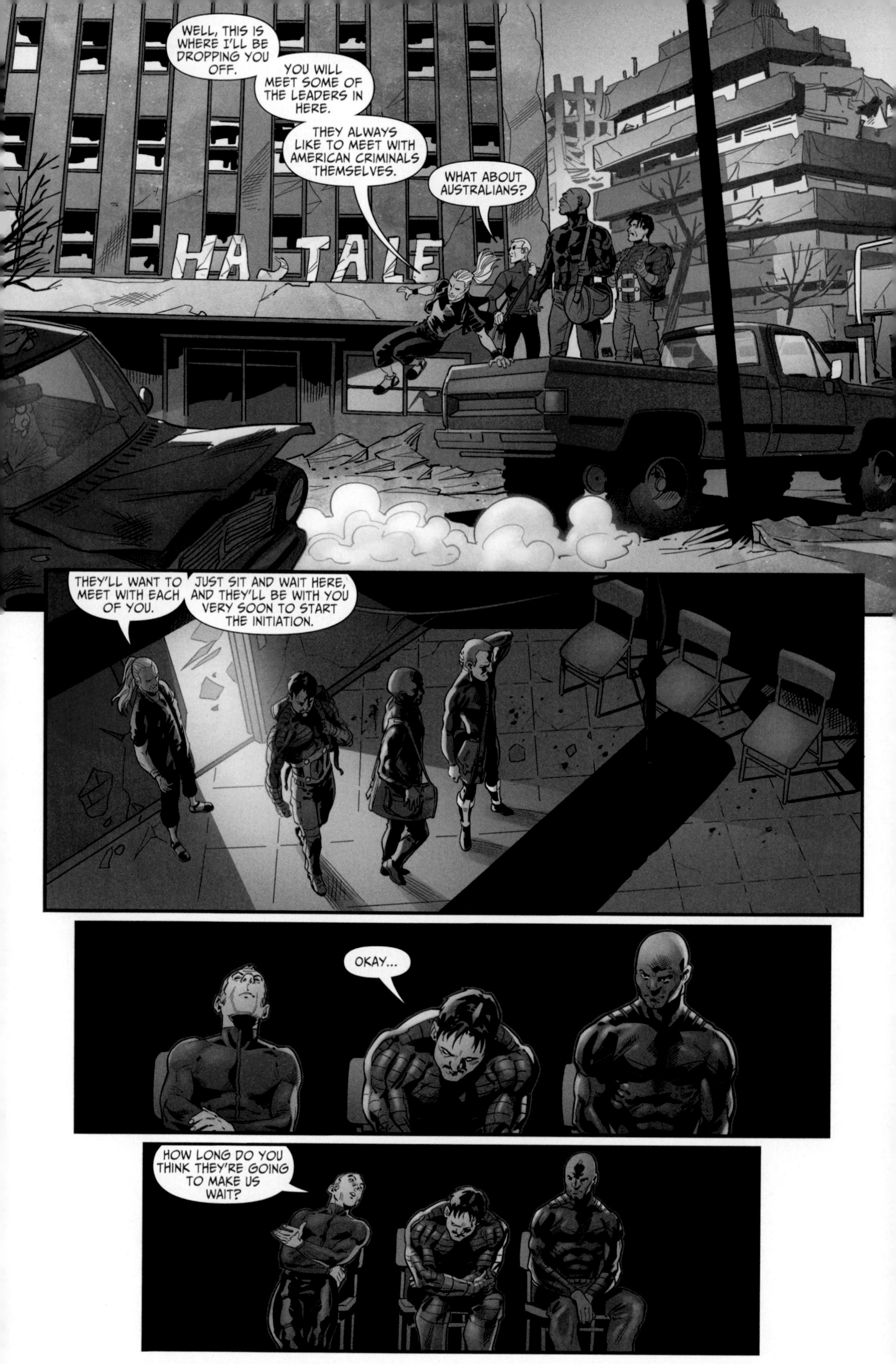
WELL, THIS IS WHERE I'LL BE DROPPING YOU OFF.
YOU WILL MEET SOME OF THE LEADERS IN HERE.
THEY ALWAYS LIKE TO MEET WITH AMERICAN CRIMINALS THEMSELVES.
WHAT ABOUT AUSTRALIANS?
HA TALE
THEY'LL WANT TO MEET WITH EACH OF YOU.
JUST SIT AND WAIT HERE, AND THEY'LL BE WITH YOU VERY SOON TO START THE INITIATION.
OKAY...
HOW LONG DO YOU THINK THEY'RE GOING TO MAKE US WAIT?

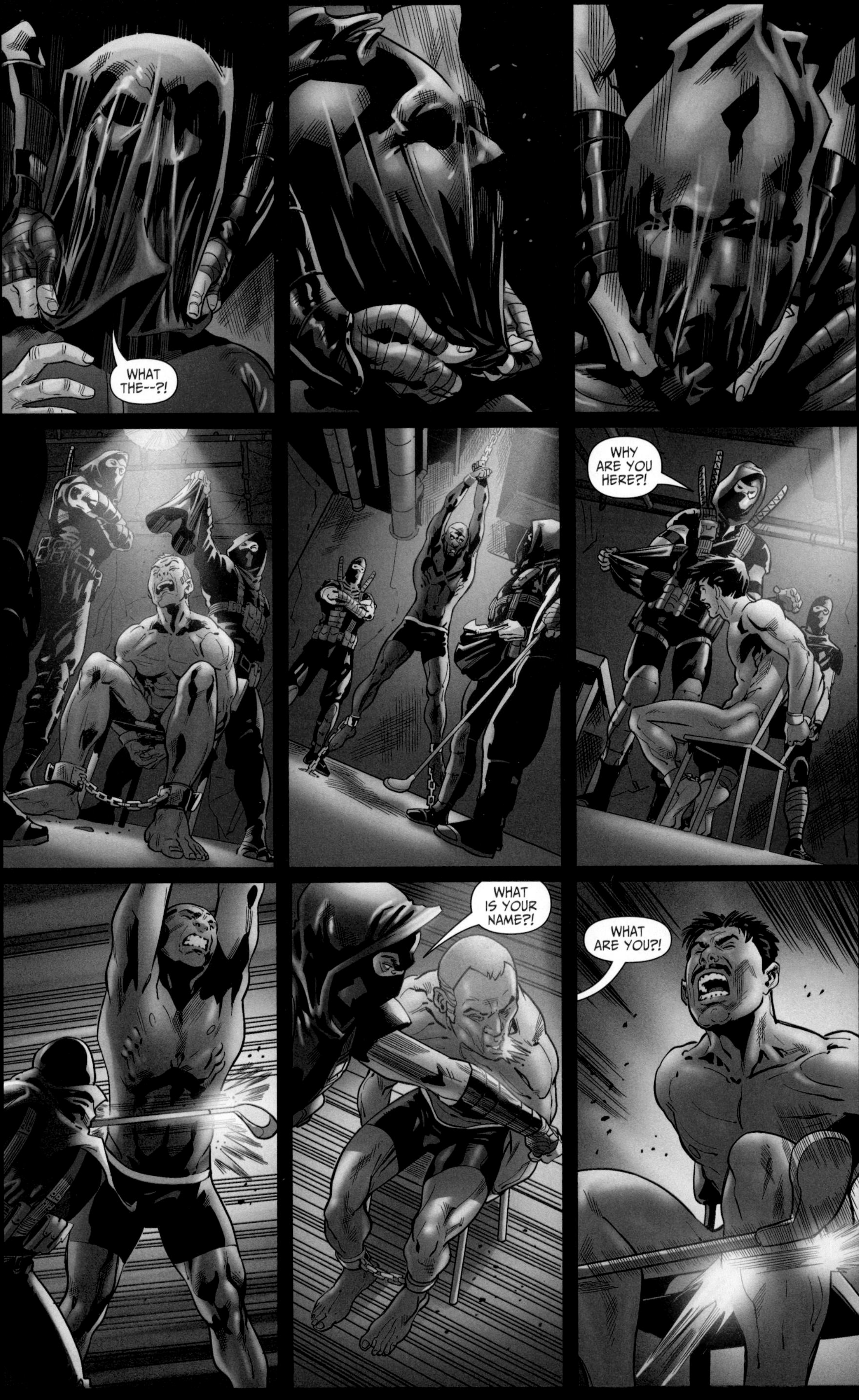
WHAT THE--?!
WHY ARE YOU HERE?!
WHAT IS YOUR NAME?!
WHAT ARE YOU?!

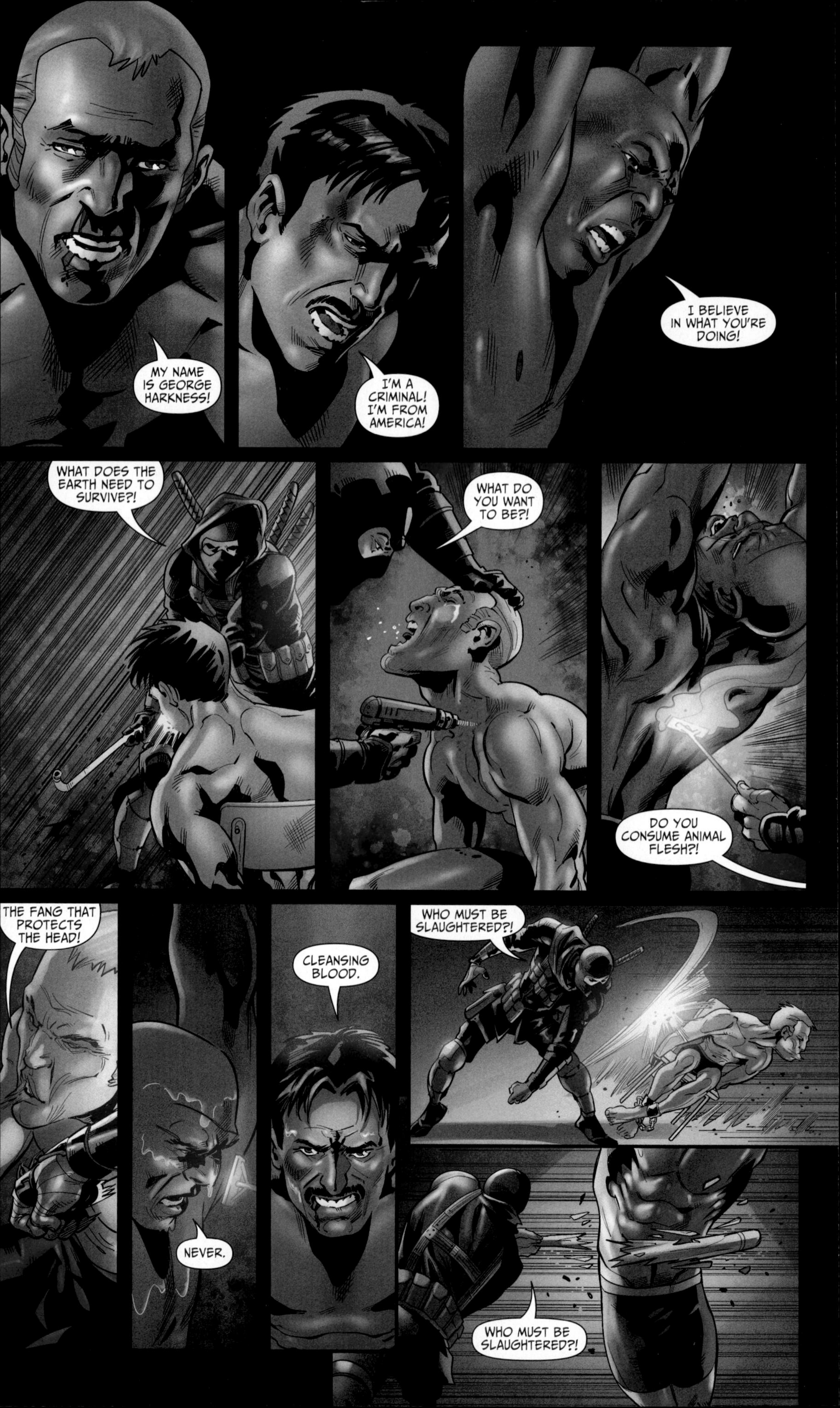
MY NAME IS GEORGE HARKNESS!
I'M A CRIMINAL! I'M FROM AMERICA!
I BELIEVE IN WHAT YOU'RE DOING!
WHAT DOES THE EARTH NEED TO SURVIVE?!
WHAT DO YOU WANT TO BE?!
DO YOU CONSUME ANIMAL FLESH?!
THE FANG THAT PROTECTS THE HEAD!
NEVER.
CLEANSING BLOOD.
WHO MUST BE SLAUGHTERED?!
WHO MUST BE SLAUGHTERED?!

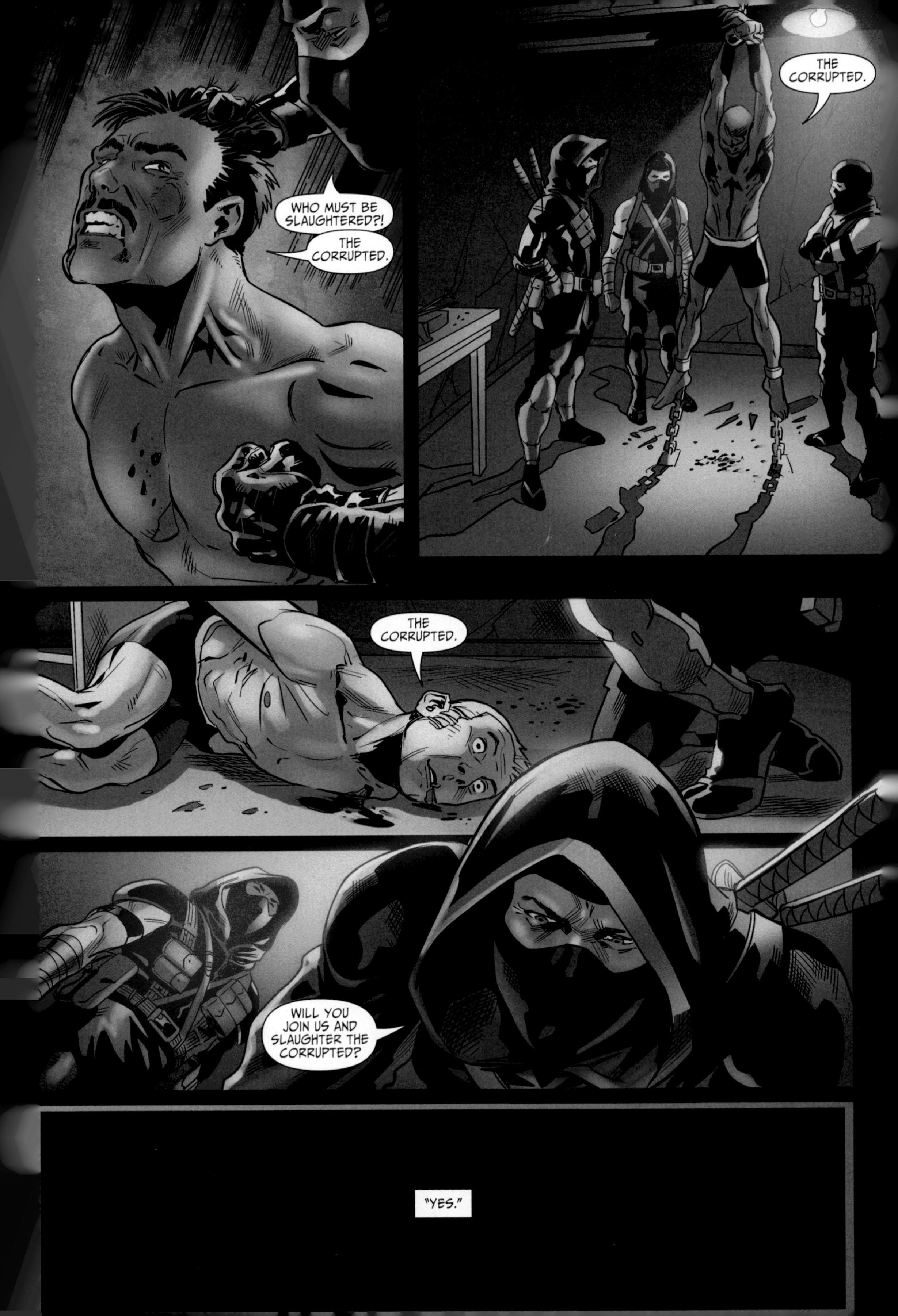
WHO MUST BE SLAUGHTERED?!
THE CORRUPTED.
THE CORRUPTED.
THE CORRUPTED.
WILL YOU JOIN US AND SLAUGHTER THE CORRUPTED?
"YES."

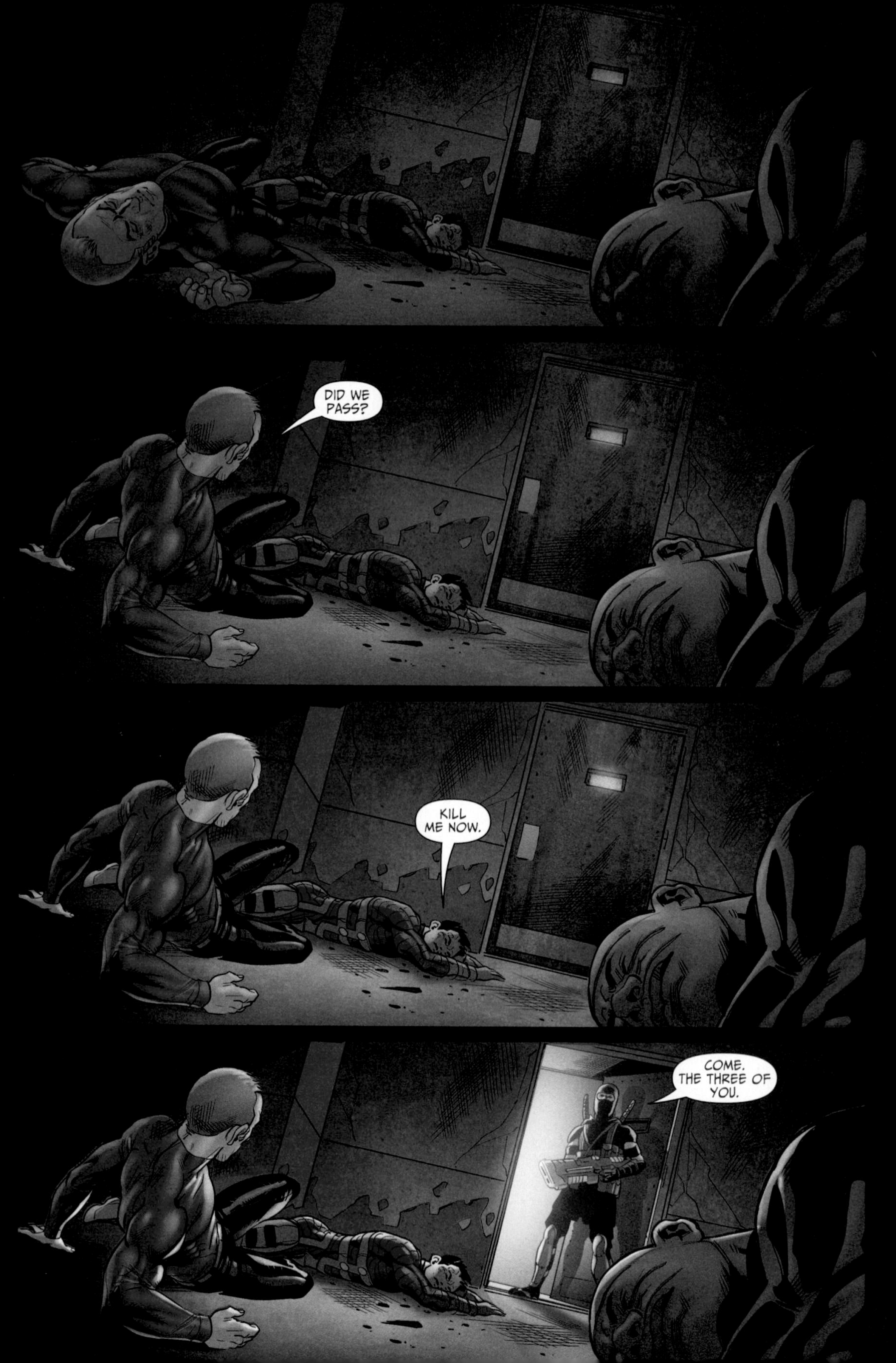
DID WE PASS?
KILL ME NOW.
COME. THE THREE OF YOU.

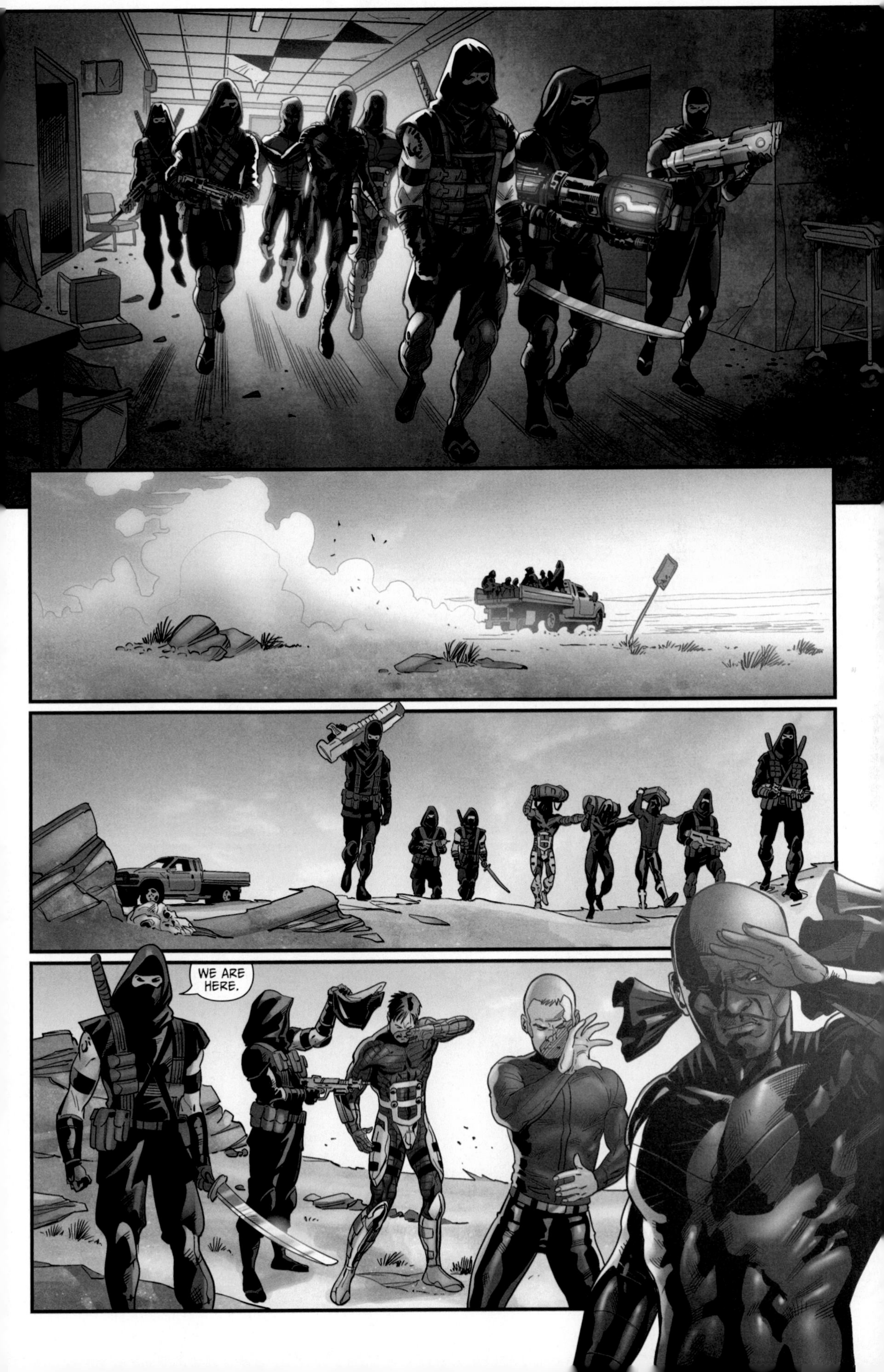
WE ARE HERE.

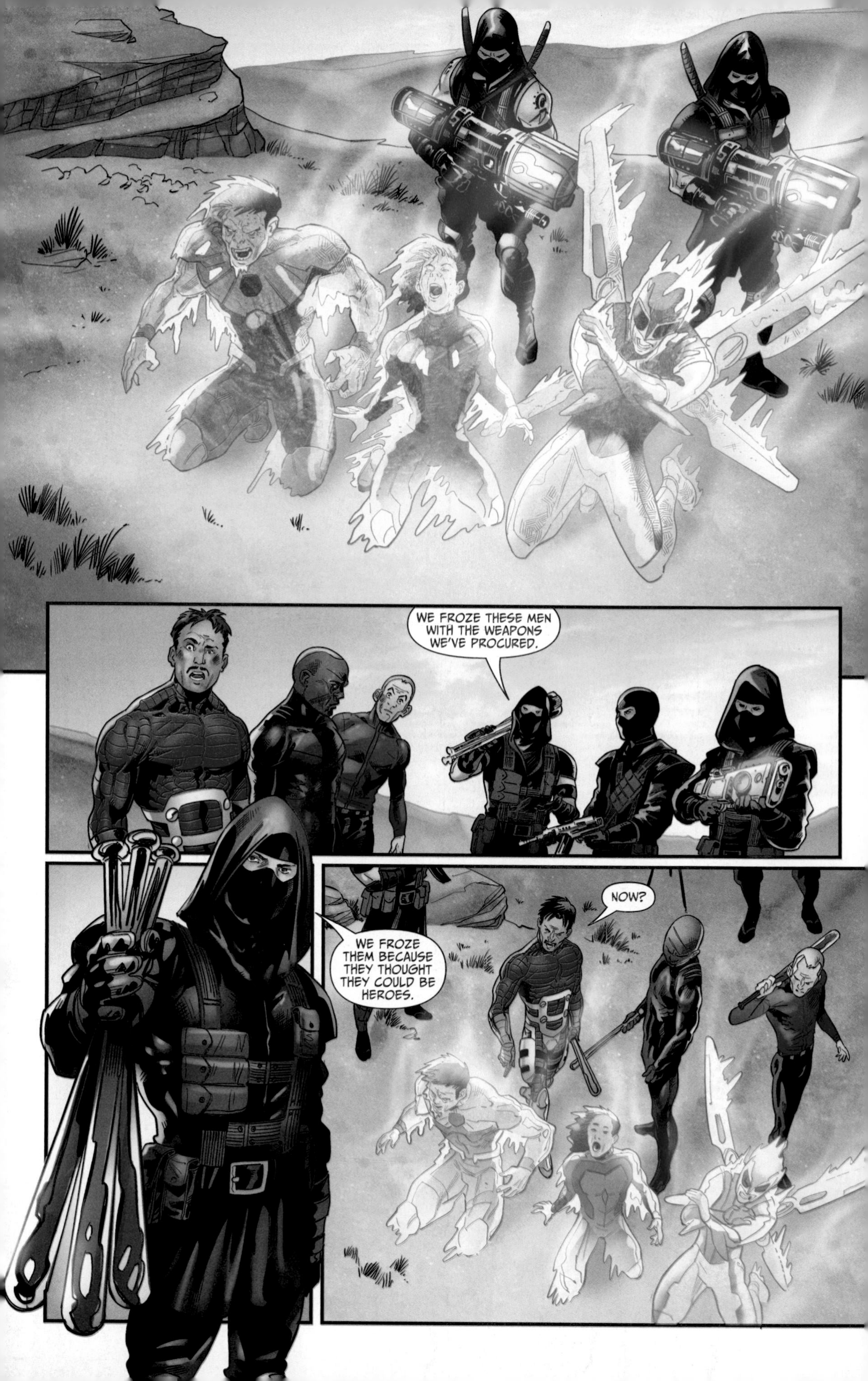
WE FROZE THESE MEN WITH THE WEAPONS WE'VE PROCURED.
WE FROZE THEM BECAUSE THEY THOUGHT THEY COULD BE HEROES.
NOW?

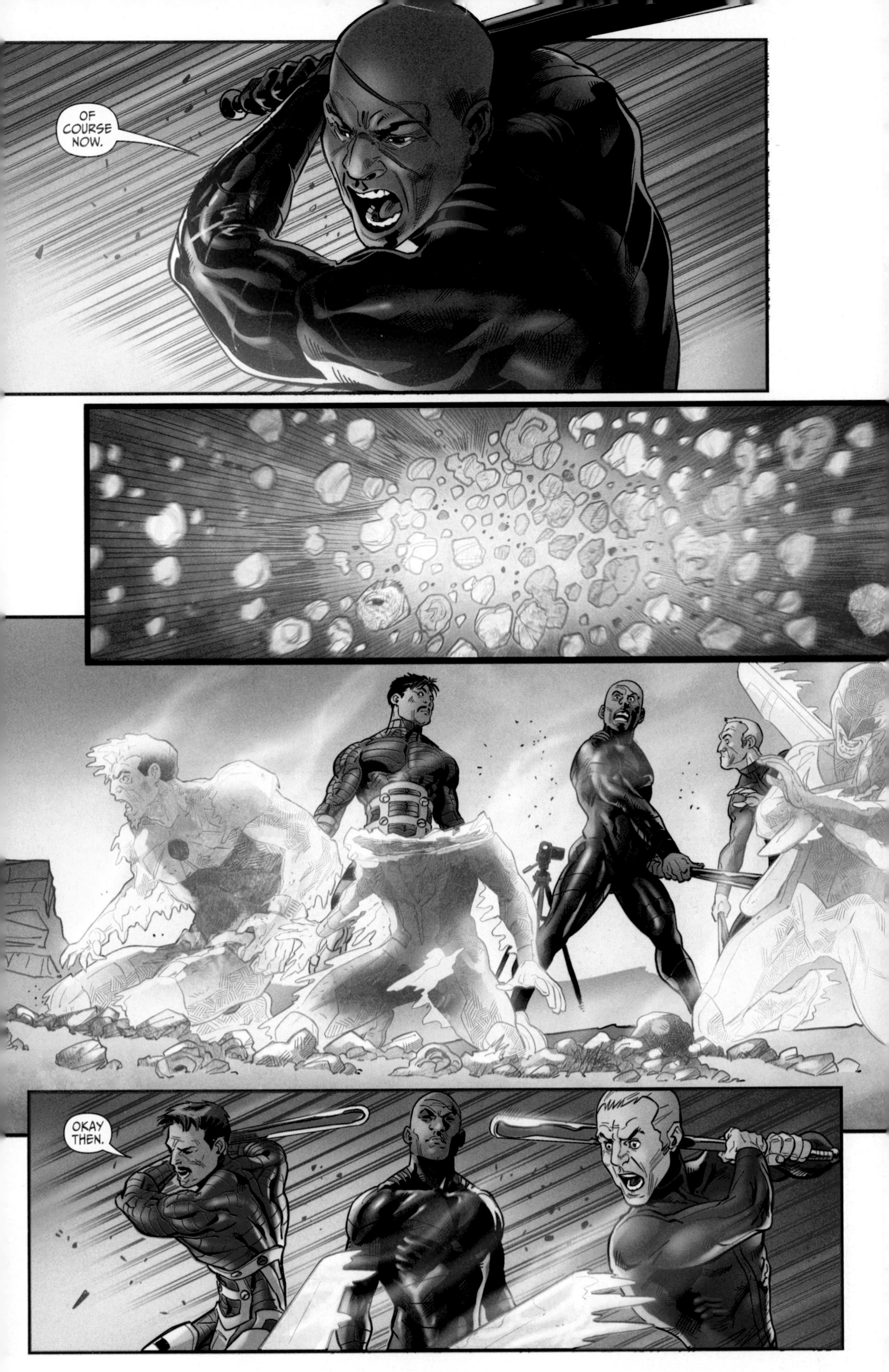
OF COURSE NOW.
OKAY THEN.

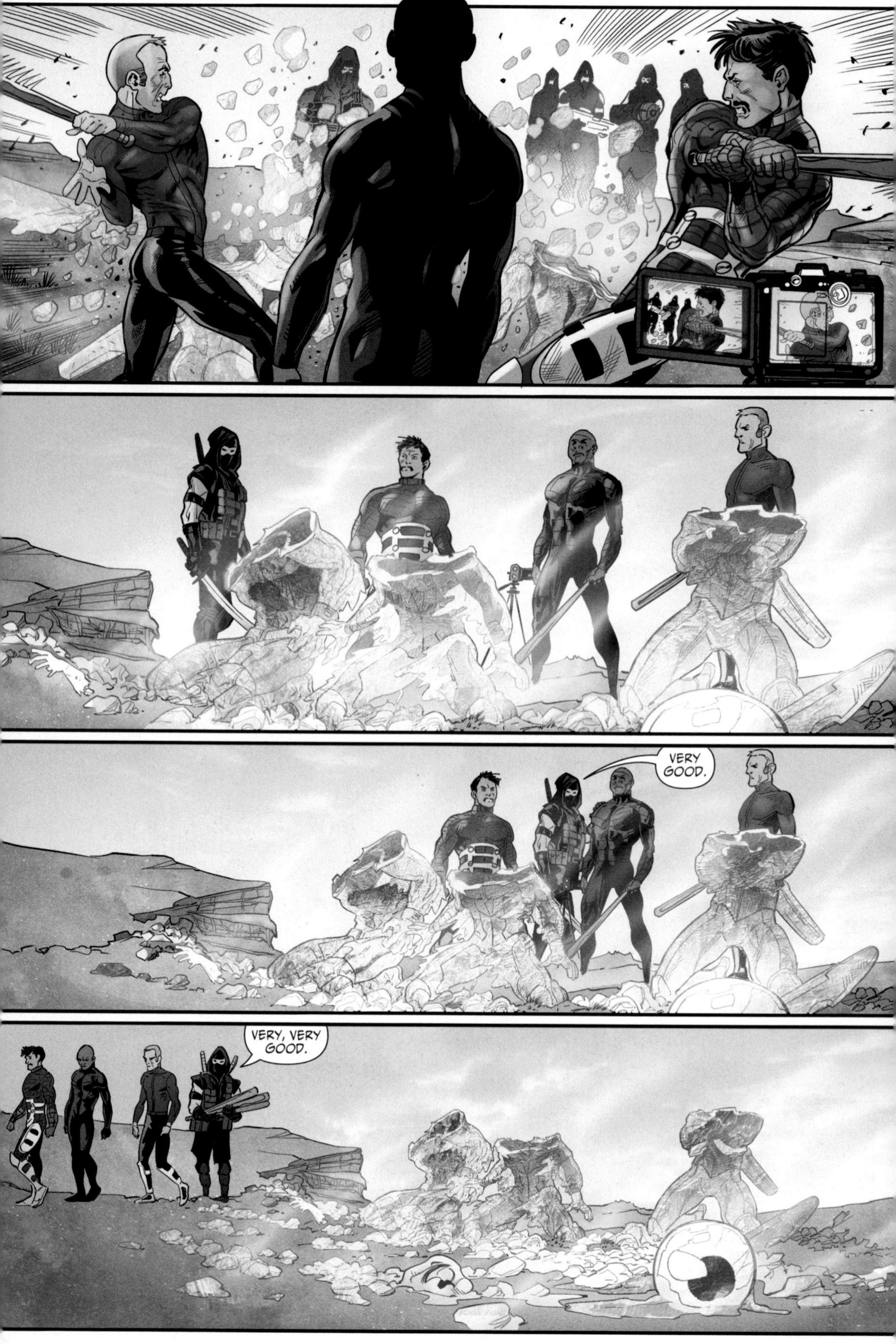
VERY GOOD.
VERY, VERY GOOD.

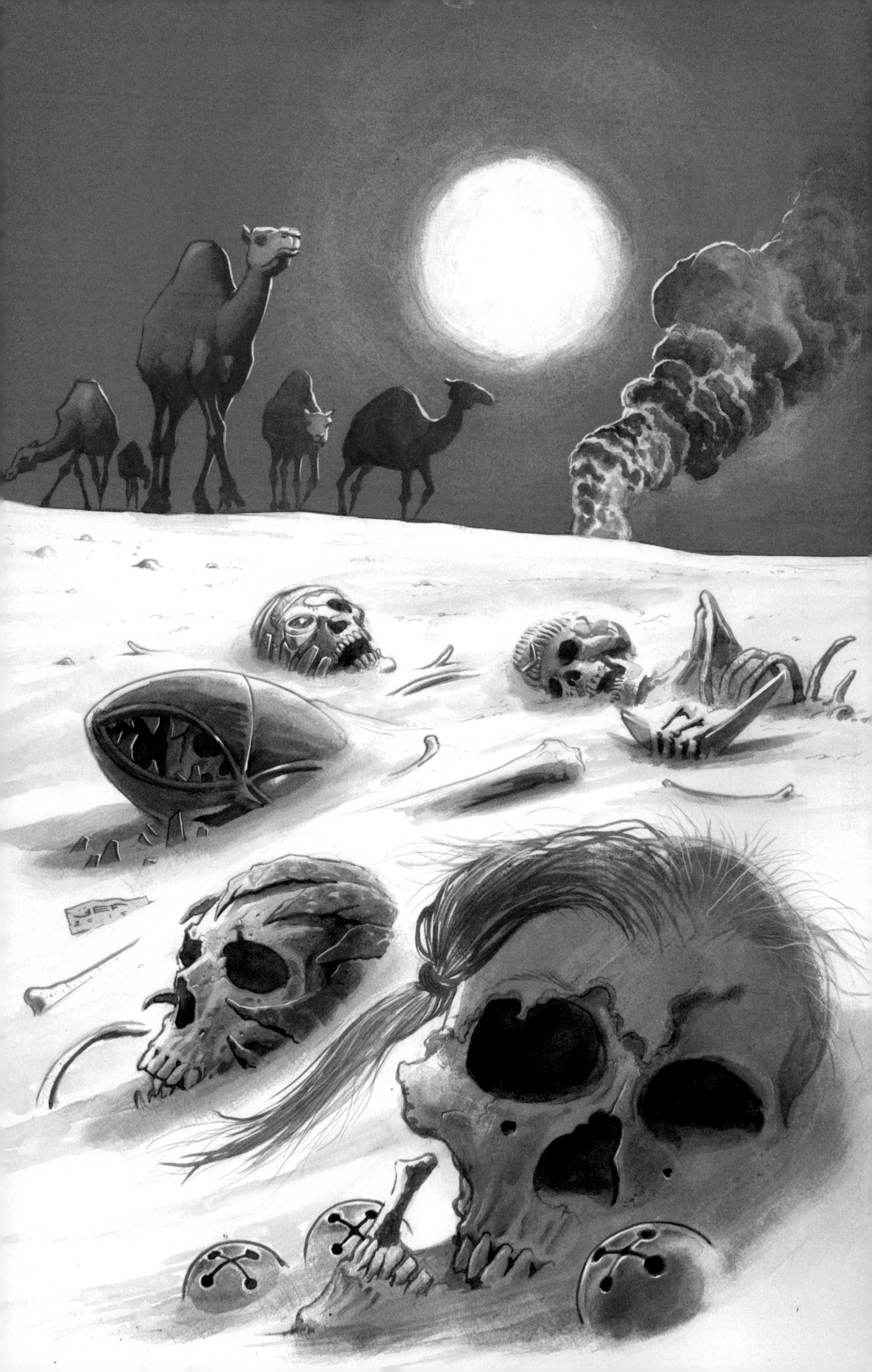

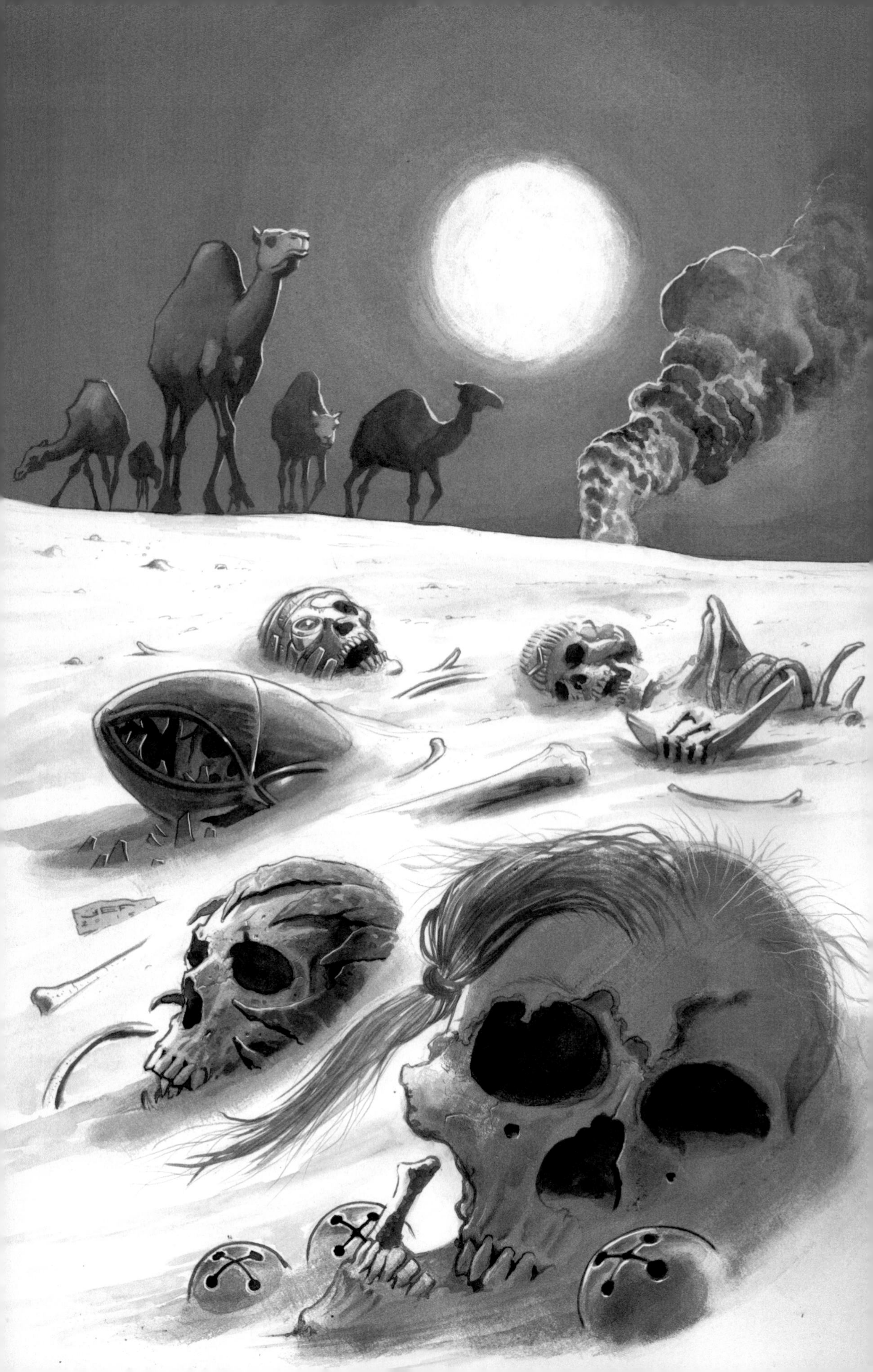

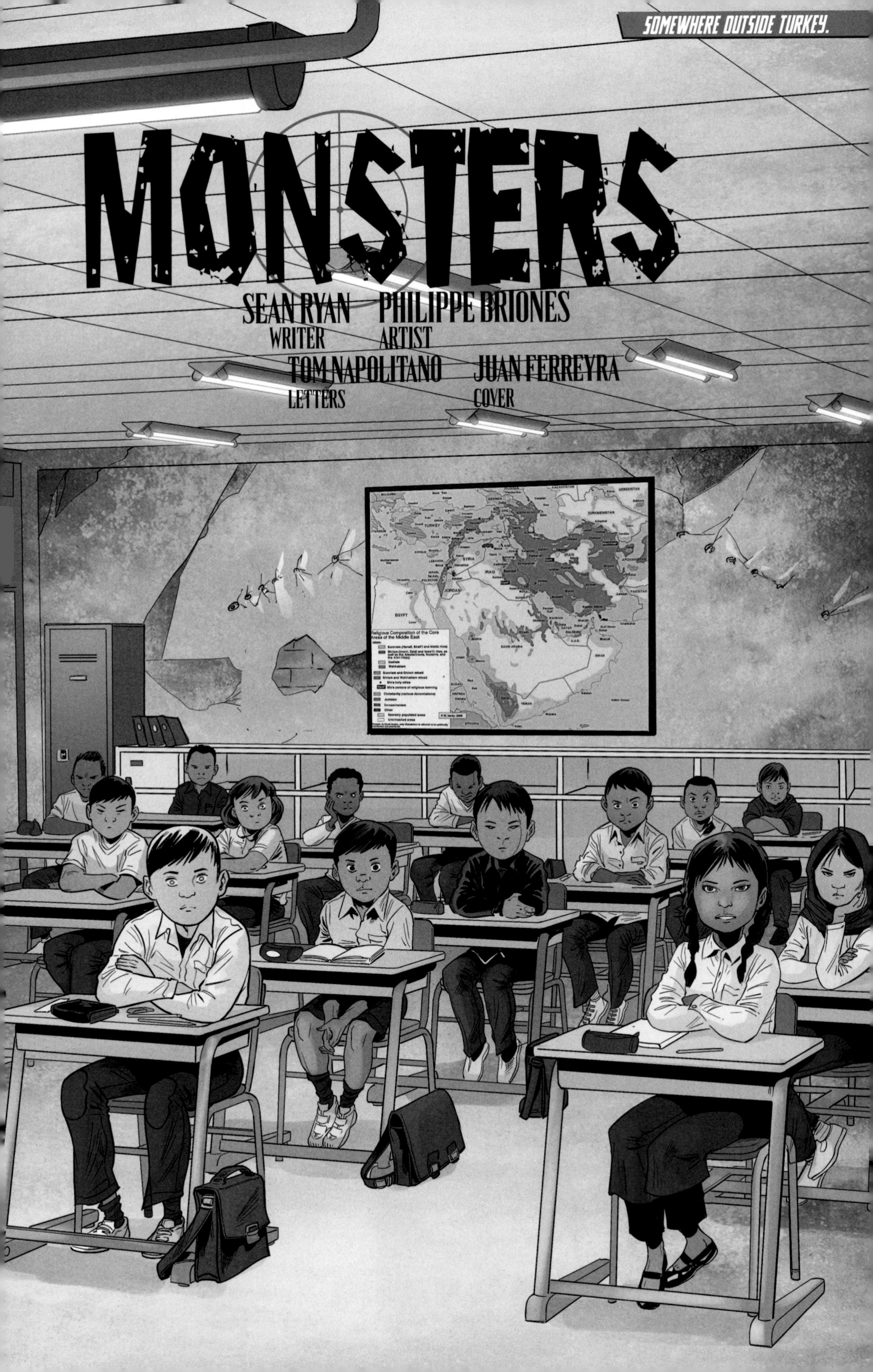
SOMEWHERE OUTSIDE TURKEY.
MONSTERS
SEAN RYAN
WRITER
PHILIPPE BRIONES
ARTIST
TOM NAPOLITANO
LETTERS
JUAN FERREYRA
COVER

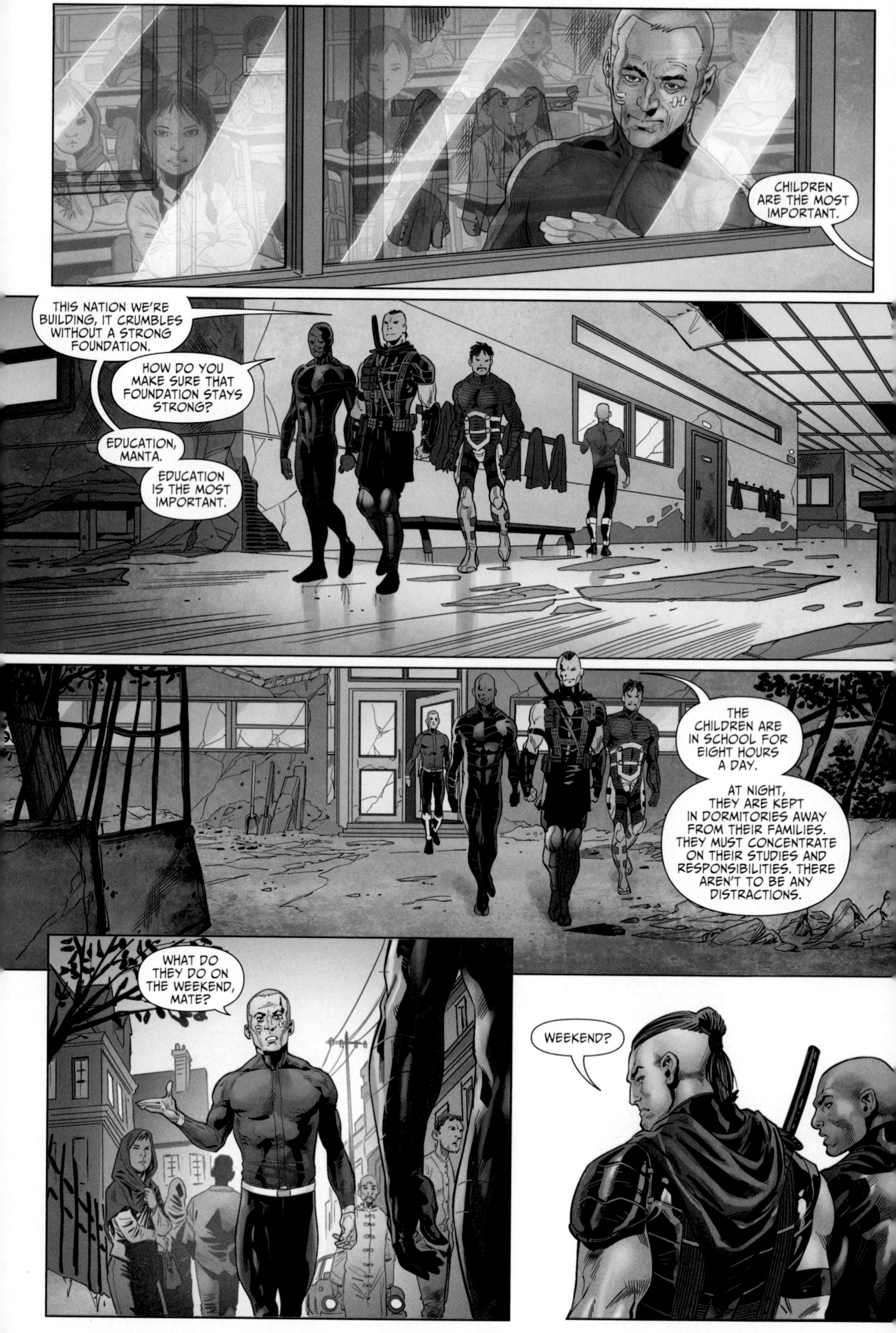
CHILDREN ARE THE MOST IMPORTANT.
THIS NATION WE'RE BUILDING, IT CRUMBLES WITHOUT A STRONG FOUNDATION.
HOW DO YOU MAKE SURE THAT FOUNDATION STAYS STRONG?
EDUCATION, MANTA.
EDUCATION IS THE MOST IMPORTANT.
THE CHILDREN ARE IN SCHOOL FOR EIGHT HOURS A DAY.
AT NIGHT, THEY ARE KEPT IN DORMITORIES AWAY FROM THEIR FAMILIES. THEY MUST CONCENTRATE ON THEIR STUDIES AND RESPONSIBILITIES. THERE AREN'T TO BE ANY DISTRACTIONS.
WHAT DO THEY DO ON THE WEEKEND, MATE?
WEEKEND?

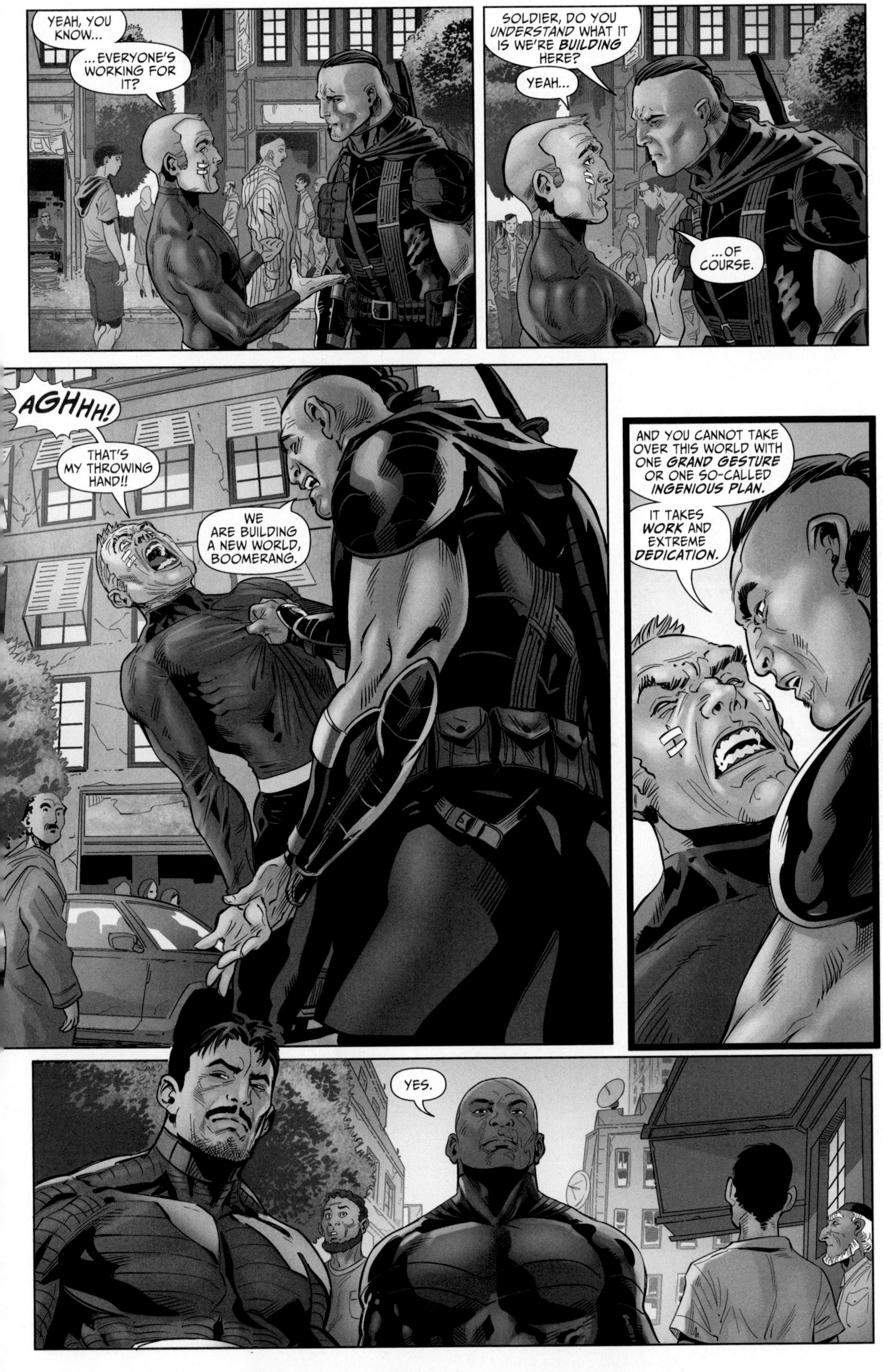
YEAH, YOU KNOW...
...EVERYONE'S WORKING FOR IT?
SOLDIER, DO YOU UNDERSTAND WHAT IT IS WE'RE BUILDING HERE?
YEAH...
...OF COURSE.
AGHHH!
THAT'S MY THROWING HAND!!
WE ARE BUILDING A NEW WORLD, BOOMERANG.
AND YOU CANNOT TAKE OVER THIS WORLD WITH ONE GRAND GESTURE OR ONE SO-CALLED INGENIOUS PLAN.
IT TAKES WORK AND EXTREME DEDICATION.
YES.

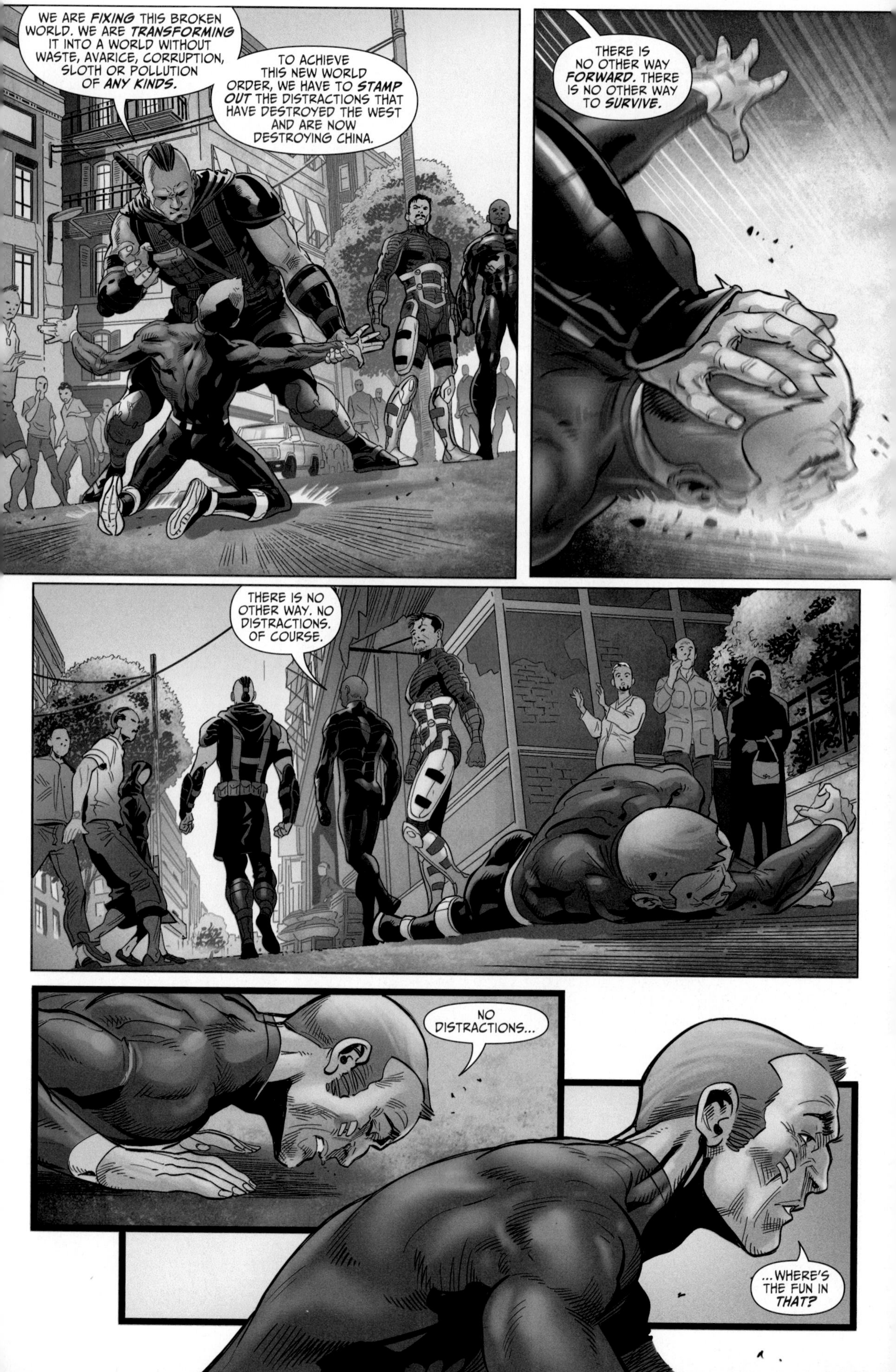

WE ARE FIXING THIS BROKEN WORLD. WE ARE TRANSFORMING IT INTO A WORLD WITHOUT WASTE, AVARICE, CORRUPTION, SLOTH OR POLLUTION OF ANY KINDS.
TO ACHIEVE THIS NEW WORLD ORDER, WE HAVE TO STAMP OUT THE DISTRACTIONS THAT HAVE DESTROYED THE WEST AND ARE NOW DESTROYING CHINA.
THERE IS NO OTHER WAY FORWARD. THERE IS NO OTHER WAY TO SURVIVE.
THERE IS NO OTHER WAY. NO DISTRACTIONS. OF COURSE.
NO DISTRACTIONS...
...WHERE'S THE FUN IN THAT?

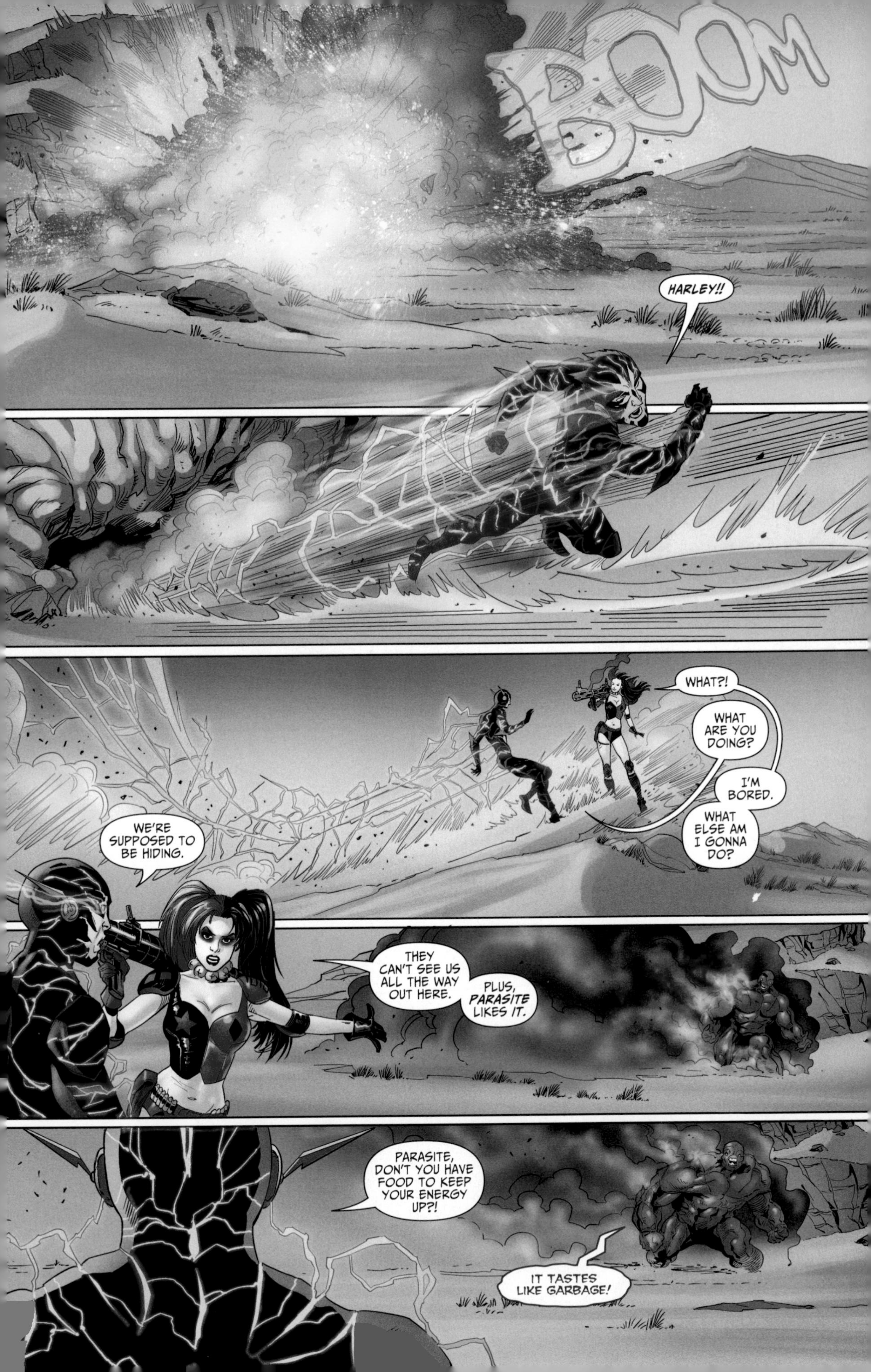
BOOM
HARLEY!!
WHAT?!
WHAT ARE YOU DOING?
I'M BORED.
WHAT ELSE AM I GONNA DO?
WE'RE SUPPOSED TO BE HIDING.
THEY CAN'T SEE US ALL THE WAY OUT HERE.
PLUS, PARASITE LIKES IT.
PARASITE, DON'T YOU HAVE FOOD TO KEEP YOUR ENERGY UP?!
IT TASTES LIKE GARBAGE!

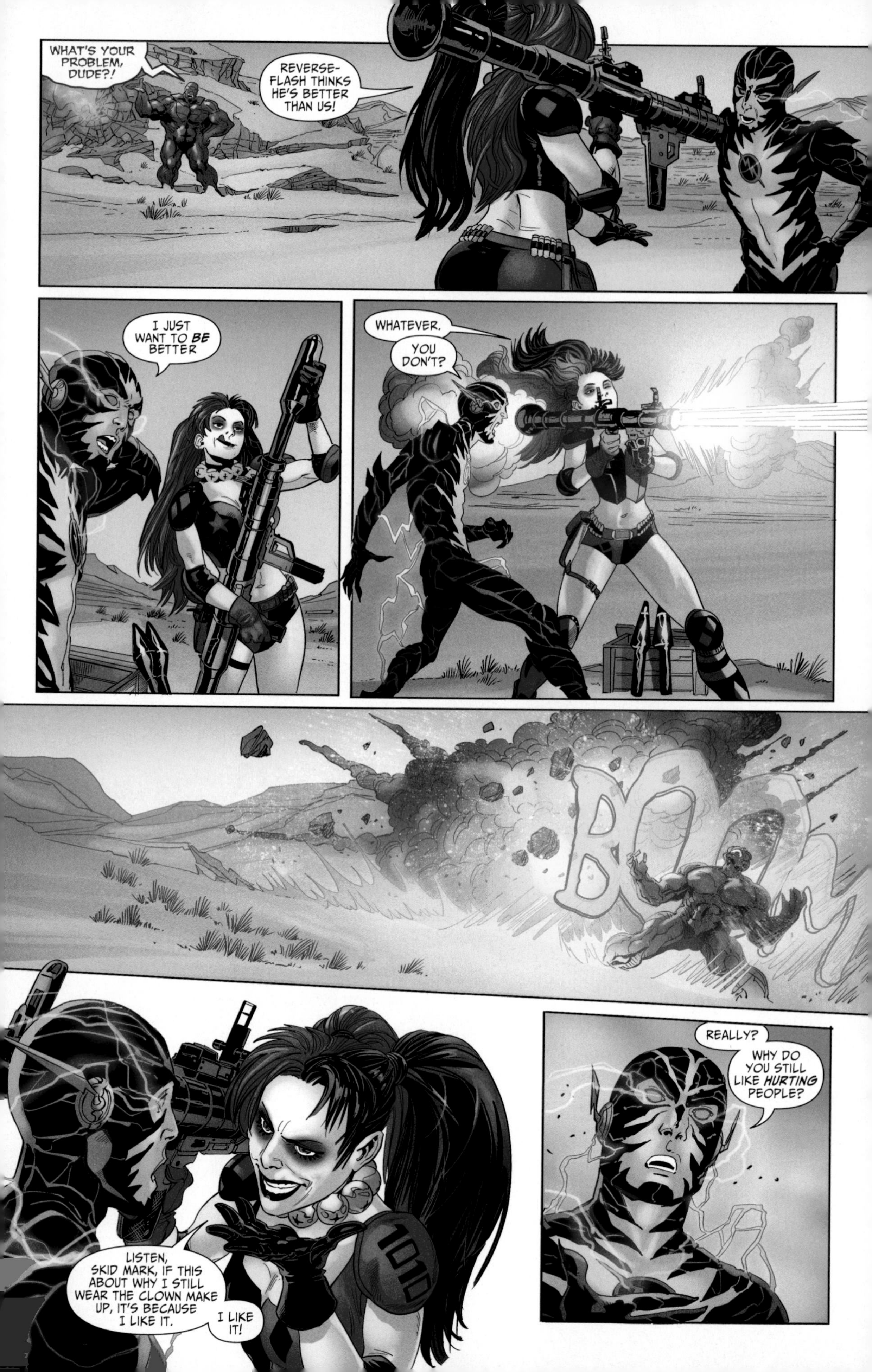
WHAT'S YOUR PROBLEM, DUDE?!
REVERSE-FLASH THINKS HE'S BETTER THAN US!
I JUST WANT TO **BE** BETTER
WHATEVER.
YOU DON'T?
LISTEN, SKID MARK, IF THIS ABOUT WHY I STILL WEAR THE CLOWN MAKE UP, IT'S BECAUSE I LIKE IT.
I LIKE IT!
REALLY?
WHY DO YOU STILL LIKE ***HURTING*** PEOPLE?

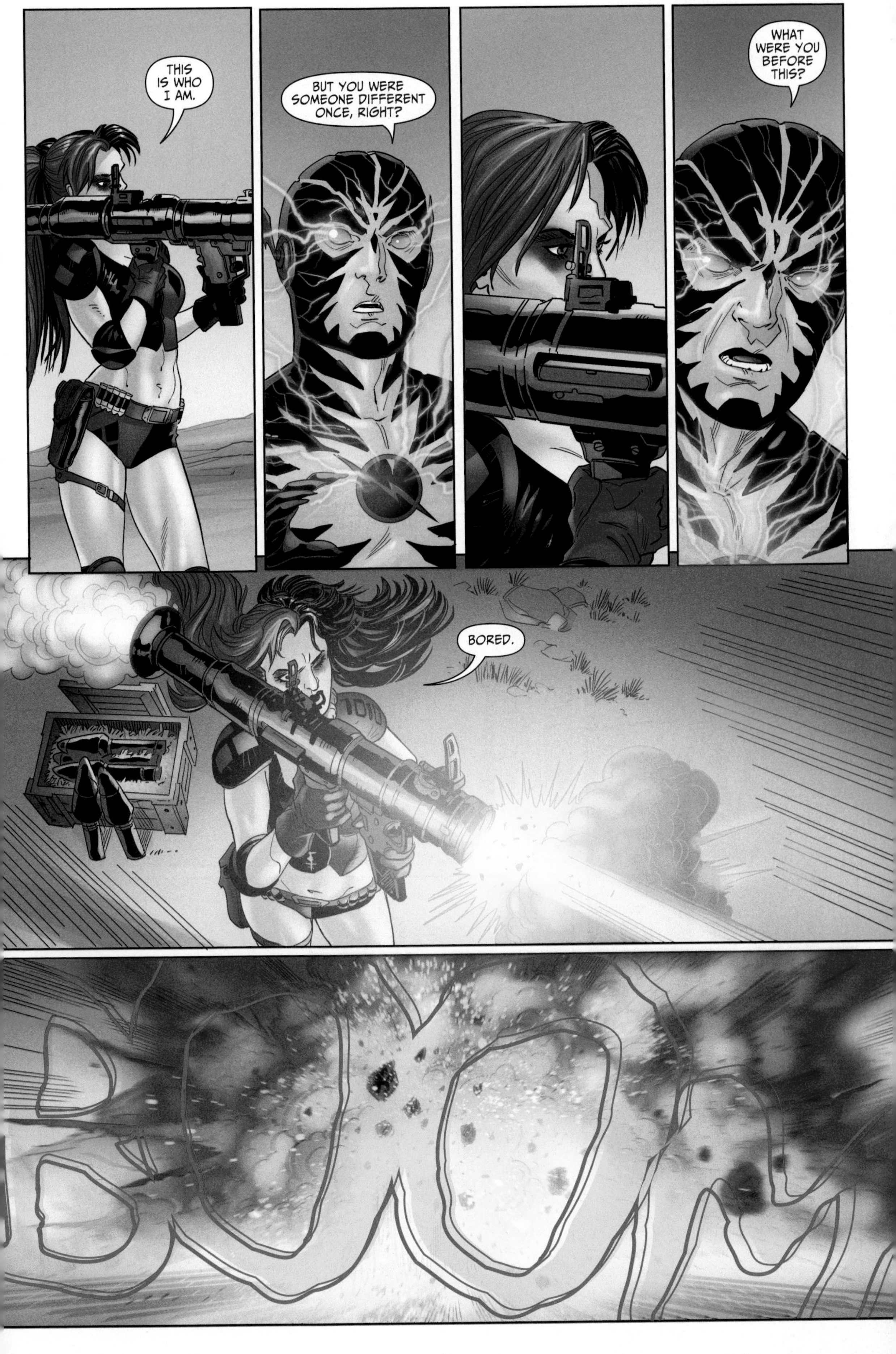
THIS IS WHO I AM.
BUT YOU WERE SOMEONE DIFFERENT ONCE, RIGHT?
WHAT WERE YOU BEFORE THIS?
BORED.
BOOM

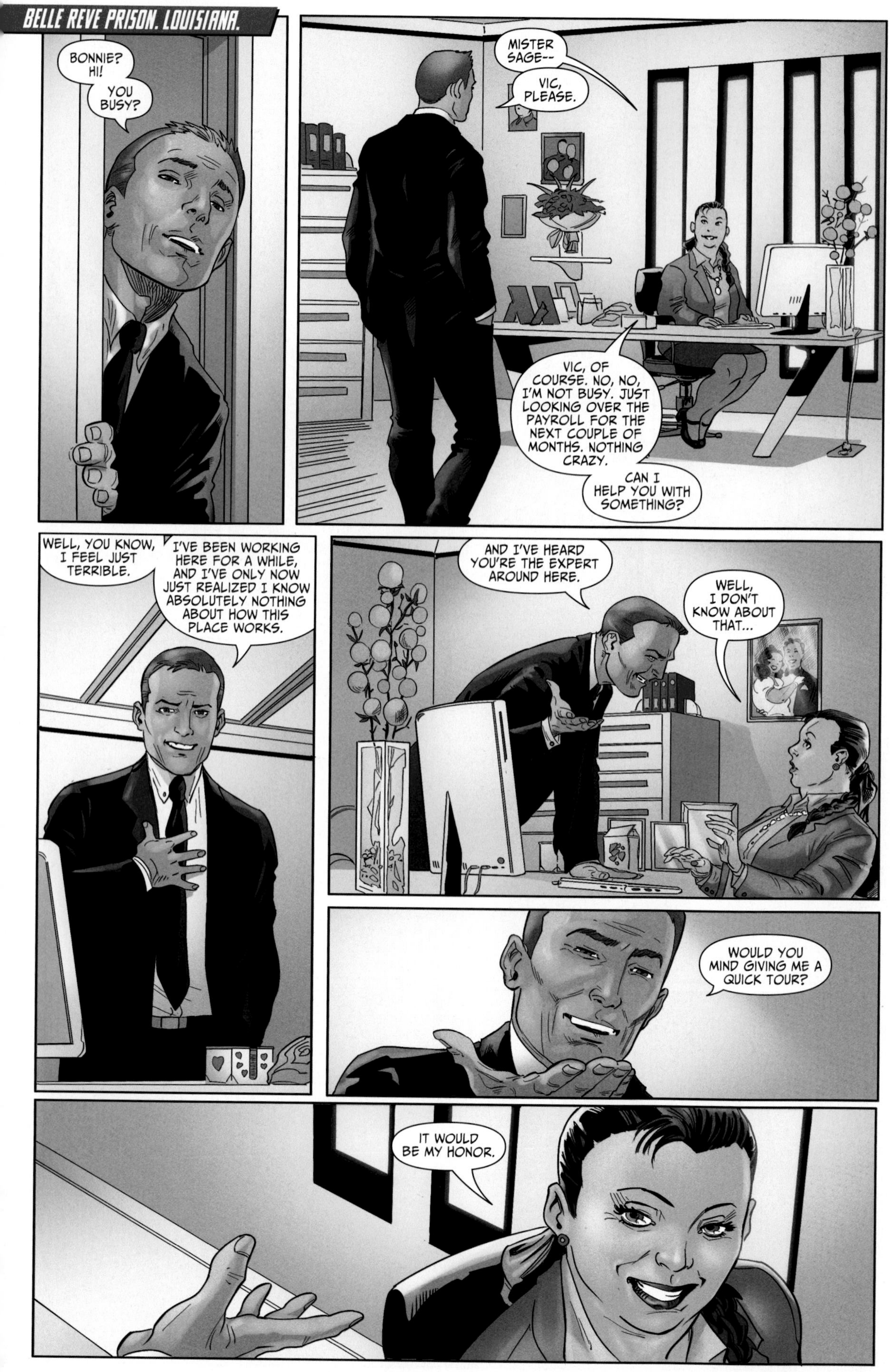
BELLE REVE PRISON. LOUISIANA.
BONNIE? HI!
YOU BUSY?
MISTER SAGE--
VIC, PLEASE.
VIC, OF COURSE. NO, NO, I'M NOT BUSY. JUST LOOKING OVER THE PAYROLL FOR THE NEXT COUPLE OF MONTHS. NOTHING CRAZY.
CAN I HELP YOU WITH SOMETHING?
WELL, YOU KNOW, I FEEL JUST TERRIBLE.
I'VE BEEN WORKING HERE FOR A WHILE, AND I'VE ONLY NOW JUST REALIZED I KNOW ABSOLUTELY NOTHING ABOUT HOW THIS PLACE WORKS.
AND I'VE HEARD YOU'RE THE EXPERT AROUND HERE.
WELL, I DON'T KNOW ABOUT THAT...
WOULD YOU MIND GIVING ME A QUICK TOUR?
IT WOULD BE MY HONOR.

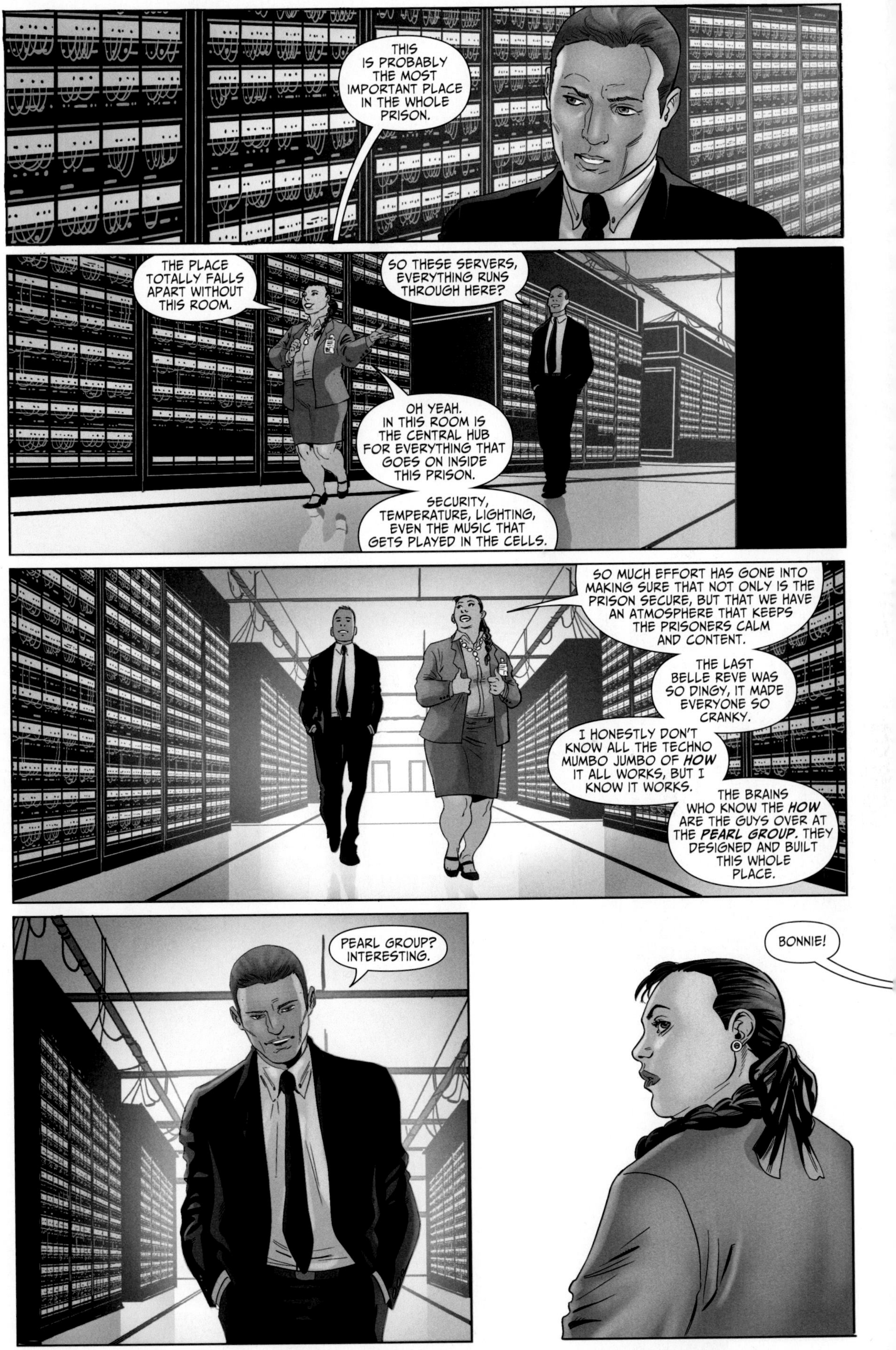
THIS IS PROBABLY THE MOST IMPORTANT PLACE IN THE WHOLE PRISON.
THE PLACE TOTALLY FALLS APART WITHOUT THIS ROOM.
SO THESE SERVERS, EVERYTHING RUNS THROUGH HERE?
OH YEAH. IN THIS ROOM IS THE CENTRAL HUB FOR EVERYTHING THAT GOES ON INSIDE THIS PRISON.
SECURITY, TEMPERATURE, LIGHTING, EVEN THE MUSIC THAT GETS PLAYED IN THE CELLS.
SO MUCH EFFORT HAS GONE INTO MAKING SURE THAT NOT ONLY IS THE PRISON SECURE, BUT THAT WE HAVE AN ATMOSPHERE THAT KEEPS THE PRISONERS CALM AND CONTENT.
THE LAST BELLE REVE WAS SO DINGY, IT MADE EVERYONE SO CRANKY.
I HONESTLY DON'T KNOW ALL THE TECHNO MUMBO JUMBO OF *HOW* IT ALL WORKS, BUT I KNOW IT WORKS.
THE BRAINS WHO KNOW THE *HOW* ARE THE GUYS OVER AT THE *PEARL GROUP.* THEY DESIGNED AND BUILT THIS WHOLE PLACE.
PEARL GROUP? INTERESTING.
BONNIE!

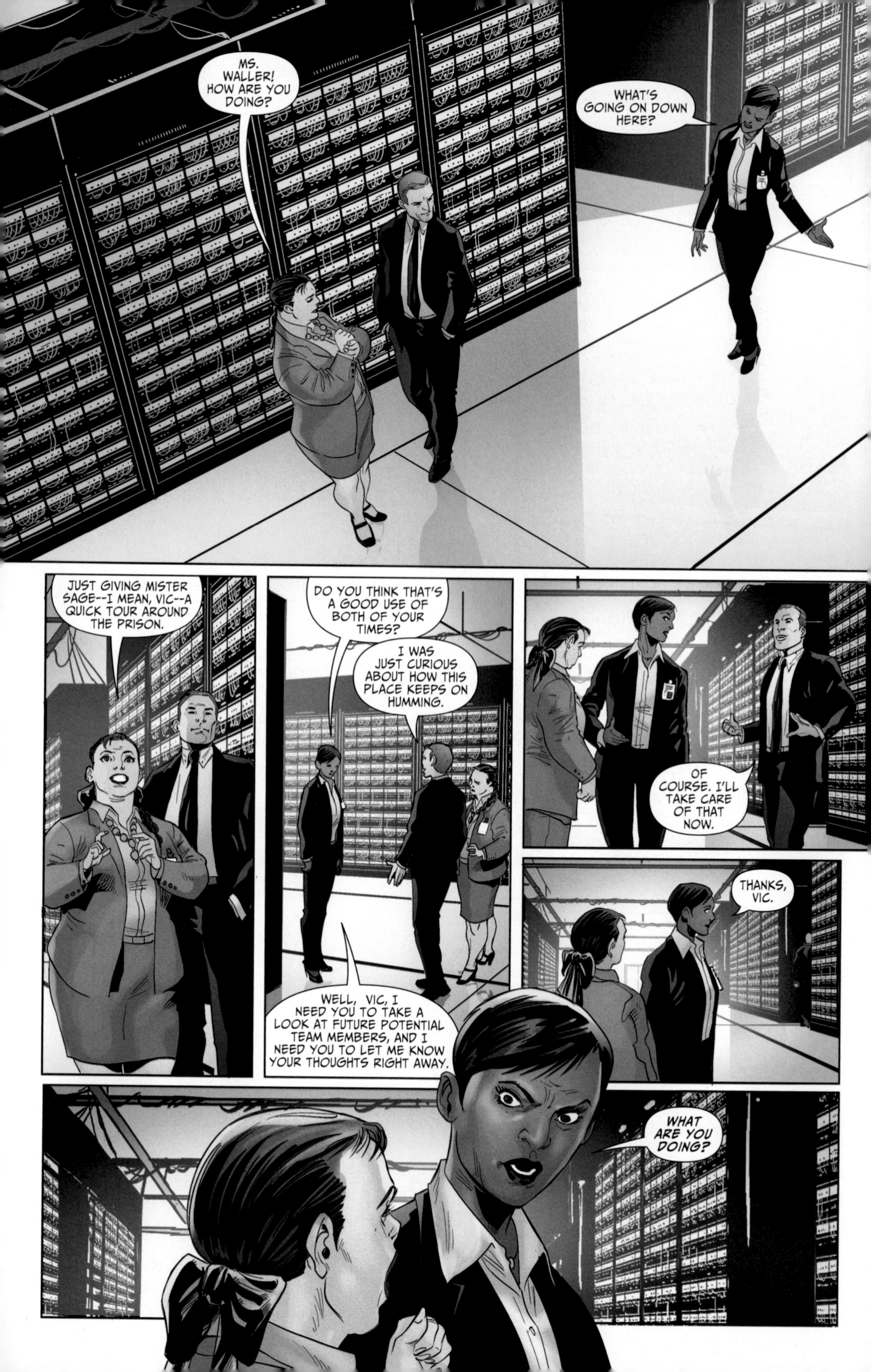
MS. WALLER! HOW ARE YOU DOING?
WHAT'S GOING ON DOWN HERE?
JUST GIVING MISTER SAGE--I MEAN, VIC--A QUICK TOUR AROUND THE PRISON.
DO YOU THINK THAT'S A GOOD USE OF BOTH OF YOUR TIMES?
I WAS JUST CURIOUS ABOUT HOW THIS PLACE KEEPS ON HUMMING.
WELL, VIC, I NEED YOU TO TAKE A LOOK AT FUTURE POTENTIAL TEAM MEMBERS, AND I NEED YOU TO LET ME KNOW YOUR THOUGHTS RIGHT AWAY.
OF COURSE. I'LL TAKE CARE OF THAT NOW.
THANKS, VIC.
WHAT ARE YOU DOING?

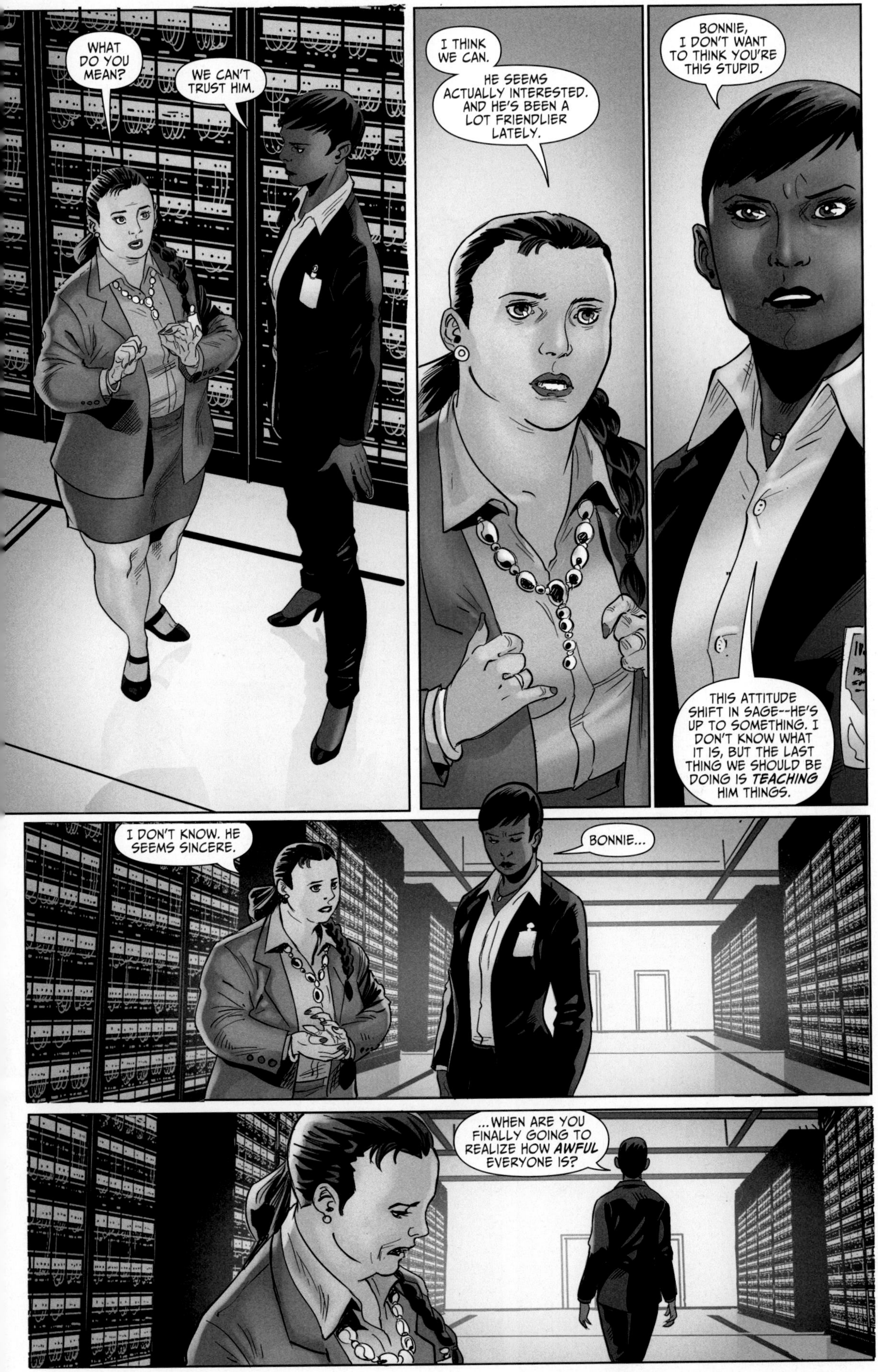
WHAT DO YOU MEAN?
WE CAN'T TRUST HIM.
I THINK WE CAN.
HE SEEMS ACTUALLY INTERESTED. AND HE'S BEEN A LOT FRIENDLIER LATELY.
BONNIE, I DON'T WANT TO THINK YOU'RE THIS STUPID.
THIS ATTITUDE SHIFT IN SAGE--HE'S UP TO SOMETHING. I DON'T KNOW WHAT IT IS, BUT THE LAST THING WE SHOULD BE DOING IS TEACHING HIM THINGS.
I DON'T KNOW. HE SEEMS SINCERE.
BONNIE...
...WHEN ARE YOU FINALLY GOING TO REALIZE HOW AWFUL EVERYONE IS?

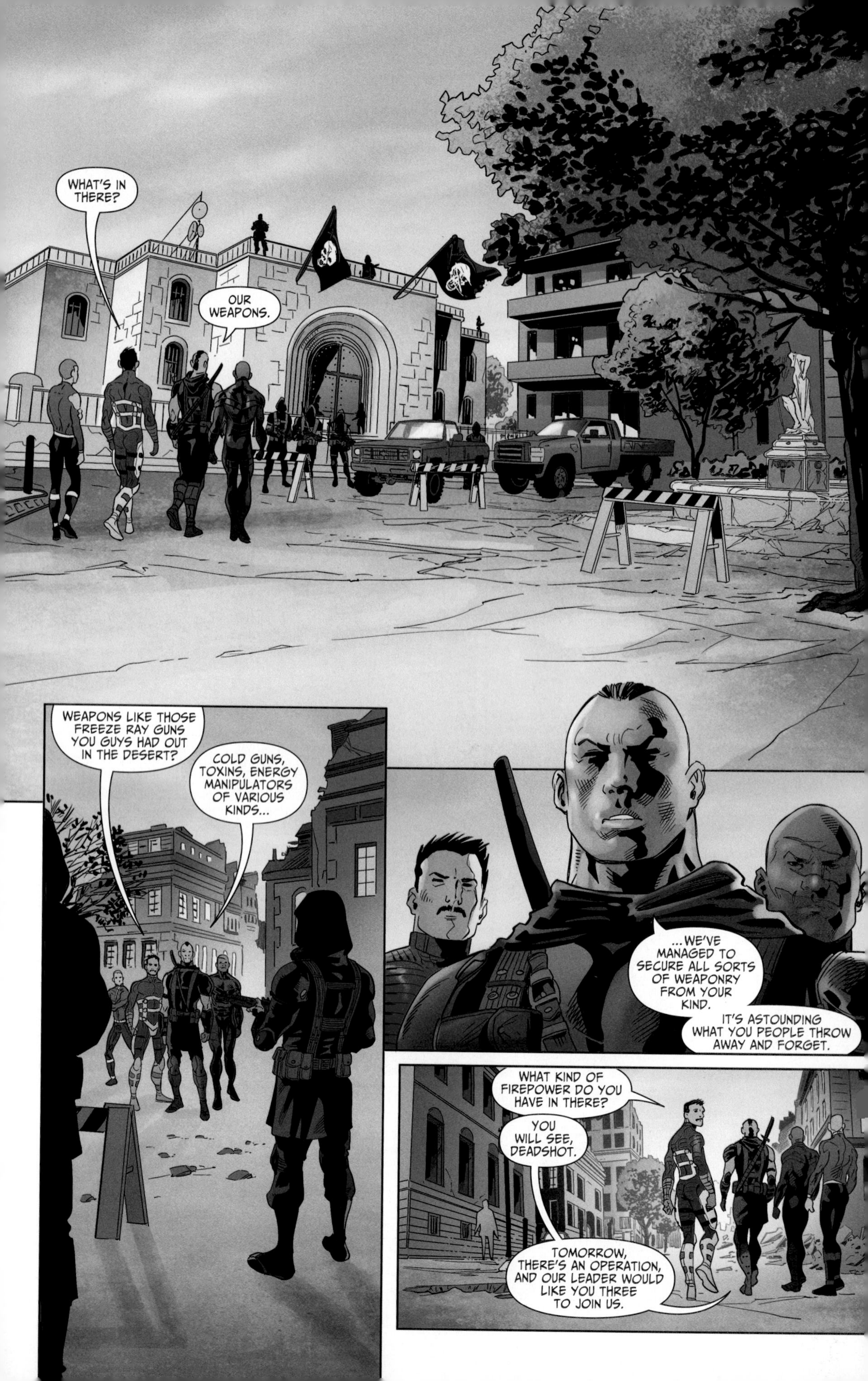
WHAT'S IN THERE?
OUR WEAPONS.
WEAPONS LIKE THOSE FREEZE RAY GUNS YOU GUYS HAD OUT IN THE DESERT?
COLD GUNS, TOXINS, ENERGY MANIPULATORS OF VARIOUS KINDS...
...WE'VE MANAGED TO SECURE ALL SORTS OF WEAPONRY FROM YOUR KIND.
IT'S ASTOUNDING WHAT YOU PEOPLE THROW AWAY AND FORGET.
WHAT KIND OF FIREPOWER DO YOU HAVE IN THERE?
YOU WILL SEE, DEADSHOT.
TOMORROW, THERE'S AN OPERATION, AND OUR LEADER WOULD LIKE YOU THREE TO JOIN US.

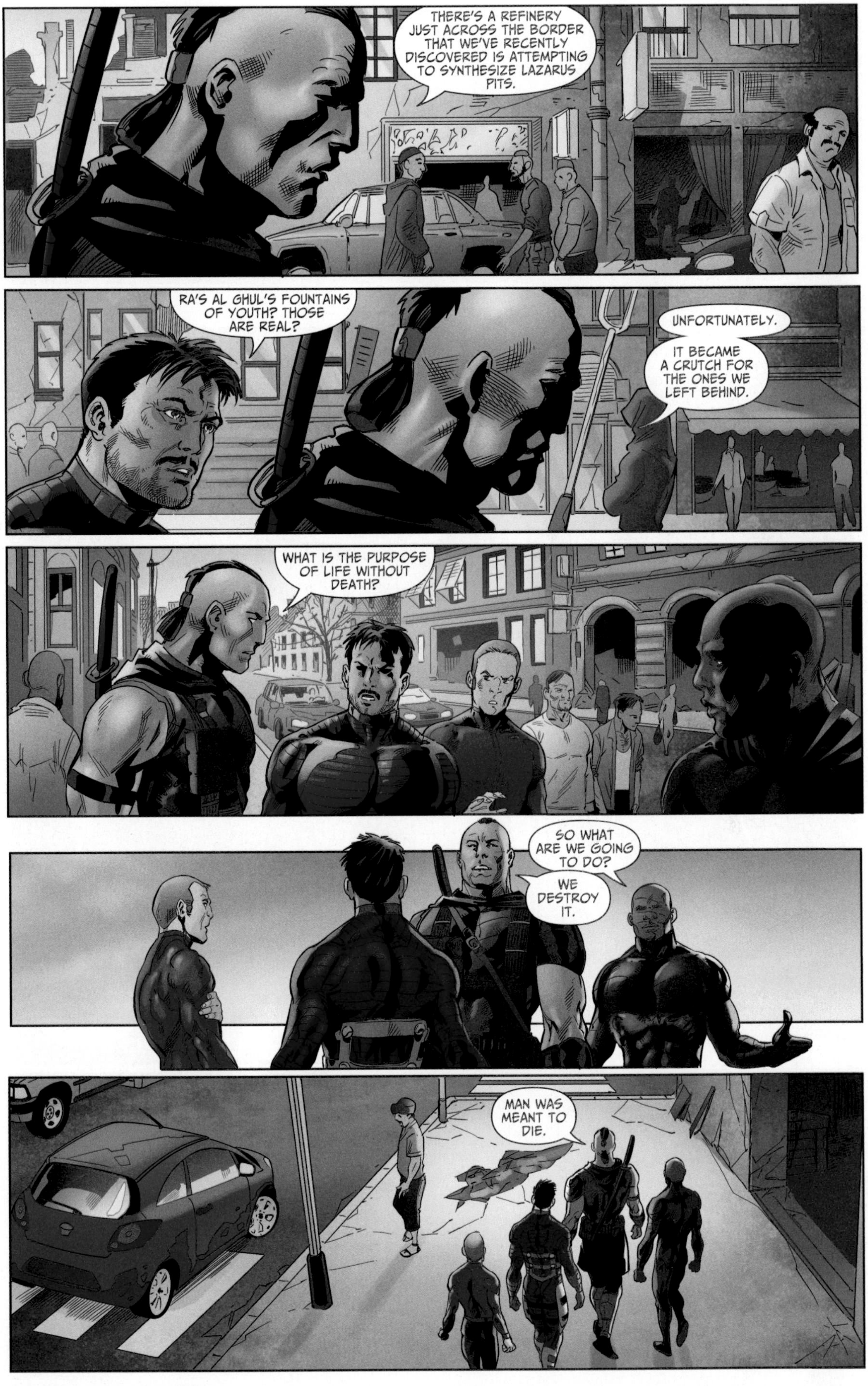
THERE'S A REFINERY JUST ACROSS THE BORDER THAT WE'VE RECENTLY DISCOVERED IS ATTEMPTING TO SYNTHESIZE LAZARUS PITS.
RA'S AL GHUL'S FOUNTAINS OF YOUTH? THOSE ARE REAL?
UNFORTUNATELY.
IT BECAME A CRUTCH FOR THE ONES WE LEFT BEHIND.
WHAT IS THE PURPOSE OF LIFE WITHOUT DEATH?
SO WHAT ARE WE GOING TO DO?
WE DESTROY IT.
MAN WAS MEANT TO DIE.

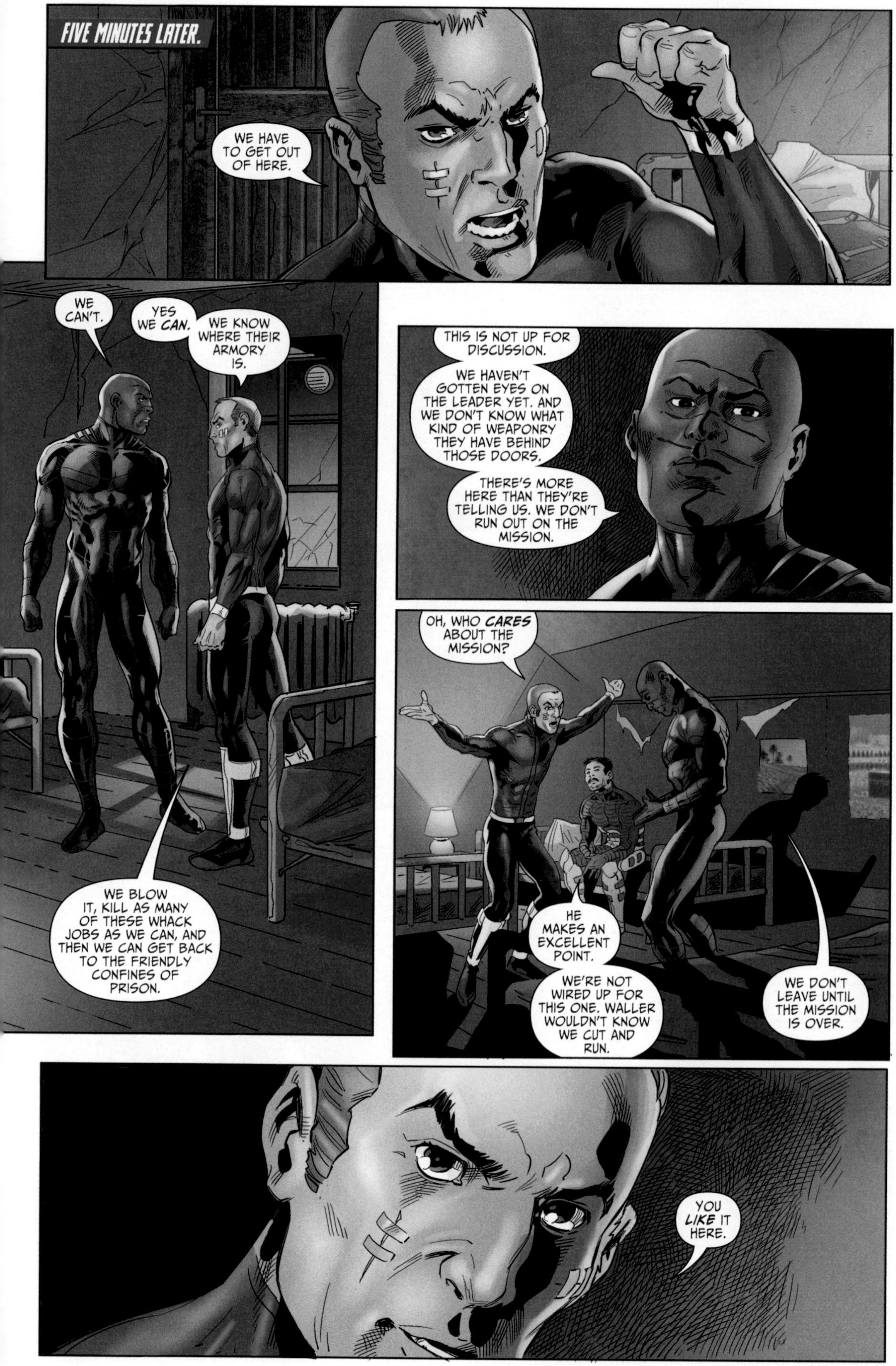
FIVE MINUTES LATER.
WE HAVE TO GET OUT OF HERE.
WE CAN'T.
YES WE CAN.
WE KNOW WHERE THEIR ARMORY IS.
WE BLOW IT, KILL AS MANY OF THESE WHACK JOBS AS WE CAN, AND THEN WE CAN GET BACK TO THE FRIENDLY CONFINES OF PRISON.
THIS IS NOT UP FOR DISCUSSION.
WE HAVEN'T GOTTEN EYES ON THE LEADER YET. AND WE DON'T KNOW WHAT KIND OF WEAPONRY THEY HAVE BEHIND THOSE DOORS.
THERE'S MORE HERE THAN THEY'RE TELLING US. WE DON'T RUN OUT ON THE MISSION.
OH, WHO CARES ABOUT THE MISSION?
HE MAKES AN EXCELLENT POINT.
WE'RE NOT WIRED UP FOR THIS ONE. WALLER WOULDN'T KNOW WE CUT AND RUN.
WE DON'T LEAVE UNTIL THE MISSION IS OVER.
YOU LIKE IT HERE.

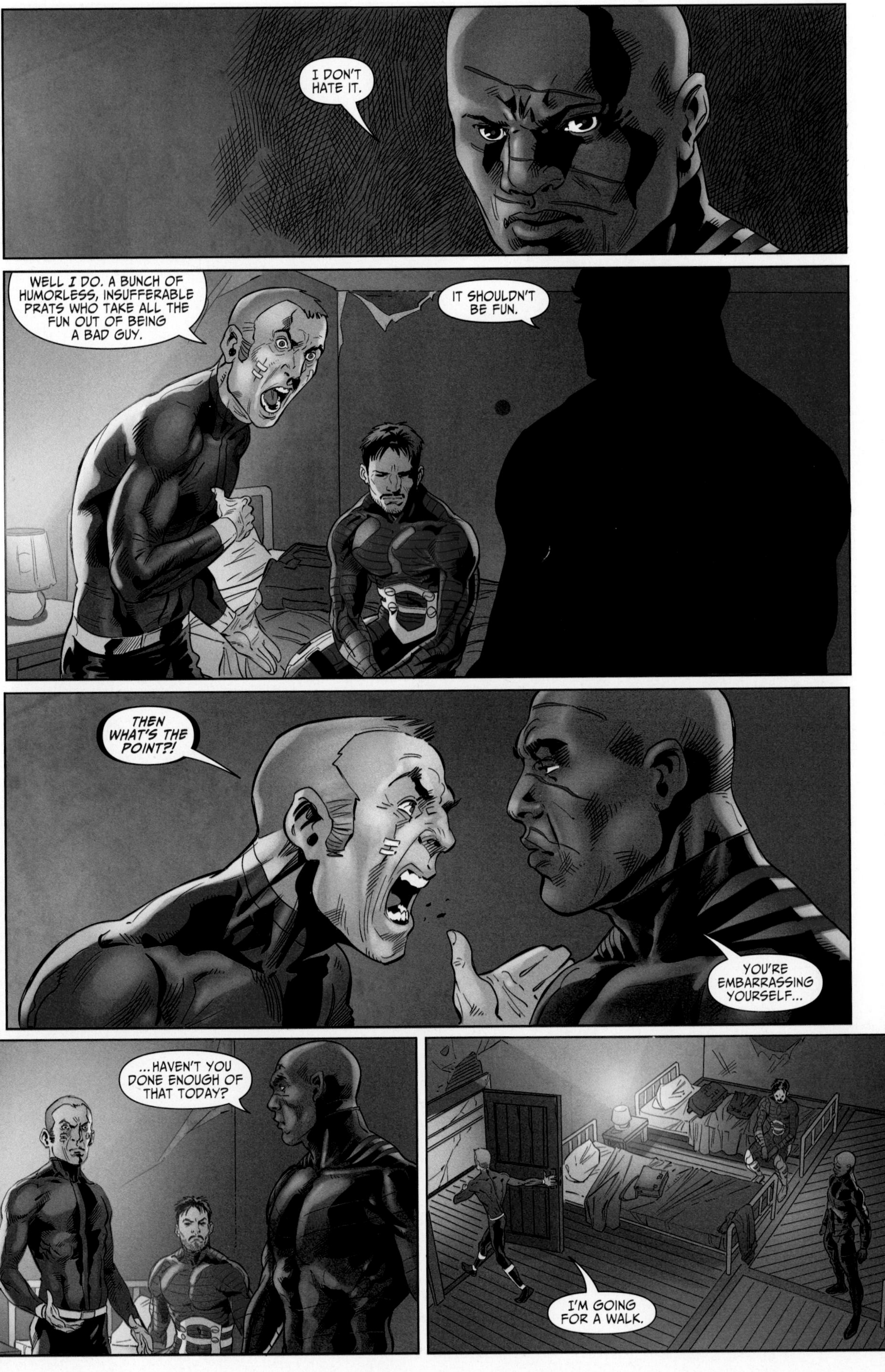
I DON'T HATE IT.
WELL I DO. A BUNCH OF HUMORLESS, INSUFFERABLE PRATS WHO TAKE ALL THE FUN OUT OF BEING A BAD GUY.
IT SHOULDN'T BE FUN.
THEN WHAT'S THE POINT?!
YOU'RE EMBARRASSING YOURSELF...
...HAVEN'T YOU DONE ENOUGH OF THAT TODAY?
I'M GOING FOR A WALK.

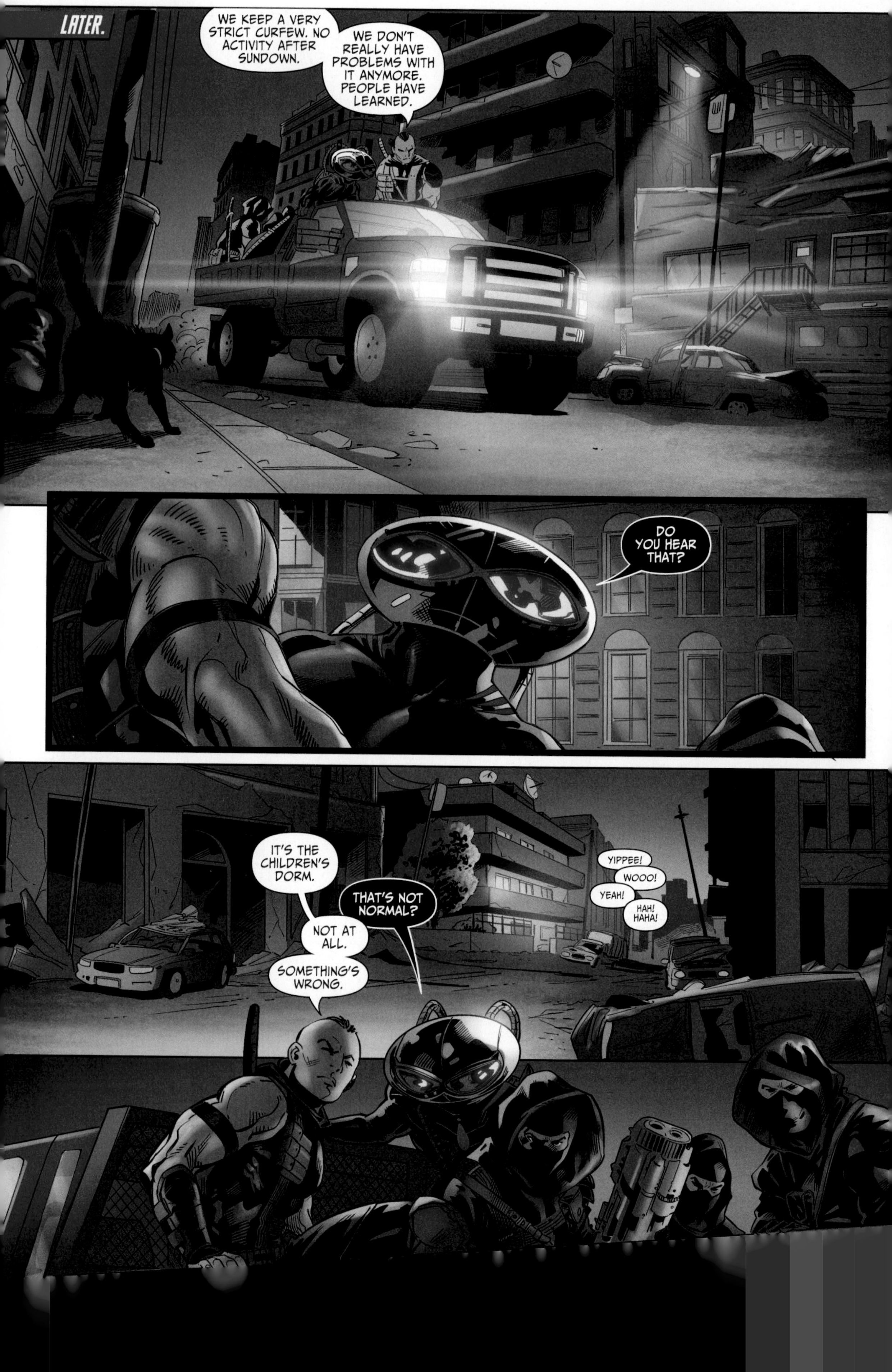
LATER.
WE KEEP A VERY STRICT CURFEW. NO ACTIVITY AFTER SUNDOWN.
WE DON'T REALLY HAVE PROBLEMS WITH IT ANYMORE. PEOPLE HAVE LEARNED.
DO YOU HEAR THAT?
YIPPEE!
WOOO!
YEAH!
HAH! HAHA!
IT'S THE CHILDREN'S DORM.
THAT'S NOT NORMAL?
NOT AT ALL.
SOMETHING'S WRONG.

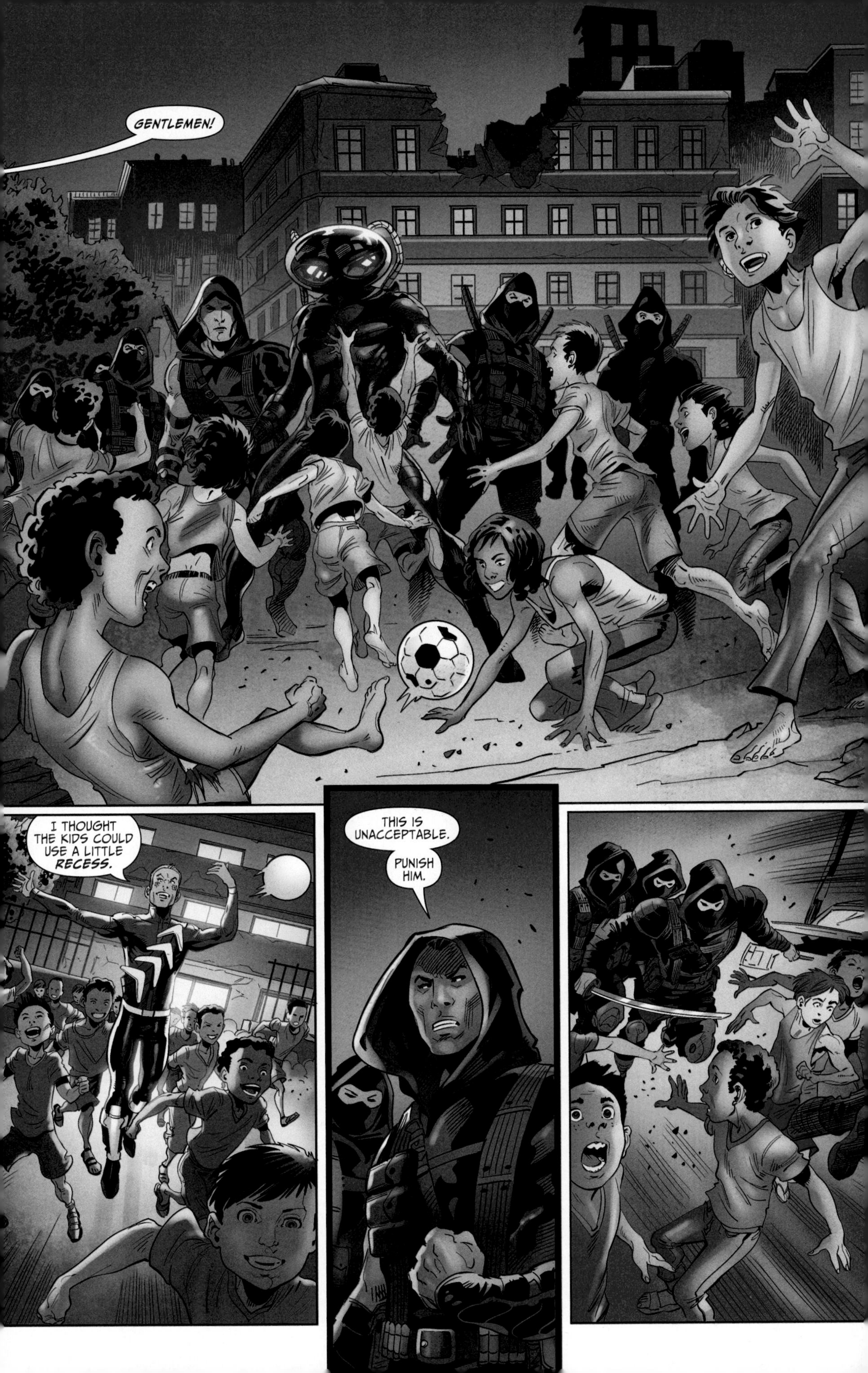
GENTLEMEN!
I THOUGHT THE KIDS COULD USE A LITTLE RECESS.
THIS IS UNACCEPTABLE.
PUNISH HIM.

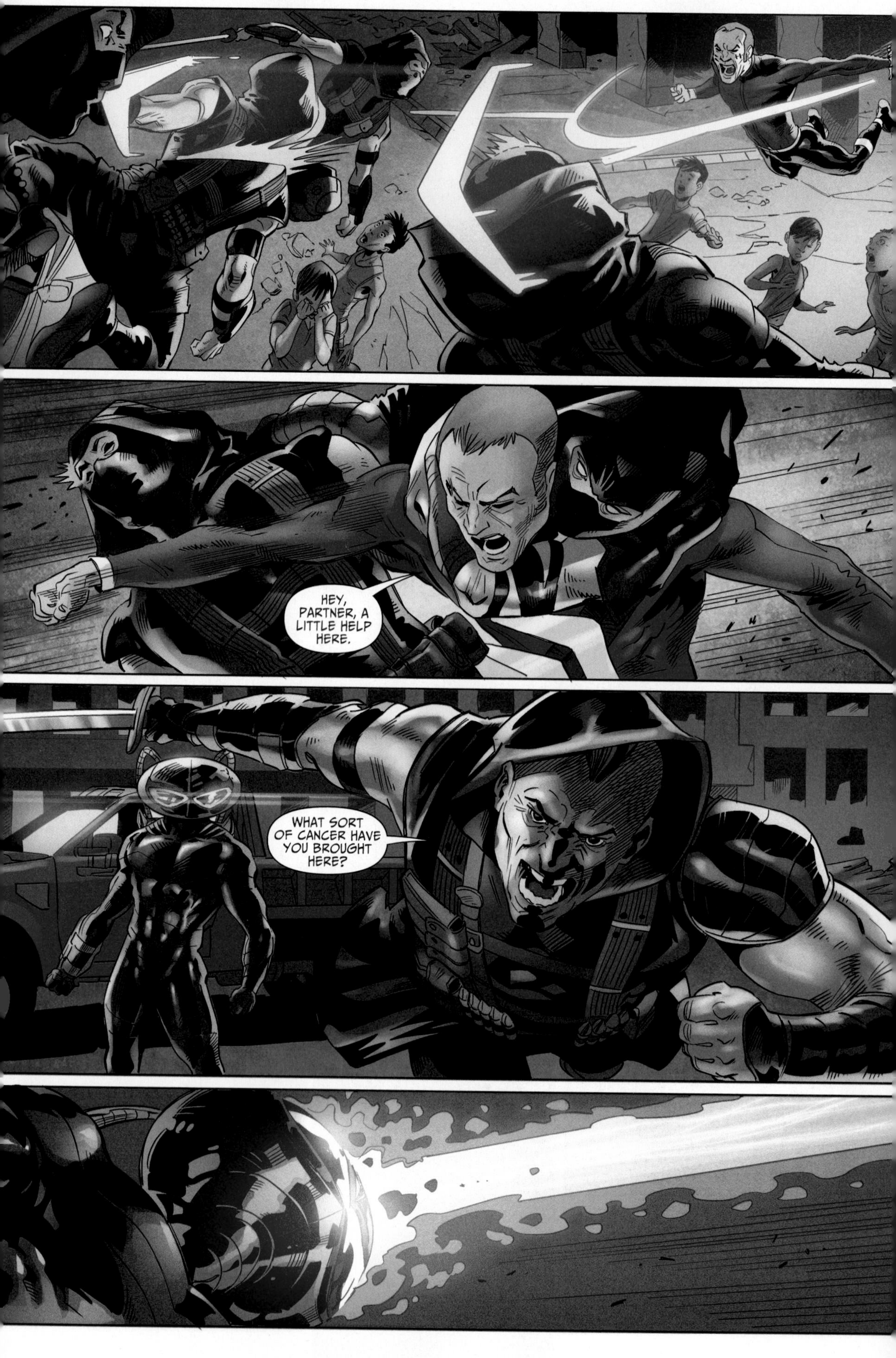
HEY, PARTNER, A LITTLE HELP HERE.
WHAT SORT OF CANCER HAVE YOU BROUGHT HERE?

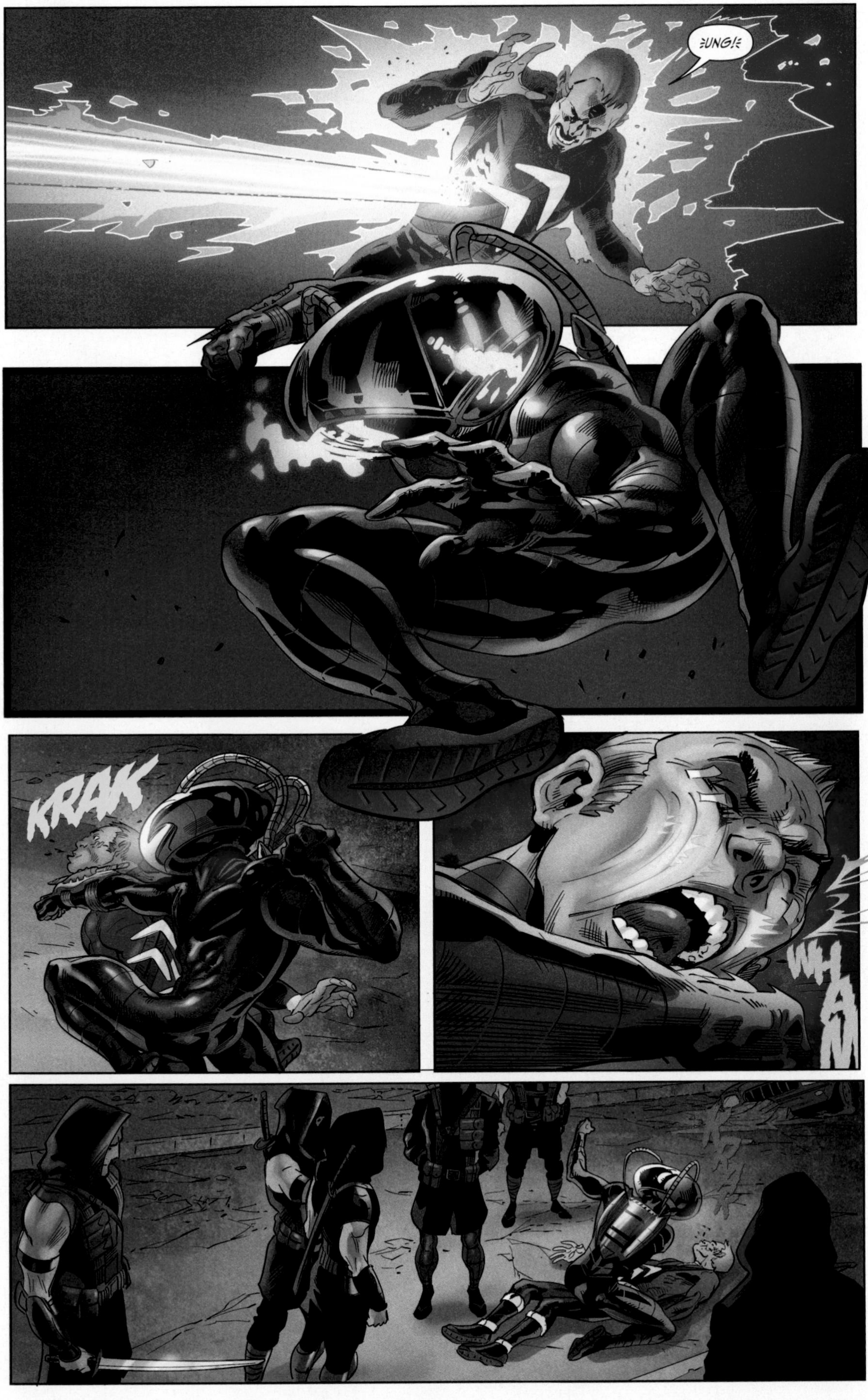
UNG!
KRAK
WHAM

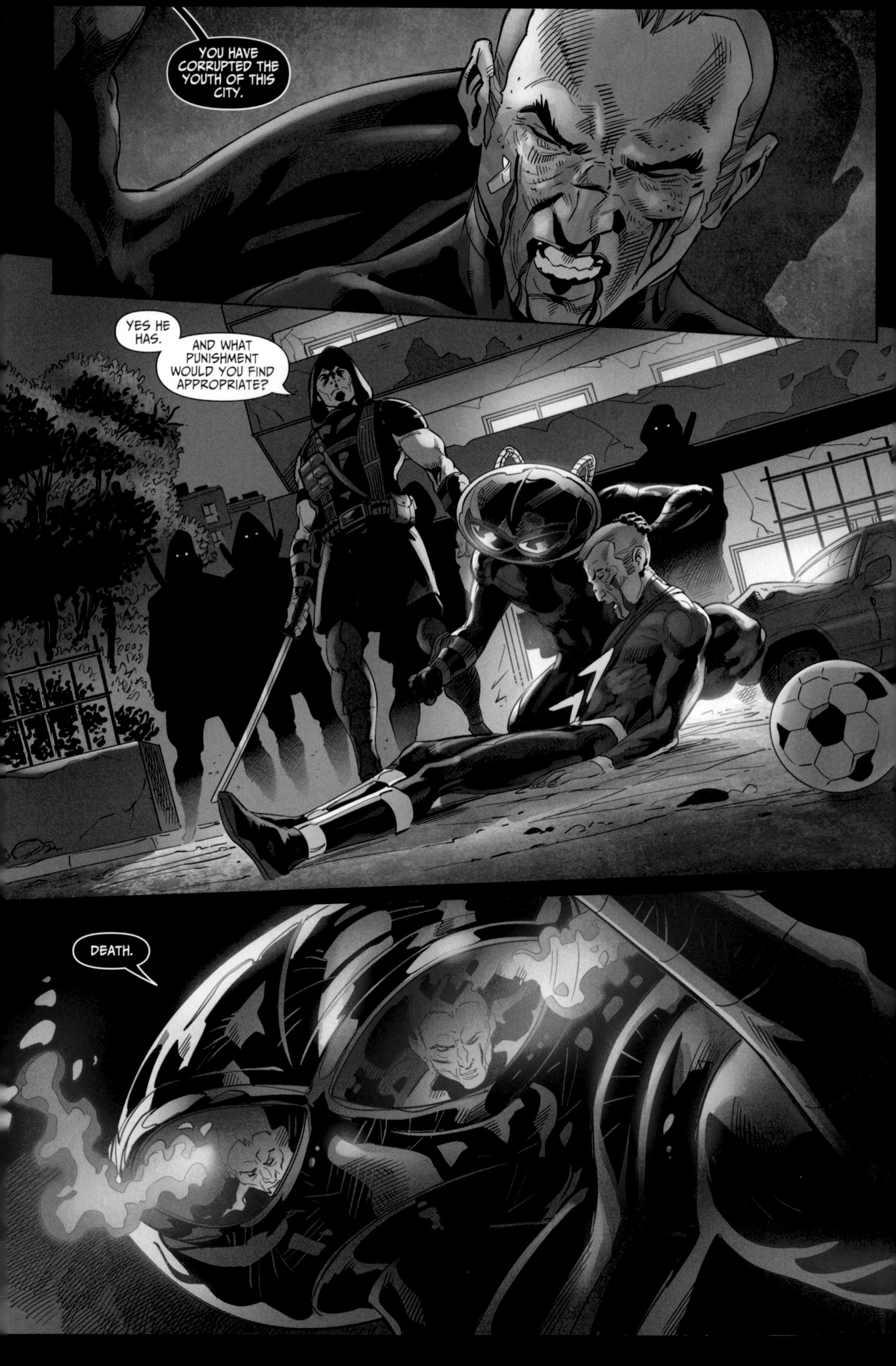
YOU HAVE CORRUPTED THE YOUTH OF THIS CITY.
YES HE HAS.
AND WHAT PUNISHMENT WOULD YOU FIND APPROPRIATE?
DEATH.

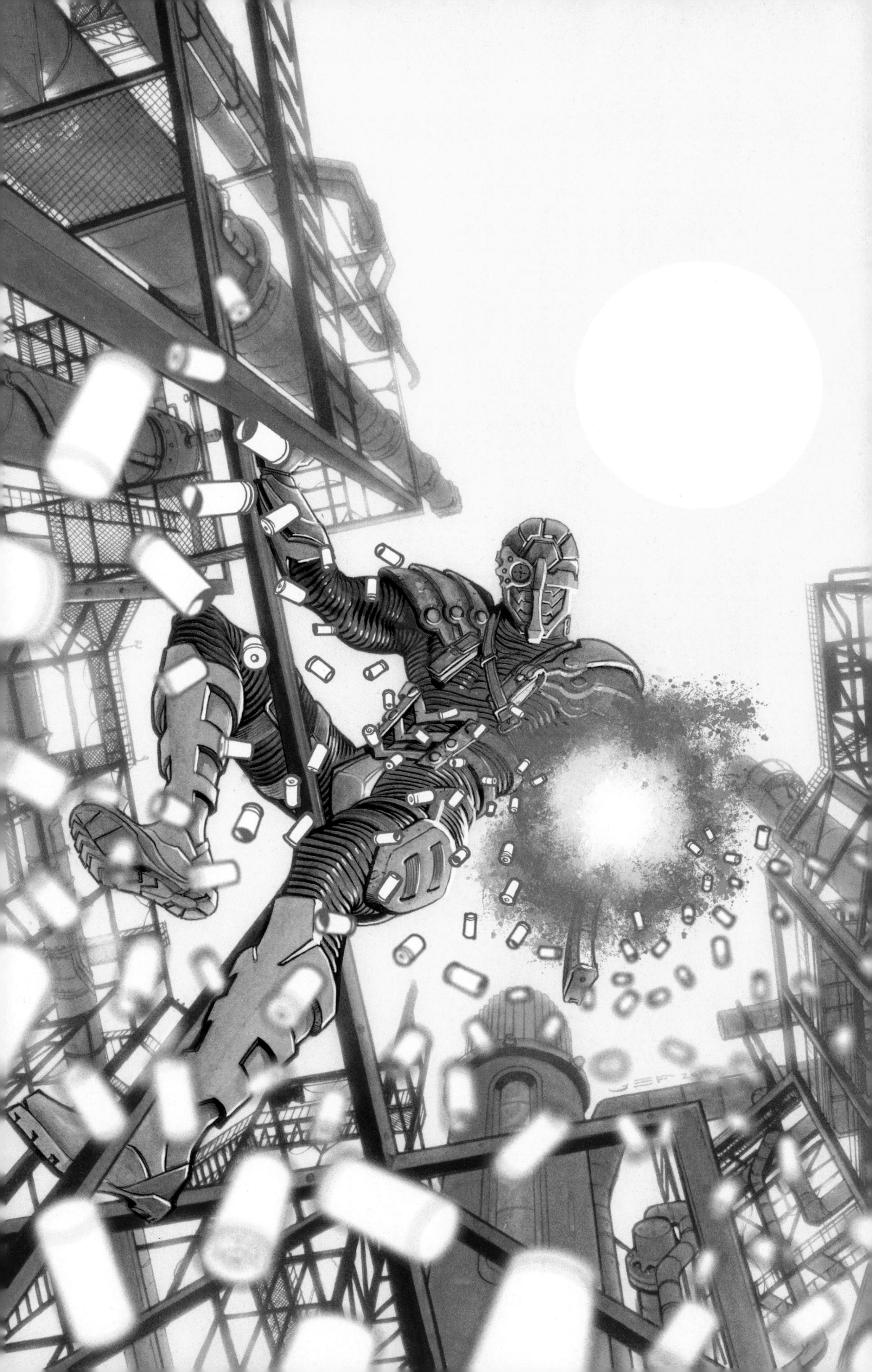

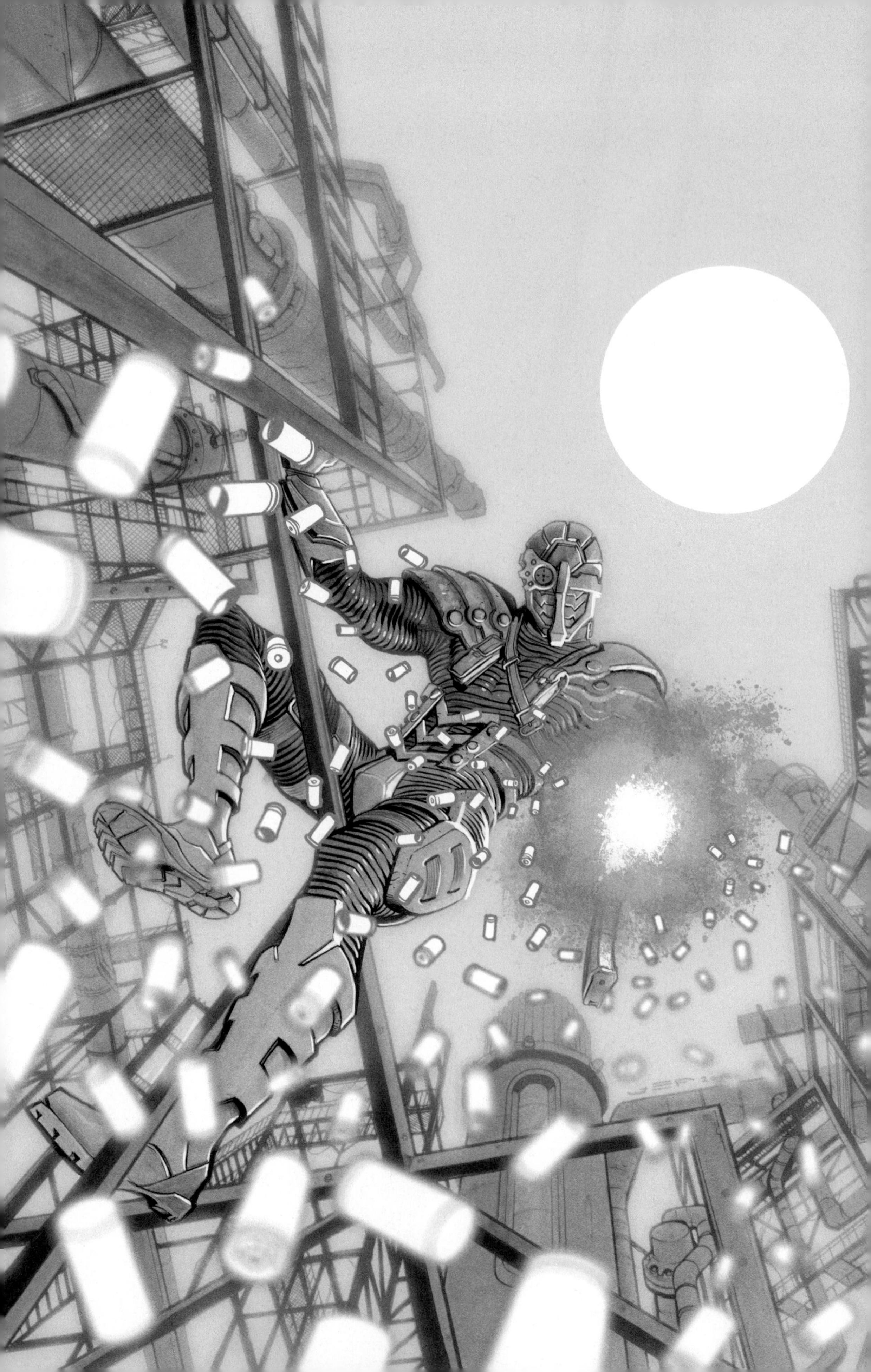

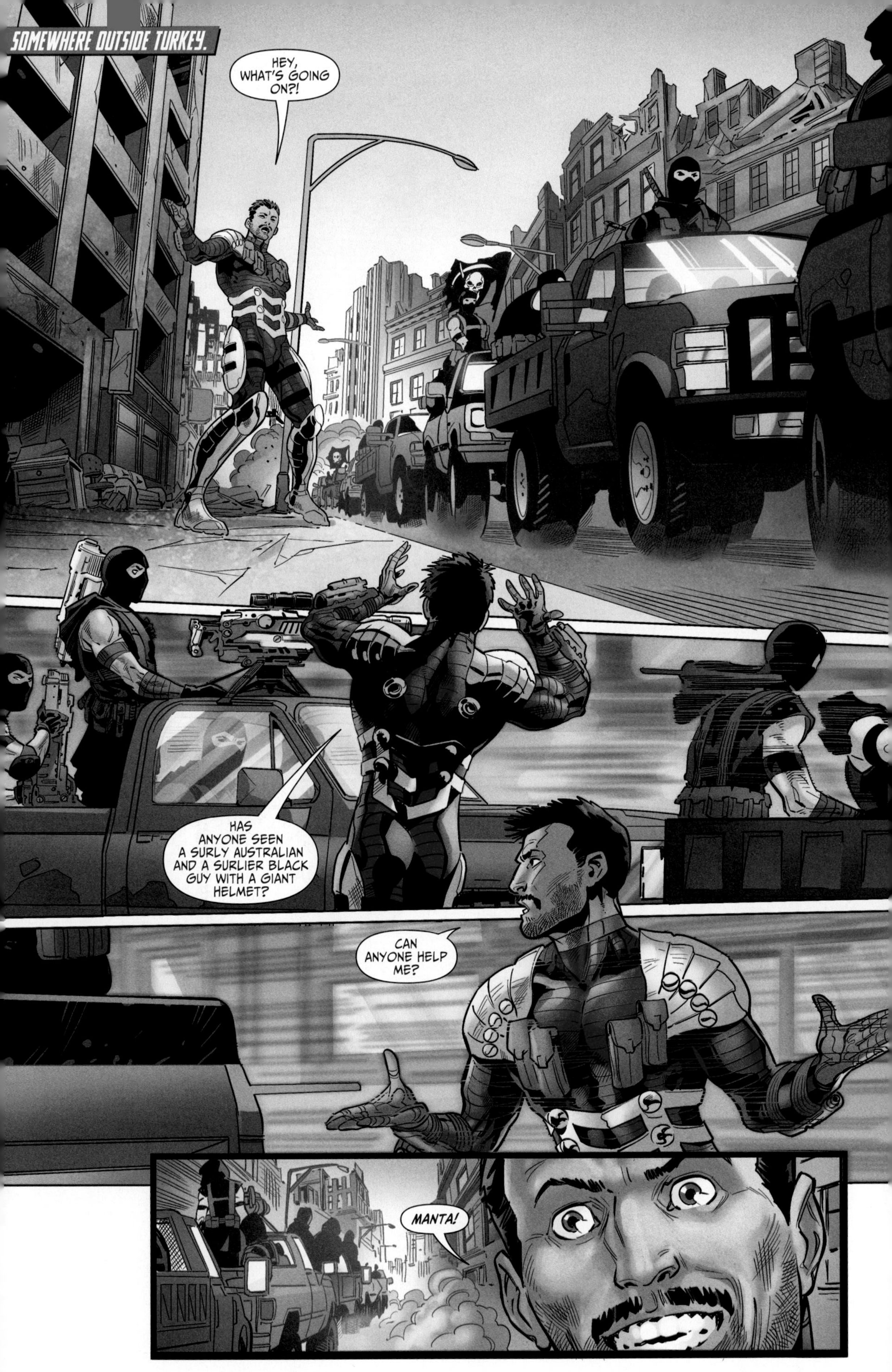
SOMEWHERE OUTSIDE TURKEY.
HEY, WHAT'S GOING ON?!
HAS ANYONE SEEN A SURLY AUSTRALIAN AND A SURLIER BLACK GUY WITH A GIANT HELMET?
CAN ANYONE HELP ME?
MANTA!

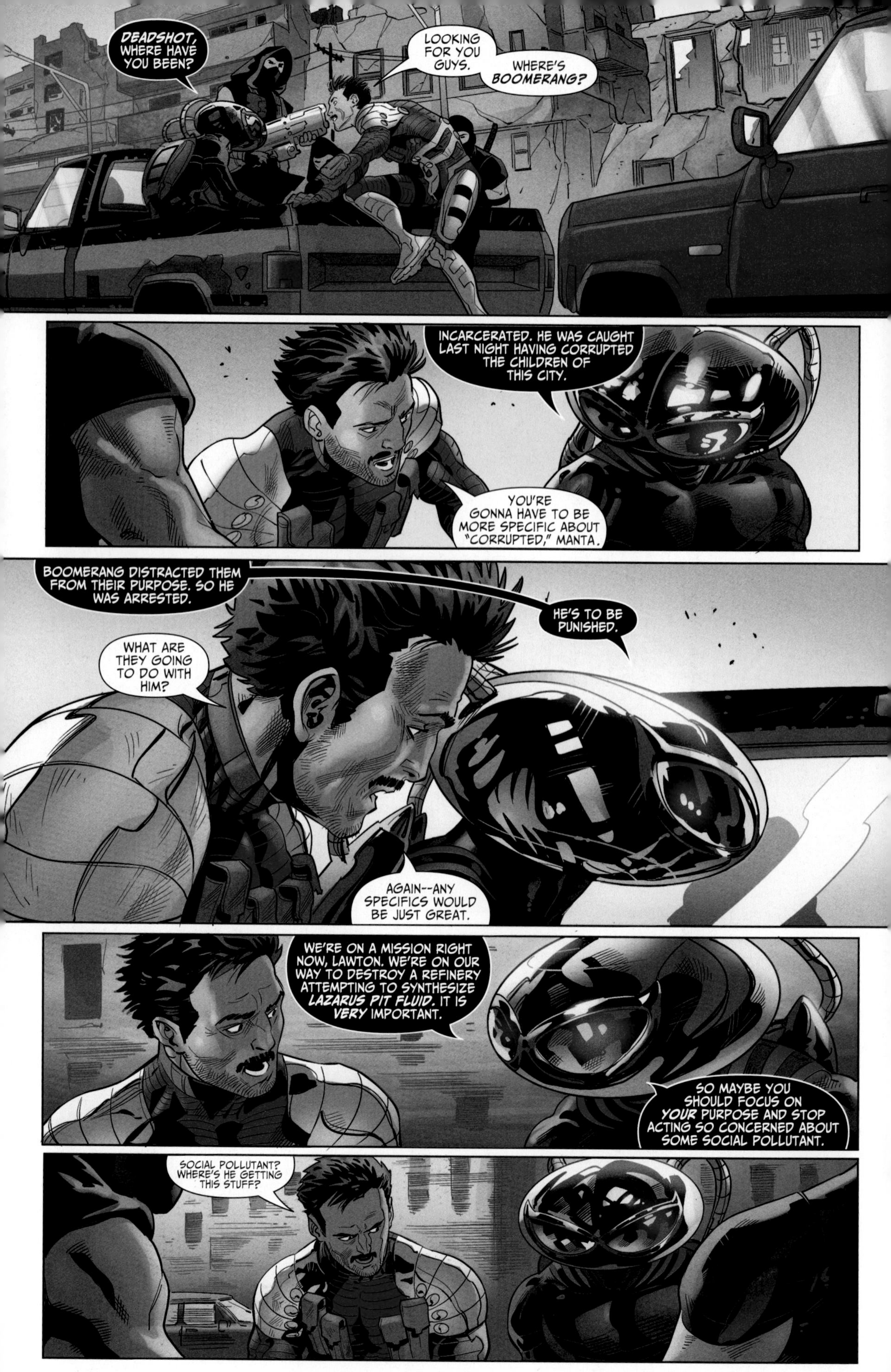
DEADSHOT, WHERE HAVE YOU BEEN?
LOOKING FOR YOU GUYS.
WHERE'S BOOMERANG?
INCARCERATED. HE WAS CAUGHT LAST NIGHT HAVING CORRUPTED THE CHILDREN OF THIS CITY.
YOU'RE GONNA HAVE TO BE MORE SPECIFIC ABOUT "CORRUPTED," MANTA.
BOOMERANG DISTRACTED THEM FROM THEIR PURPOSE. SO HE WAS ARRESTED.
HE'S TO BE PUNISHED.
WHAT ARE THEY GOING TO DO WITH HIM?
AGAIN--ANY SPECIFICS WOULD BE JUST GREAT.
WE'RE ON A MISSION RIGHT NOW, LAWTON. WE'RE ON OUR WAY TO DESTROY A REFINERY ATTEMPTING TO SYNTHESIZE LAZARUS PIT FLUID. IT IS VERY IMPORTANT.
SO MAYBE YOU SHOULD FOCUS ON YOUR PURPOSE AND STOP ACTING SO CONCERNED ABOUT SOME SOCIAL POLLUTANT.
SOCIAL POLLUTANT? WHERE'S HE GETTING THIS STUFF?

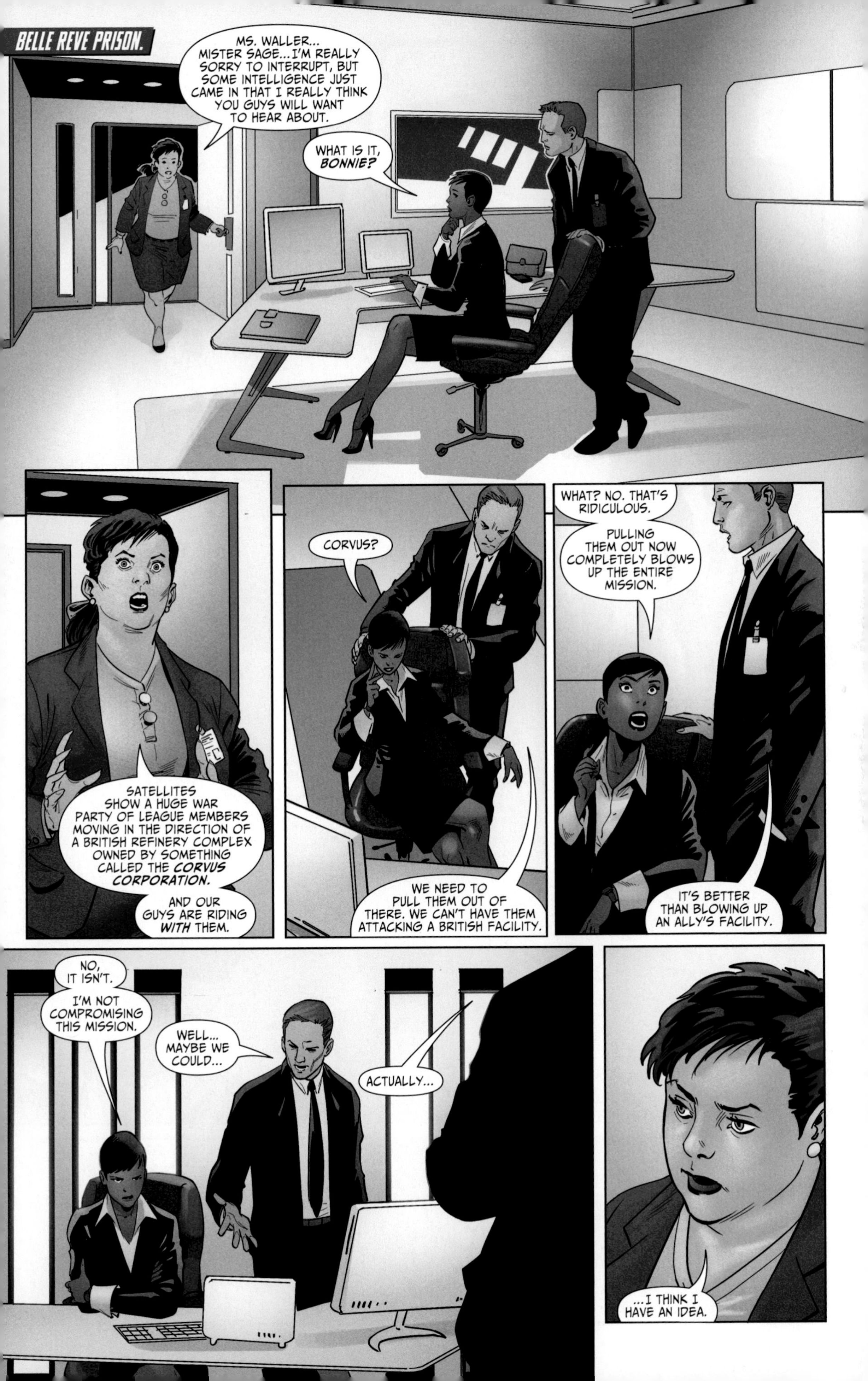
BELLE REVE PRISON.
MS. WALLER... MISTER SAGE... I'M REALLY SORRY TO INTERRUPT, BUT SOME INTELLIGENCE JUST CAME IN THAT I REALLY THINK YOU GUYS WILL WANT TO HEAR ABOUT.
WHAT IS IT, BONNIE?
SATELLITES SHOW A HUGE WAR PARTY OF LEAGUE MEMBERS MOVING IN THE DIRECTION OF A BRITISH REFINERY COMPLEX OWNED BY SOMETHING CALLED THE CORVUS CORPORATION.
AND OUR GUYS ARE RIDING WITH THEM.
CORVUS?
WE NEED TO PULL THEM OUT OF THERE. WE CAN'T HAVE THEM ATTACKING A BRITISH FACILITY.
WHAT? NO. THAT'S RIDICULOUS.
PULLING THEM OUT NOW COMPLETELY BLOWS UP THE ENTIRE MISSION.
IT'S BETTER THAN BLOWING UP AN ALLY'S FACILITY.
NO, IT ISN'T.
I'M NOT COMPROMISING THIS MISSION.
WELL... MAYBE WE COULD...
ACTUALLY...
...I THINK I HAVE AN IDEA.

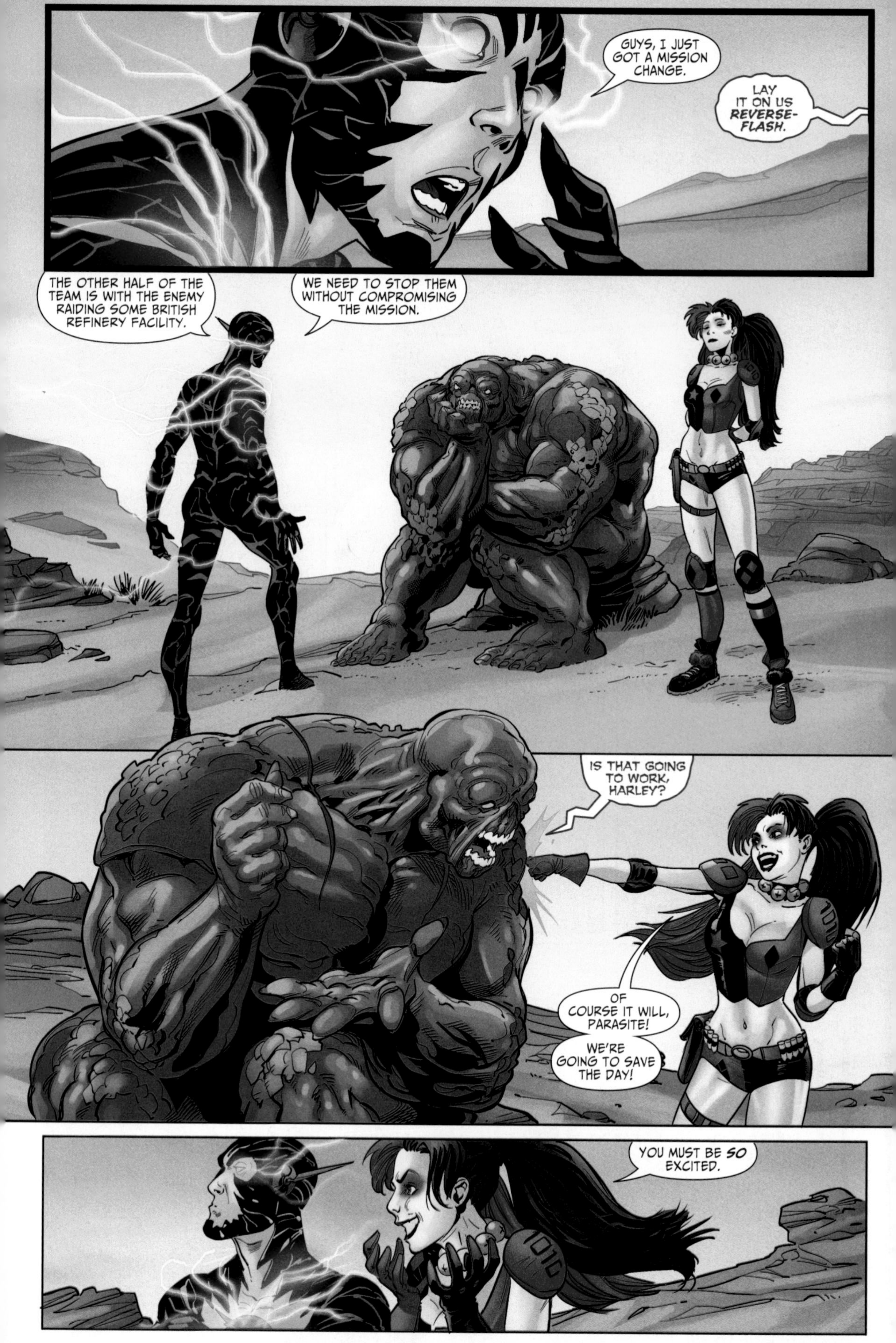
GUYS, I JUST GOT A MISSION CHANGE.
LAY IT ON US REVERSE-FLASH.
THE OTHER HALF OF THE TEAM IS WITH THE ENEMY RAIDING SOME BRITISH REFINERY FACILITY.
WE NEED TO STOP THEM WITHOUT COMPROMISING THE MISSION.
IS THAT GOING TO WORK, HARLEY?
OF COURSE IT WILL, PARASITE!
WE'RE GOING TO SAVE THE DAY!
YOU MUST BE SO EXCITED.

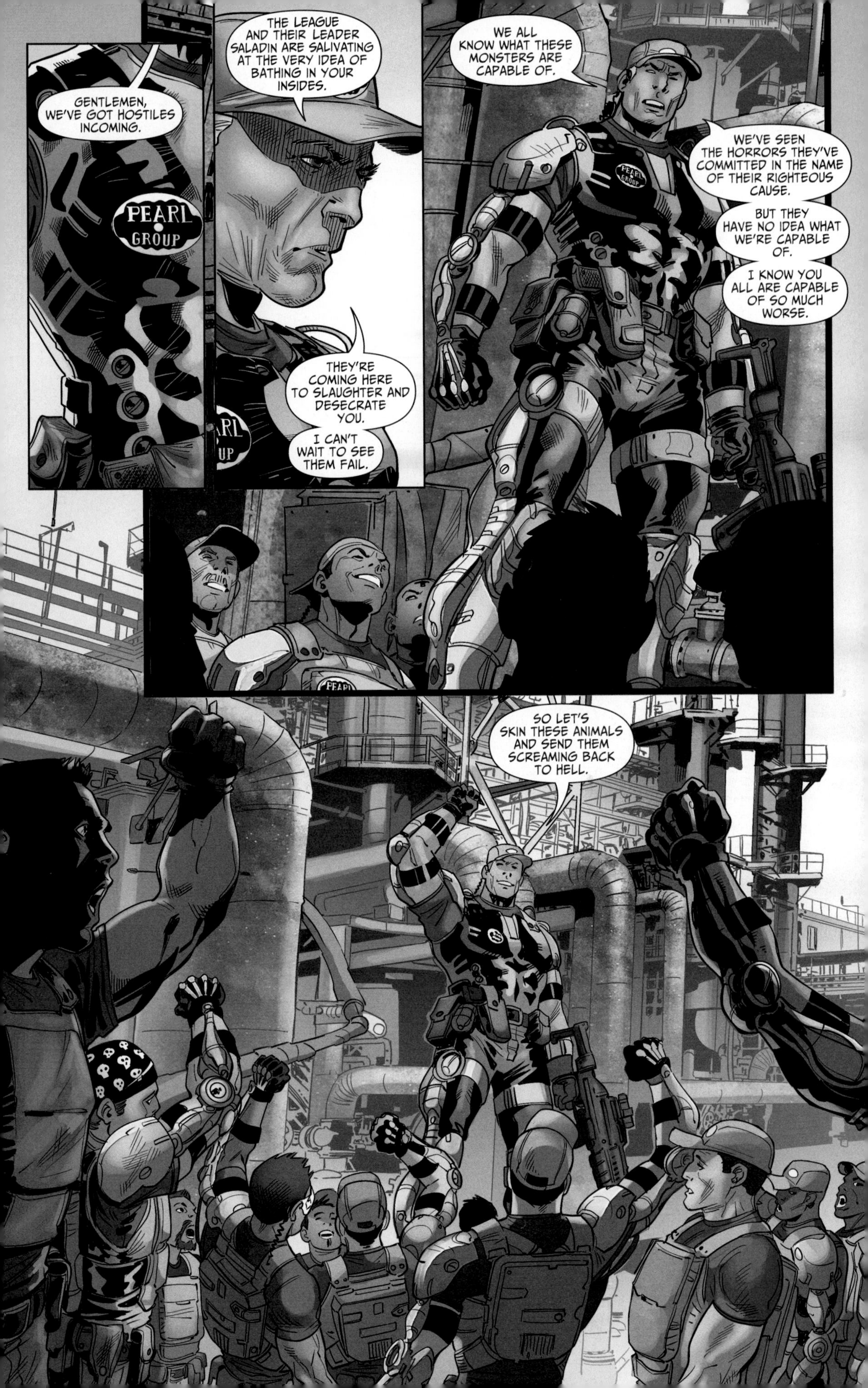
GENTLEMEN, WE'VE GOT HOSTILES INCOMING.
PEARL GROUP
THE LEAGUE AND THEIR LEADER SALADIN ARE SALIVATING AT THE VERY IDEA OF BATHING IN YOUR INSIDES.
THEY'RE COMING HERE TO SLAUGHTER AND DESECRATE YOU.
I CAN'T WAIT TO SEE THEM FAIL.
WE ALL KNOW WHAT THESE MONSTERS ARE CAPABLE OF.
WE'VE SEEN THE HORRORS THEY'VE COMMITTED IN THE NAME OF THEIR RIGHTEOUS CAUSE.
BUT THEY HAVE NO IDEA WHAT WE'RE CAPABLE OF.
I KNOW YOU ALL ARE CAPABLE OF SO MUCH WORSE.
SO LET'S SKIN THESE ANIMALS AND SEND THEM SCREAMING BACK TO HELL.

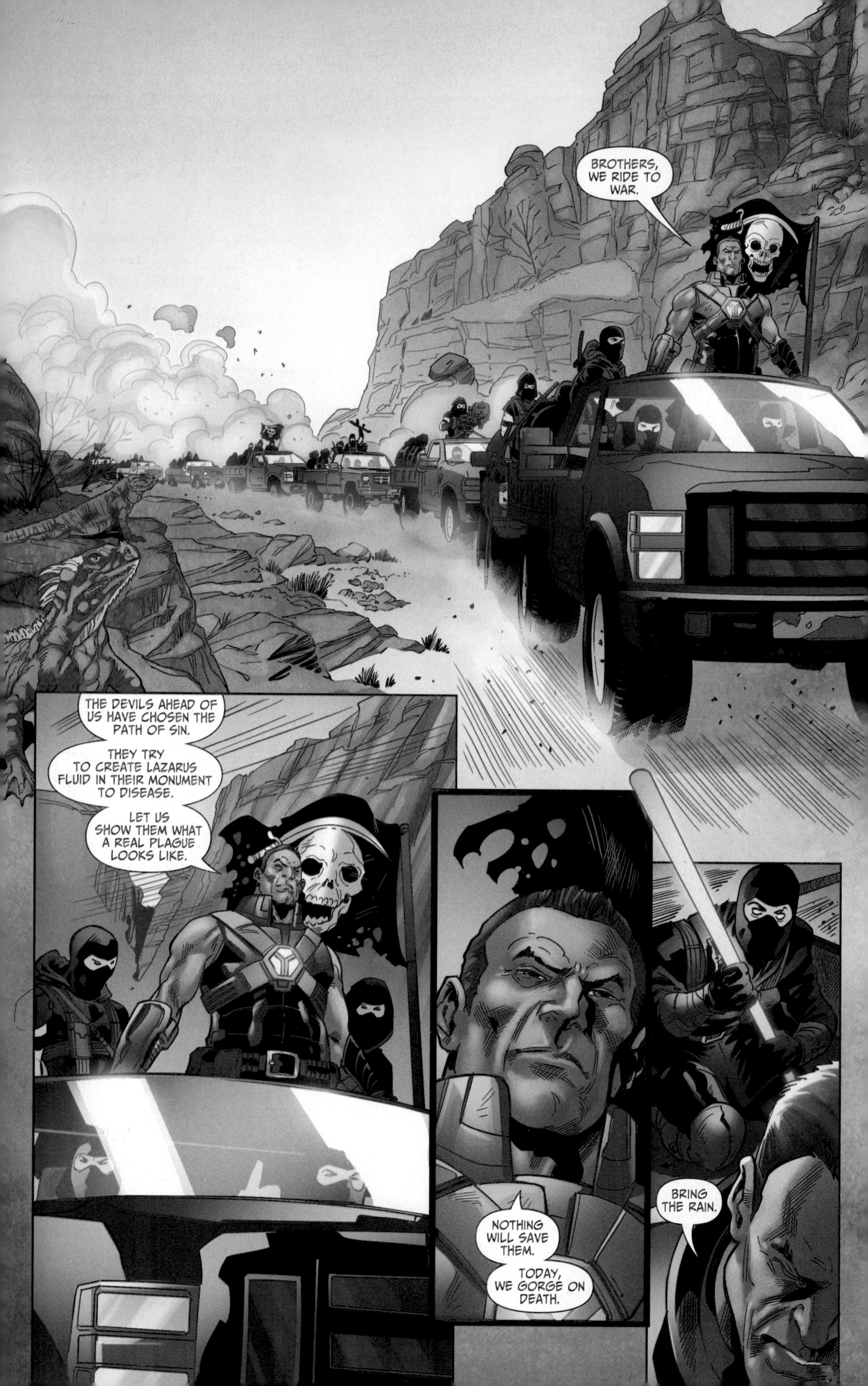
BROTHERS, WE RIDE TO WAR.
THE DEVILS AHEAD OF US HAVE CHOSEN THE PATH OF SIN.
THEY TRY TO CREATE LAZARUS FLUID IN THEIR MONUMENT TO DISEASE.
LET US SHOW THEM WHAT A REAL PLAGUE LOOKS LIKE.
NOTHING WILL SAVE THEM.
TODAY, WE GORGE ON DEATH.
BRING THE RAIN.

SCIENTIFIC
RESEARCH
FACILITY
OPERATED AND RUN
BY CORPUS...

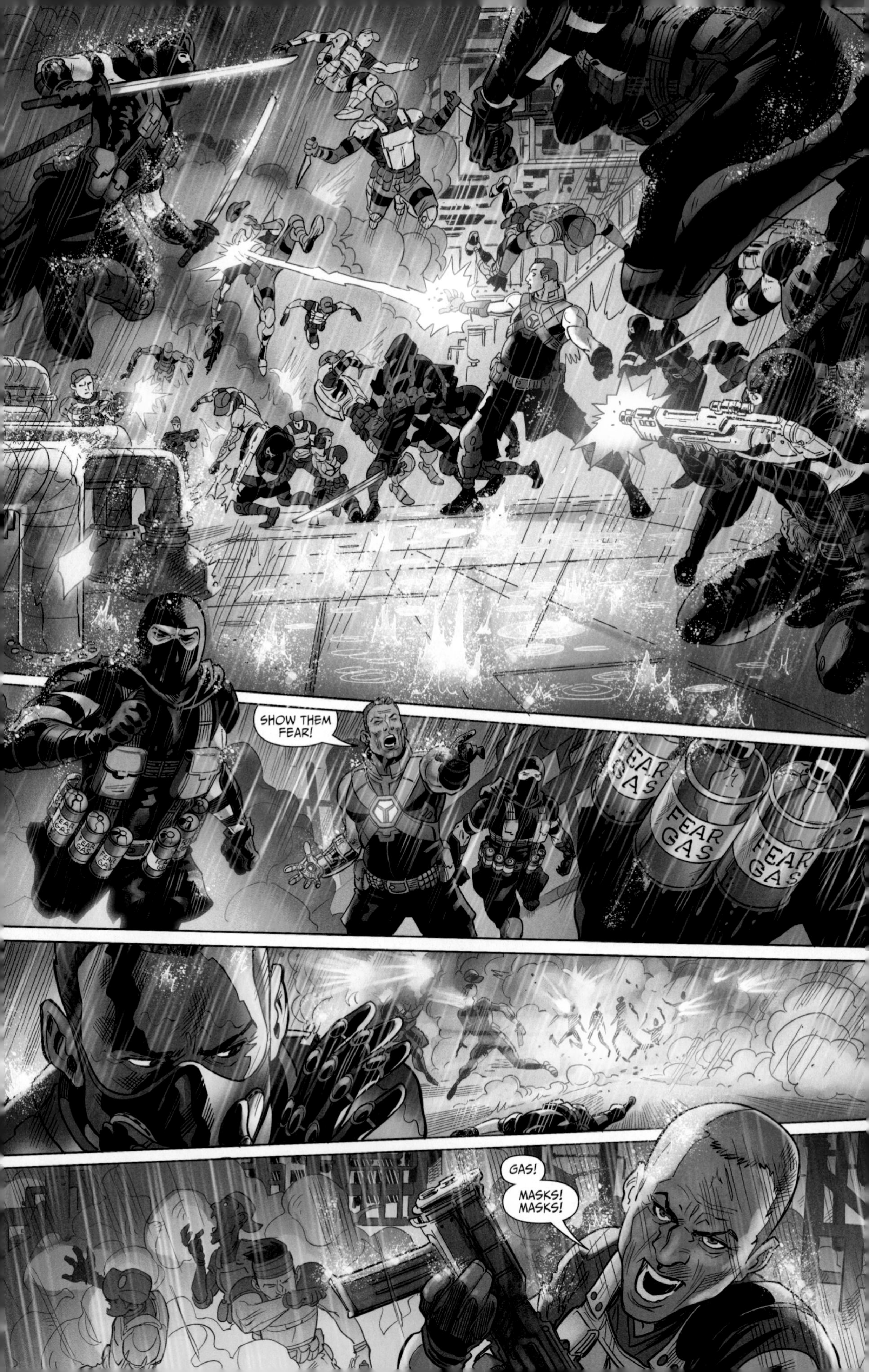
SHOW THEM FEAR!
FEAR GAS
FEAR GAS
FEAR GAS
FEAR GAS
FEAR GAS
GAS!
MASKS! MASKS!

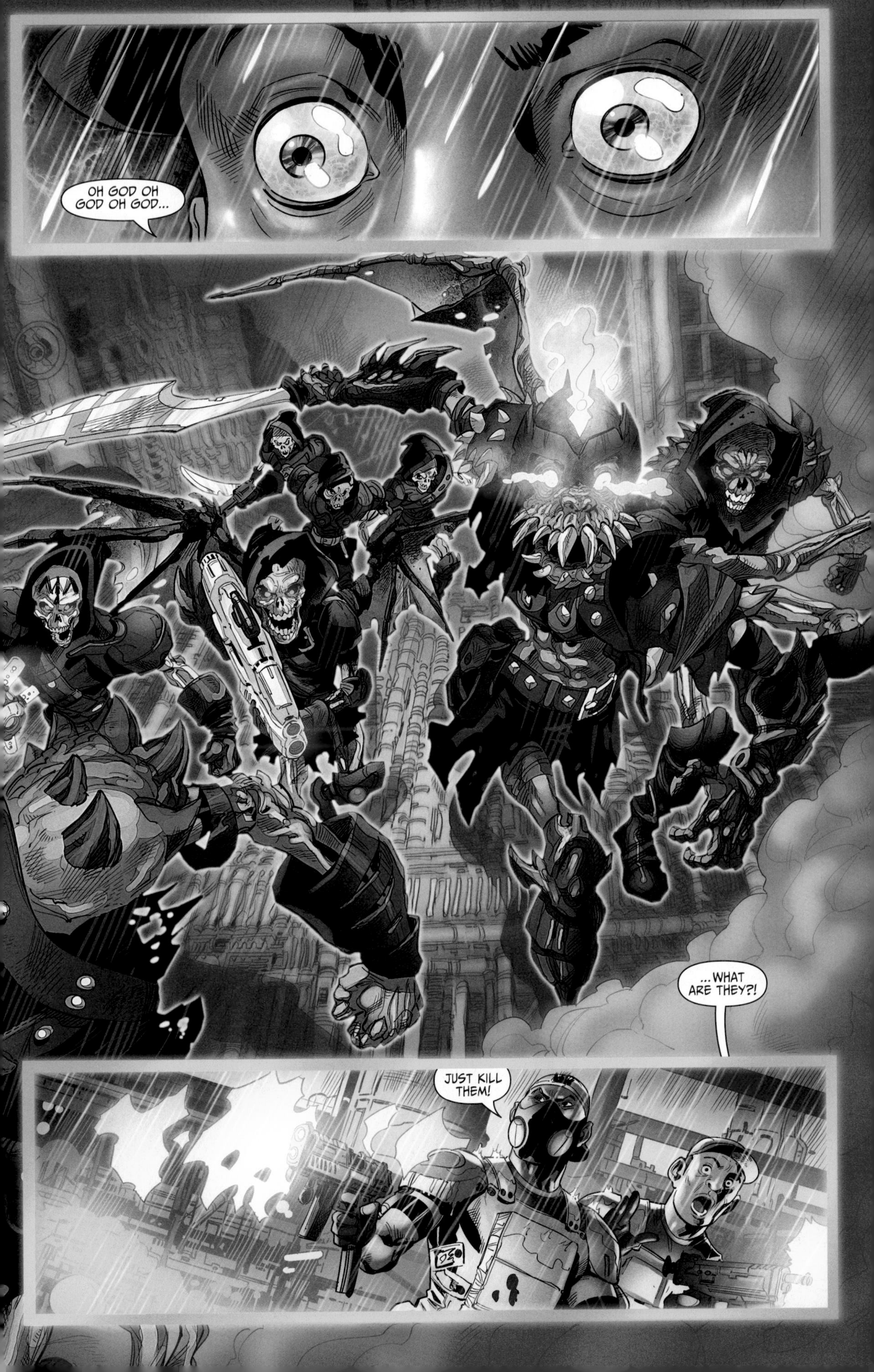
OH GOD OH GOD OH GOD...
...WHAT ARE THEY?!
JUST KILL THEM!

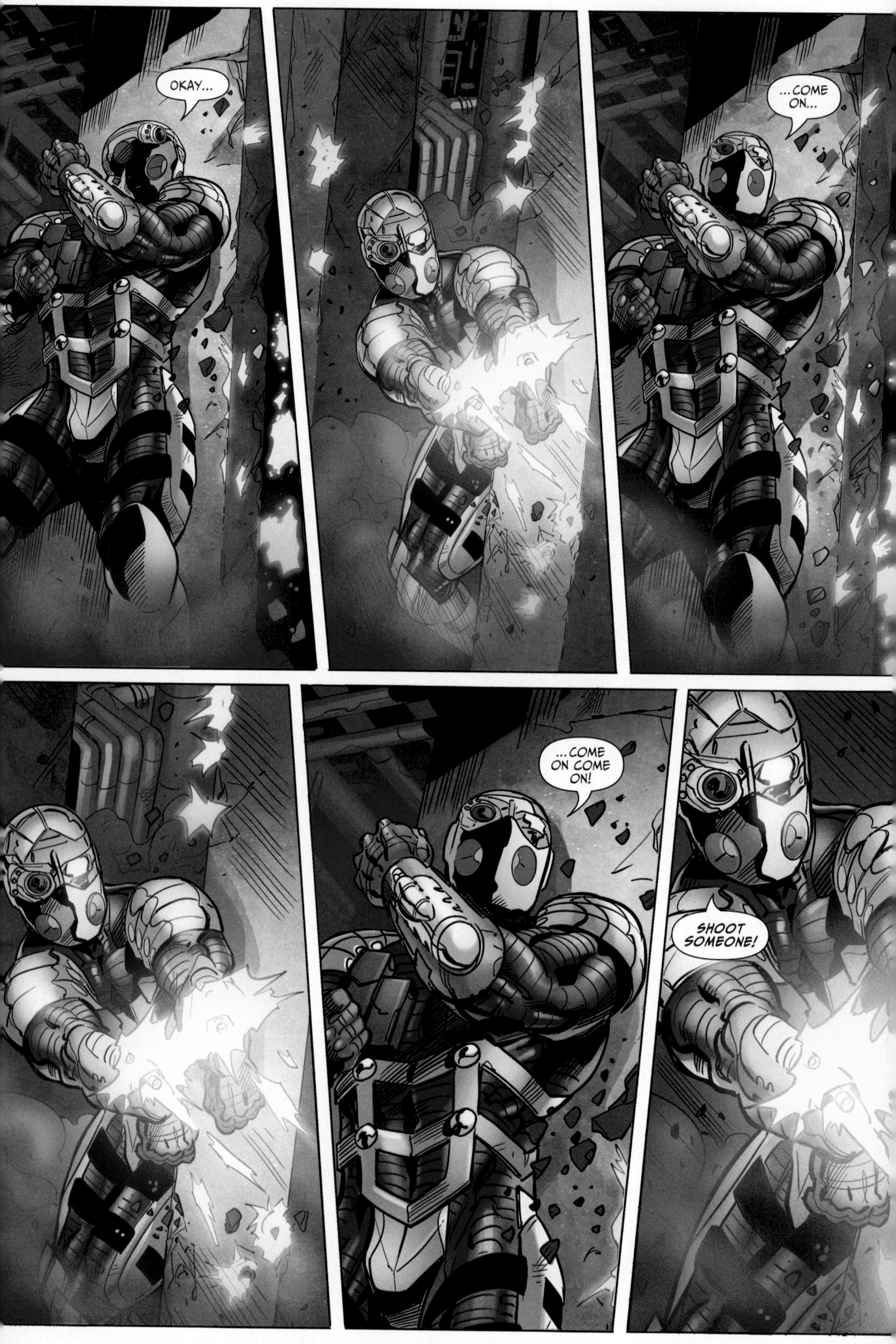
OKAY...
...COME ON...
...COME ON COME ON!
SHOOT SOMEONE!

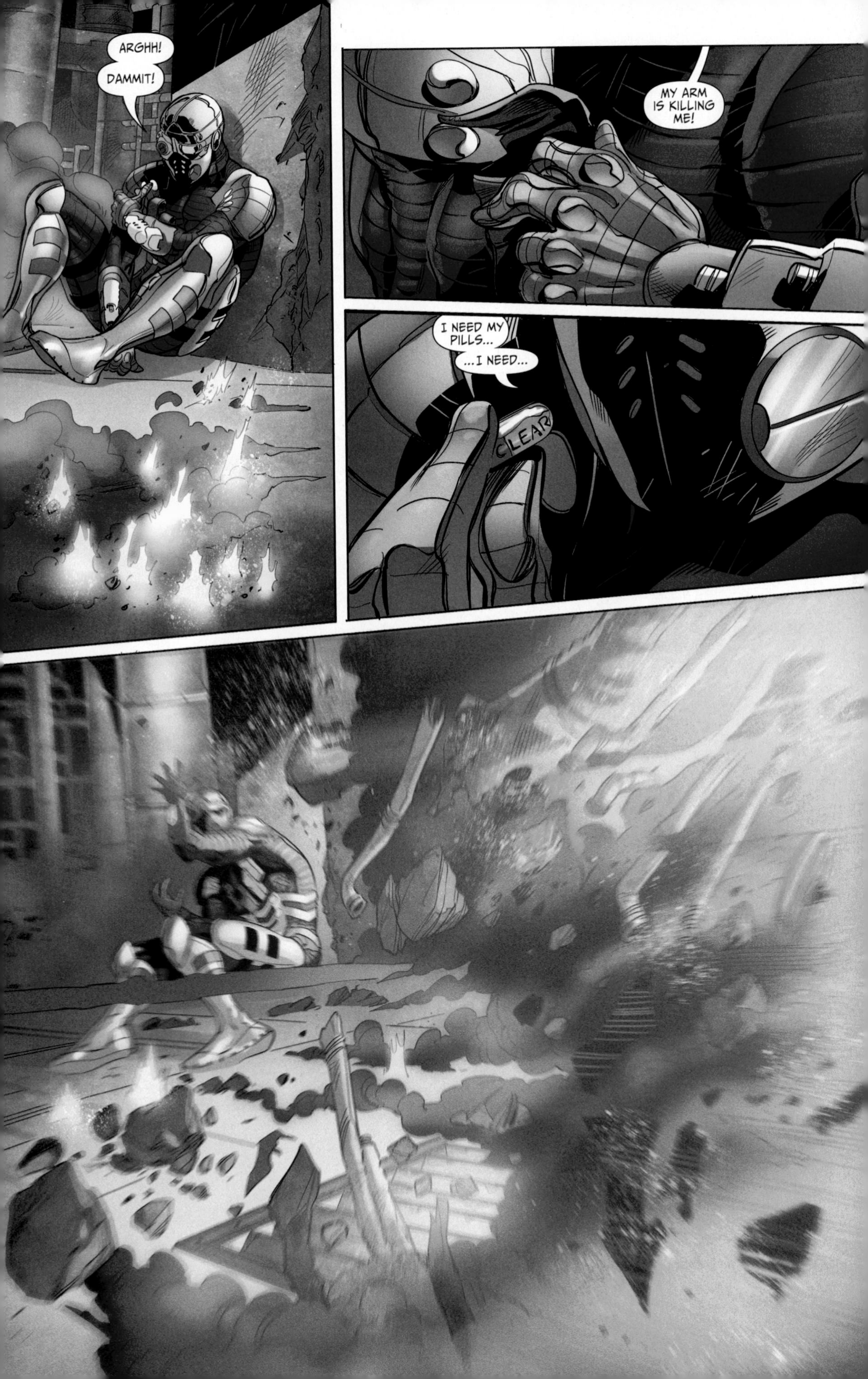
ARGHH!
DAMMIT!
MY ARM IS KILLING ME!
I NEED MY PILLS...
...I NEED...
CLEAR

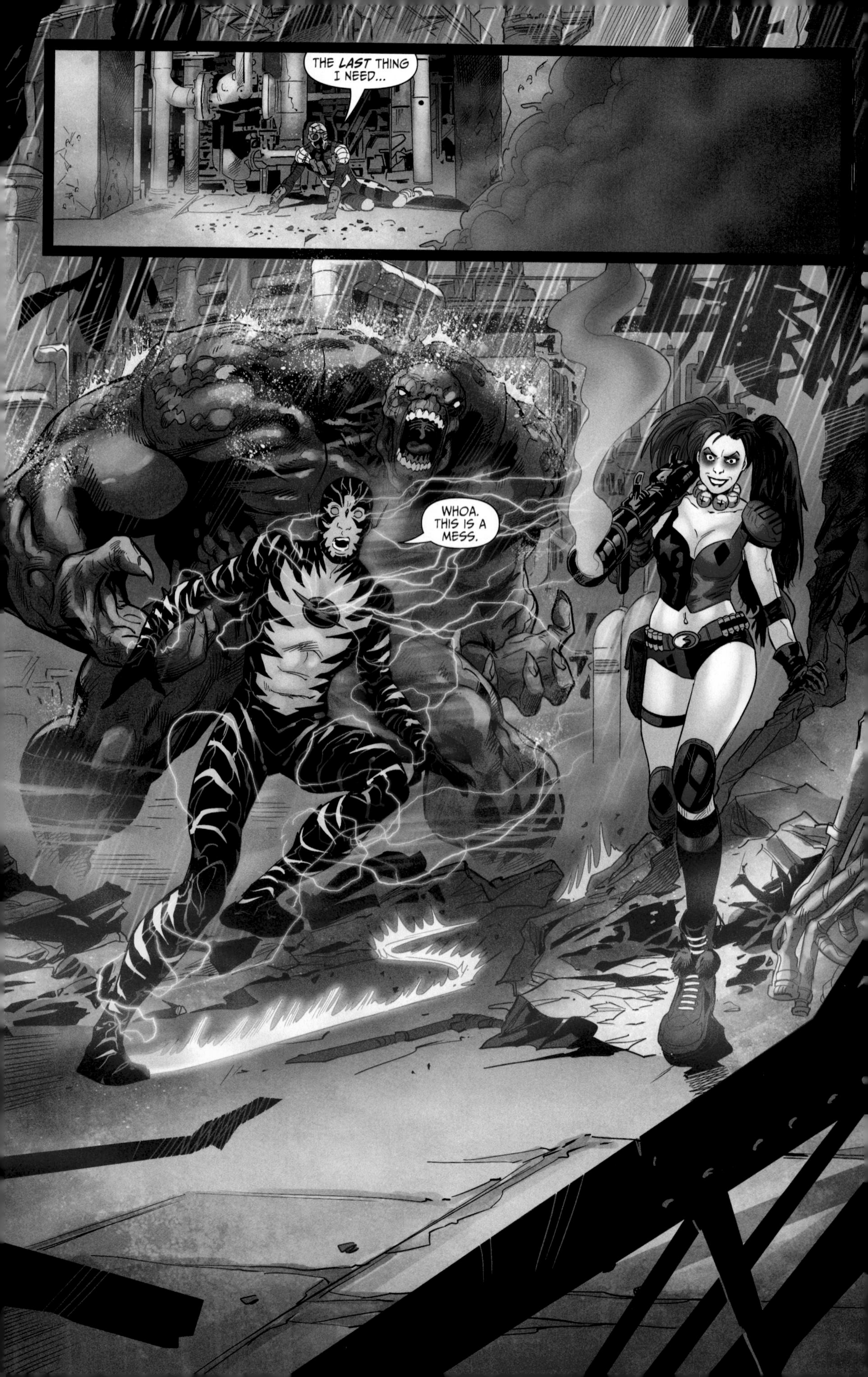
THE *LAST* THING I NEED...
WHOA. THIS IS A MESS.

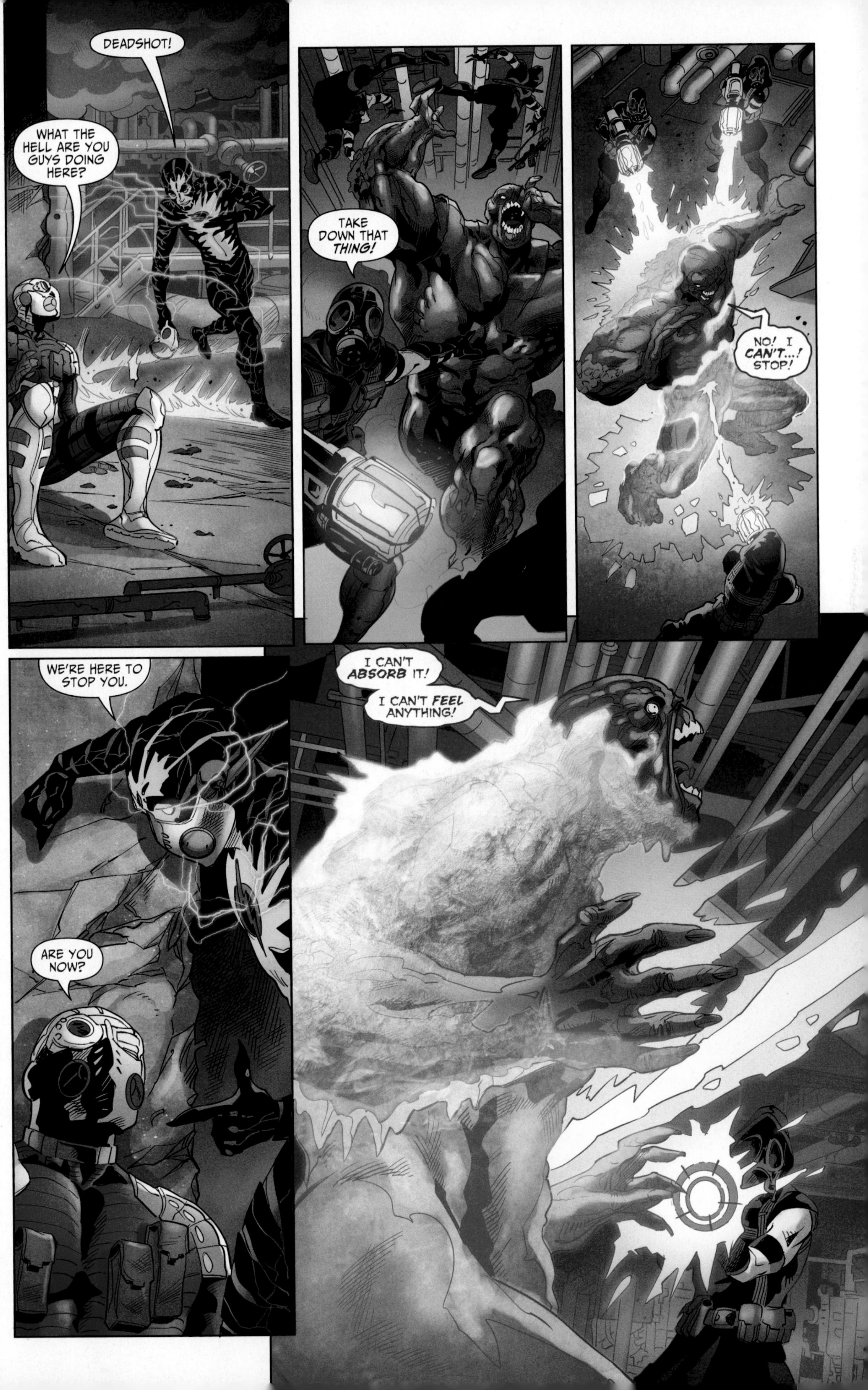
DEADSHOT!
WHAT THE HELL ARE YOU GUYS DOING HERE?
TAKE DOWN THAT *THING!*
NO! I *CAN'T...!* STOP!
WE'RE HERE TO STOP YOU.
ARE YOU NOW?
I CAN'T *ABSORB* IT!
I CAN'T *FEEL* ANYTHING!

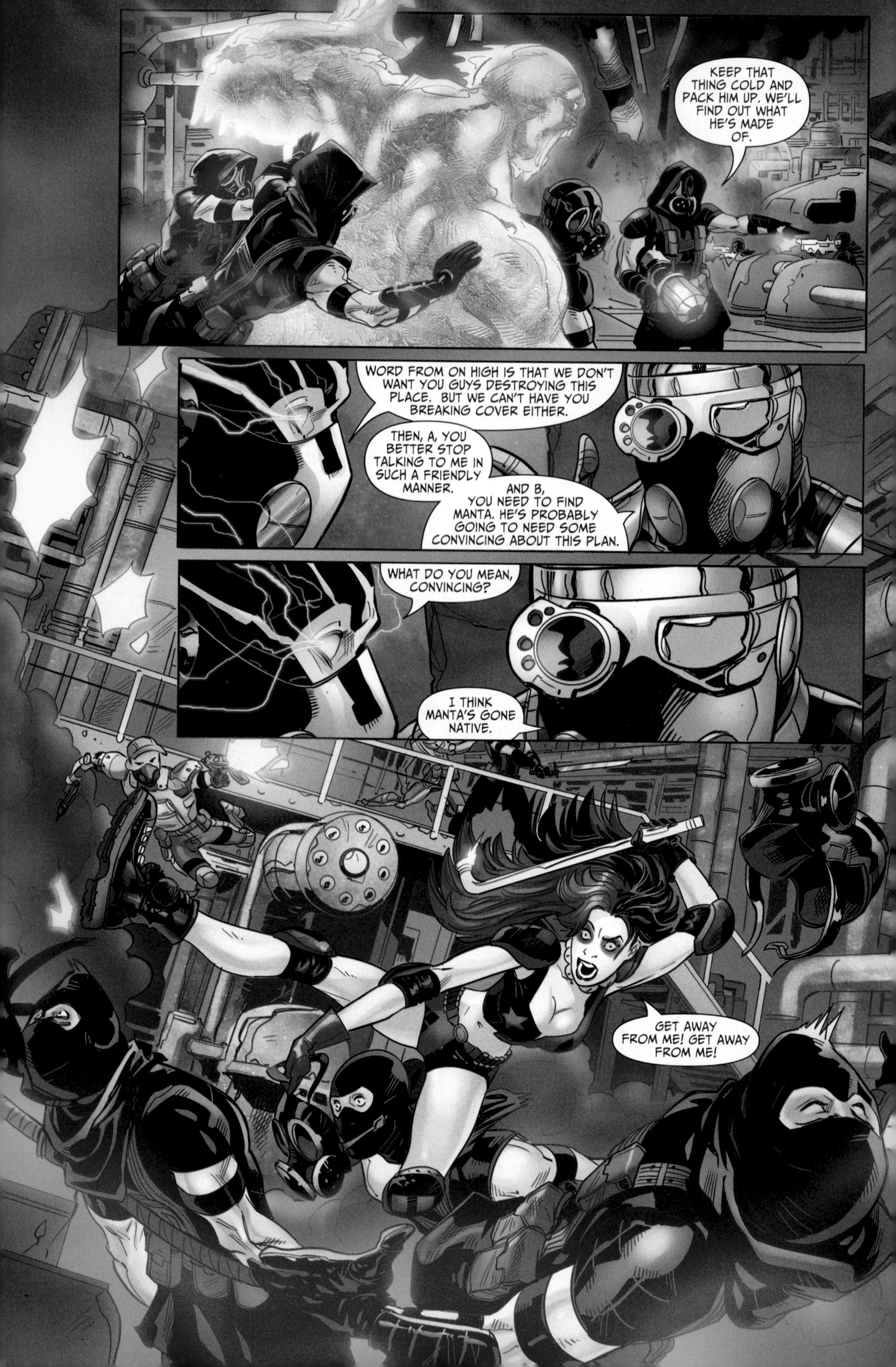
KEEP THAT THING COLD AND PACK HIM UP. WE'LL FIND OUT WHAT HE'S MADE OF.
WORD FROM ON HIGH IS THAT WE DON'T WANT YOU GUYS DESTROYING THIS PLACE. BUT WE CAN'T HAVE YOU BREAKING COVER EITHER.
THEN, A, YOU BETTER STOP TALKING TO ME IN SUCH A FRIENDLY MANNER.
AND B, YOU NEED TO FIND MANTA. HE'S PROBABLY GOING TO NEED SOME CONVINCING ABOUT THIS PLAN.
WHAT DO YOU MEAN, CONVINCING?
I THINK MANTA'S GONE NATIVE.
GET AWAY FROM ME! GET AWAY FROM ME!

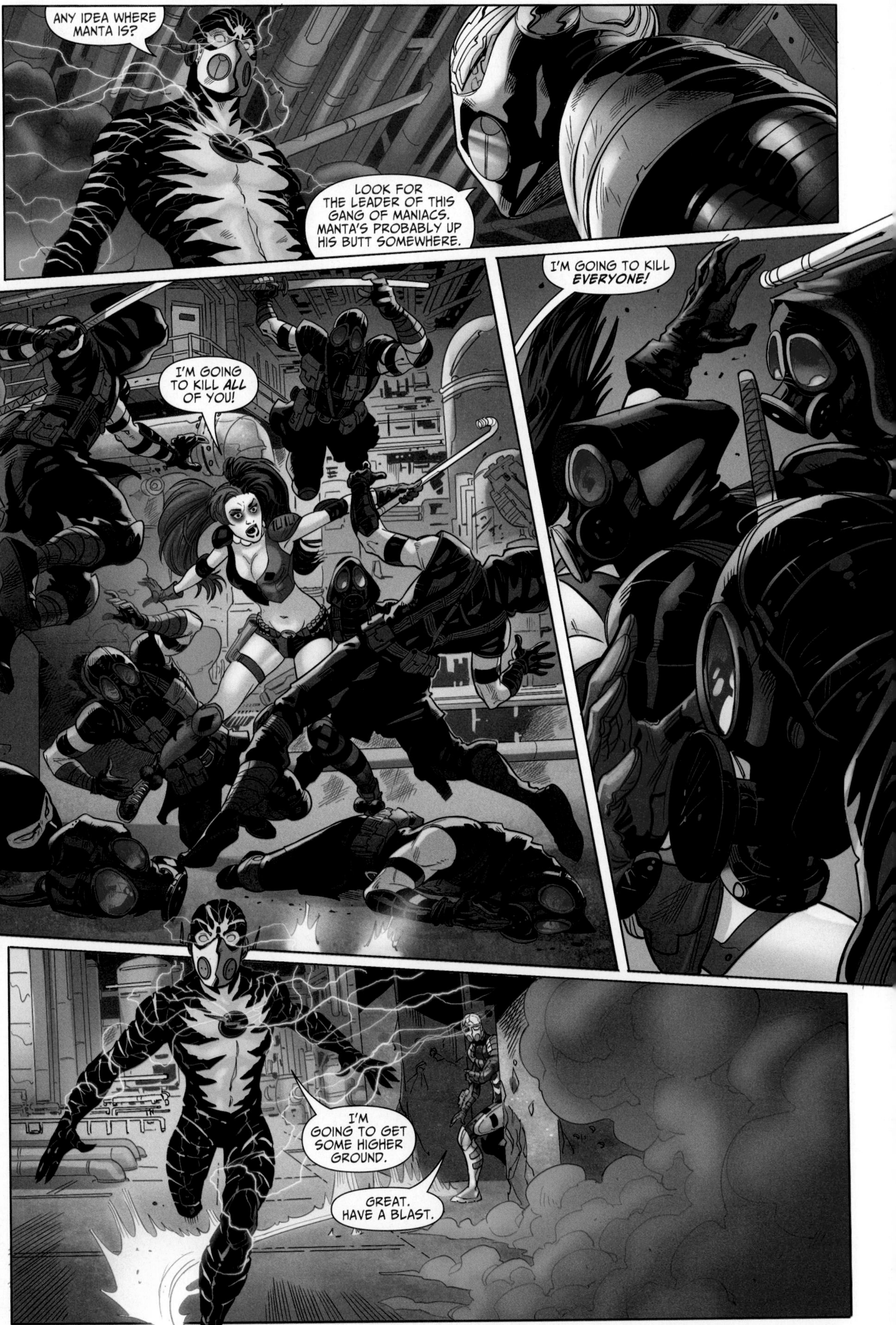
ANY IDEA WHERE MANTA IS?
LOOK FOR THE LEADER OF THIS GANG OF MANIACS. MANTA'S PROBABLY UP HIS BUTT SOMEWHERE.
I'M GOING TO KILL ALL OF YOU!
I'M GOING TO KILL EVERYONE!
I'M GOING TO GET SOME HIGHER GROUND.
GREAT. HAVE A BLAST.

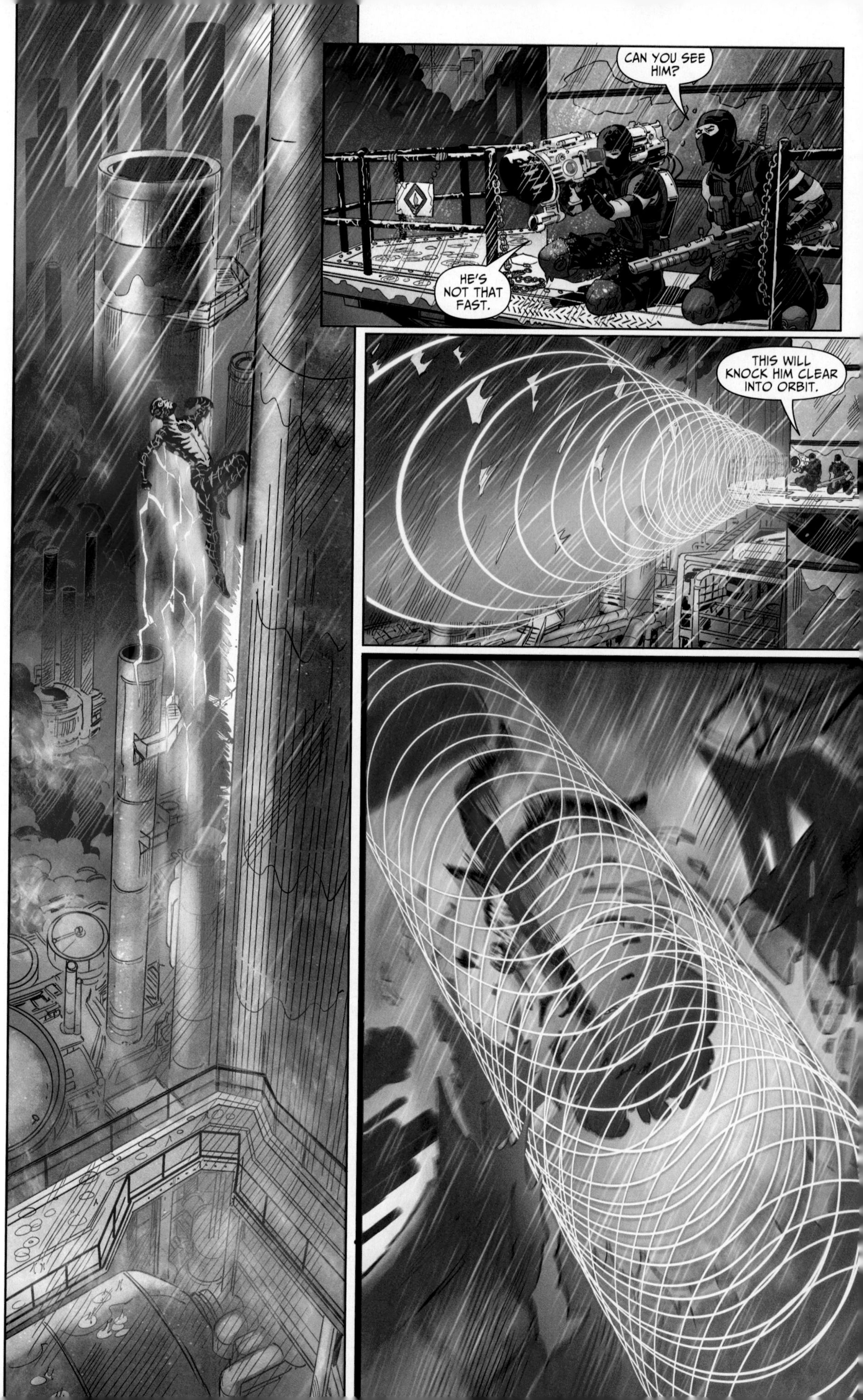
CAN YOU SEE HIM?
HE'S NOT THAT FAST.
THIS WILL KNOCK HIM CLEAR INTO ORBIT.

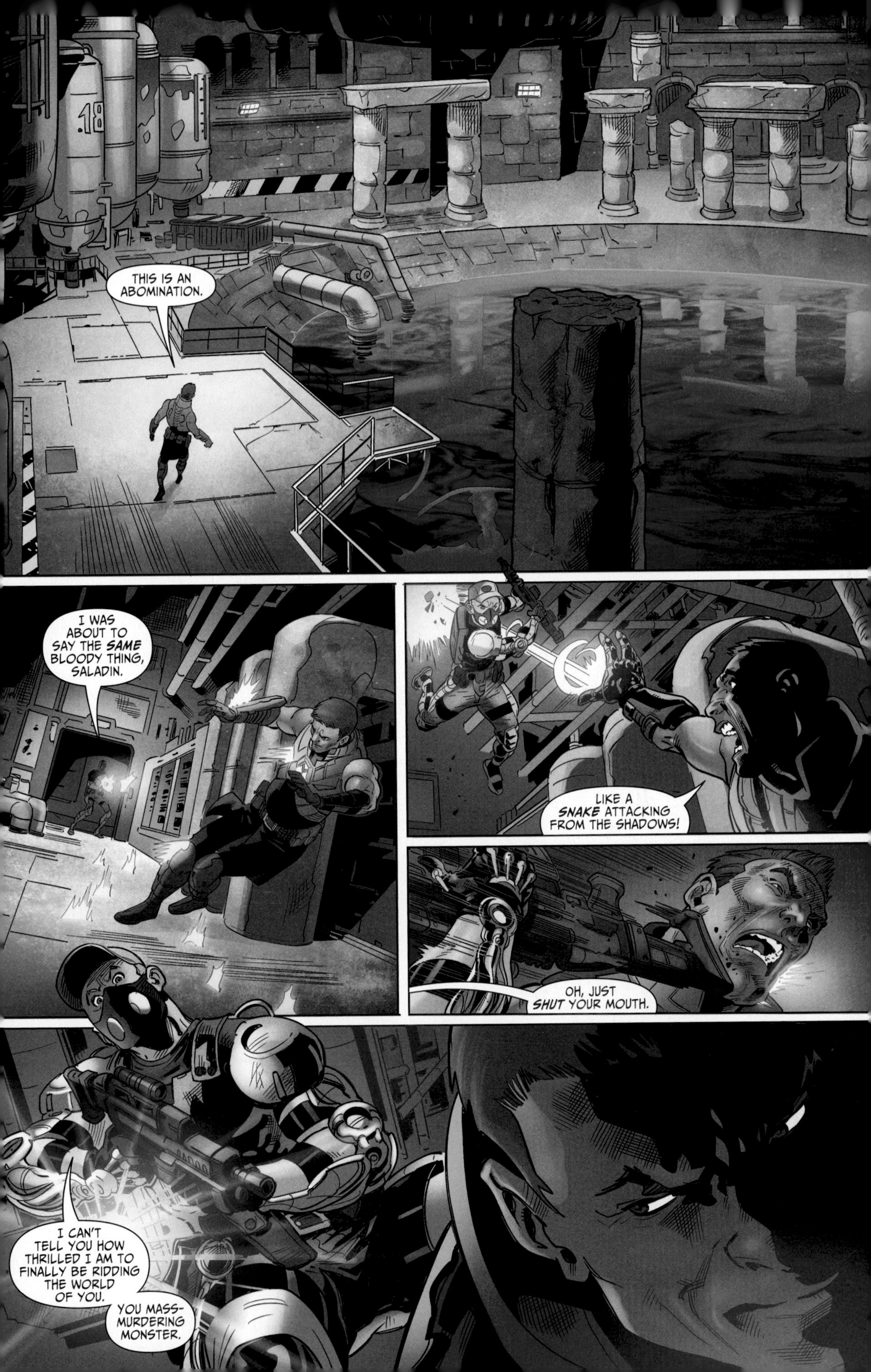
THIS IS AN ABOMINATION.
I WAS ABOUT TO SAY THE SAME BLOODY THING, SALADIN.
LIKE A SNAKE ATTACKING FROM THE SHADOWS!
OH, JUST SHUT YOUR MOUTH.
I CAN'T TELL YOU HOW THRILLED I AM TO FINALLY BE RIDDING THE WORLD OF YOU.
YOU MASS-MURDERING MONSTER.

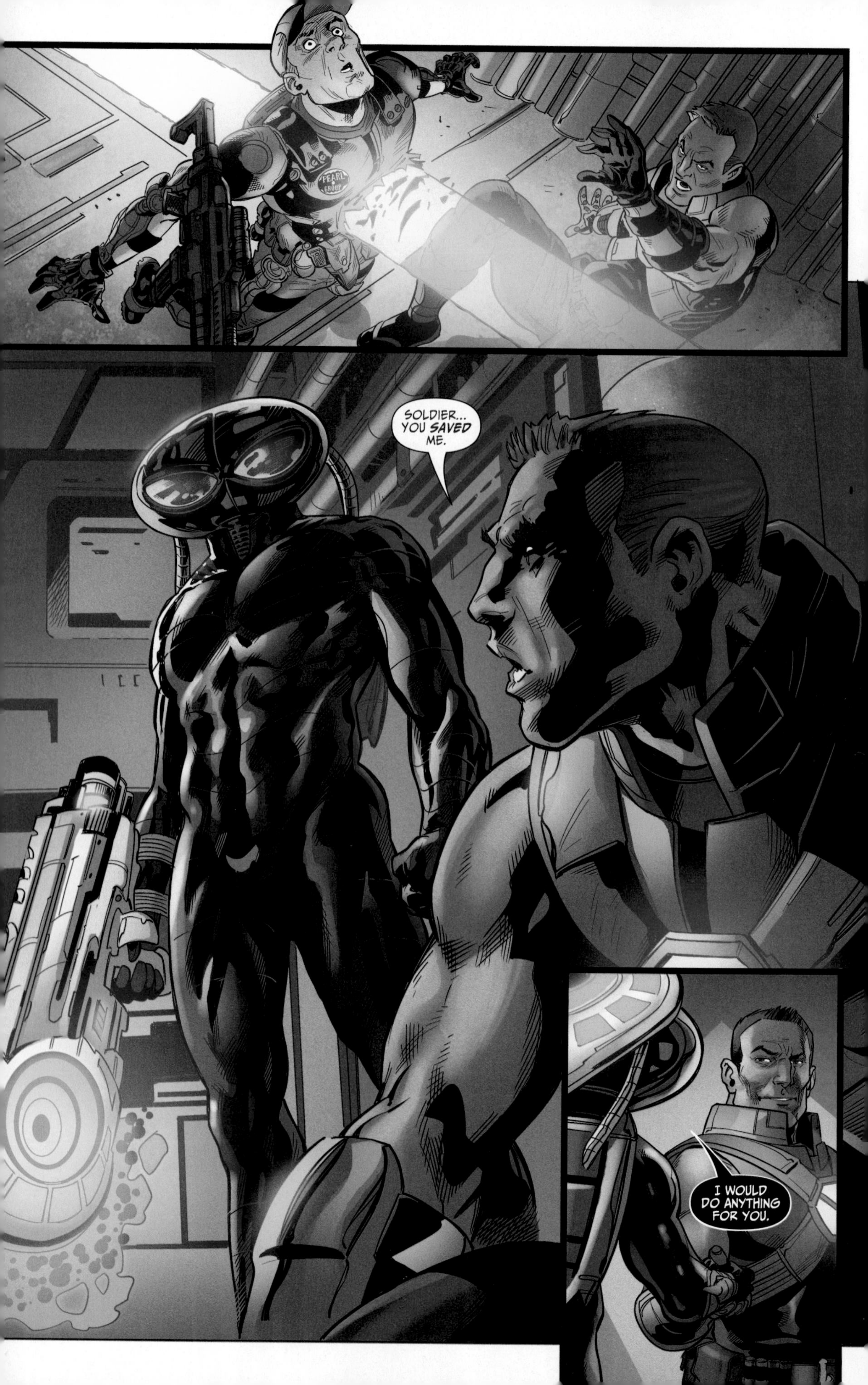
PEARL GROUP
SOLDIER... YOU SAVED ME.
I WOULD DO ANYTHING FOR YOU.

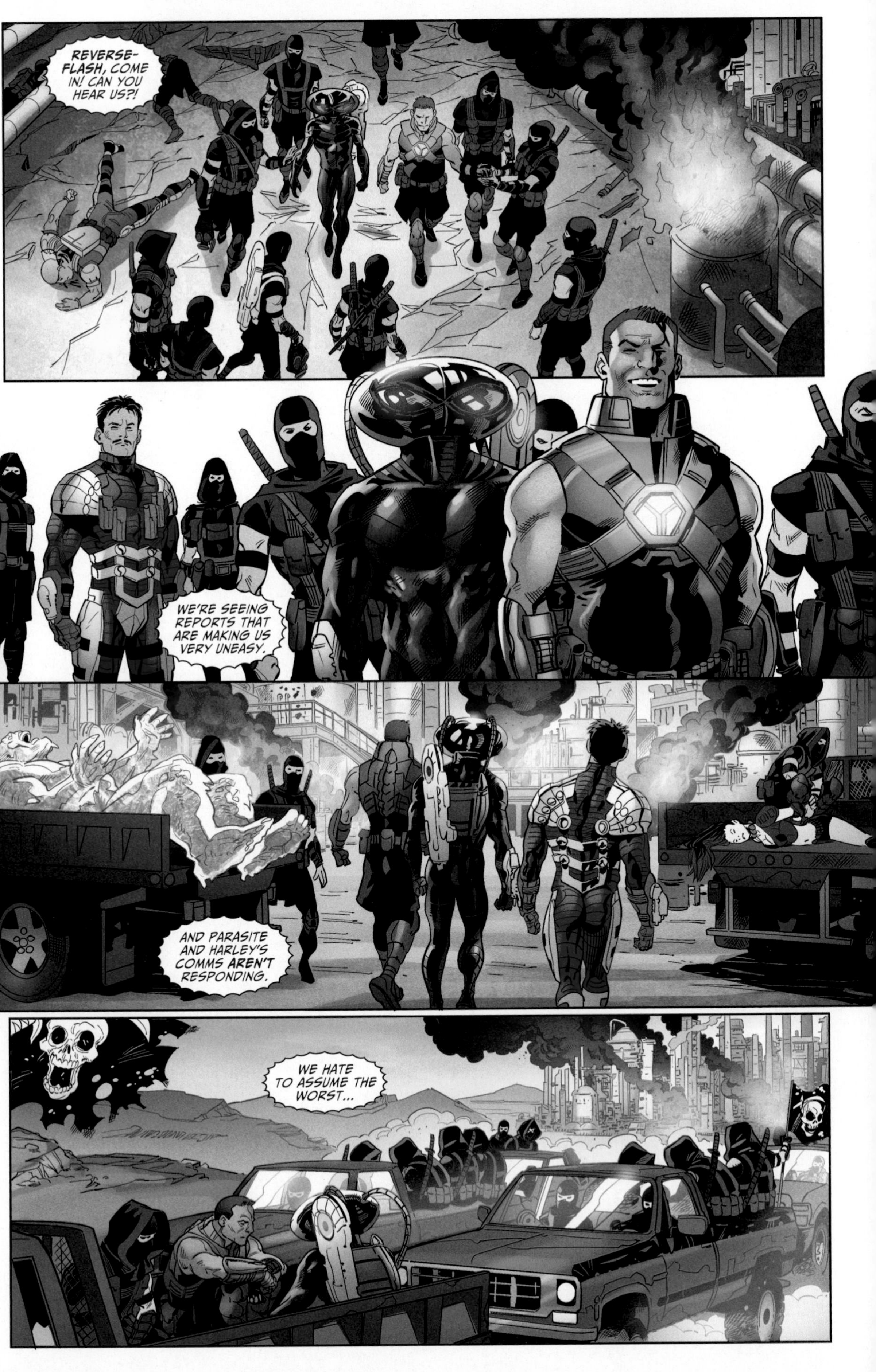
REVERSE-FLASH, COME IN! CAN YOU HEAR US?!
WE'RE SEEING REPORTS THAT ARE MAKING US VERY UNEASY.
AND PARASITE AND HARLEY'S COMMS AREN'T RESPONDING.
WE HATE TO ASSUME THE WORST...

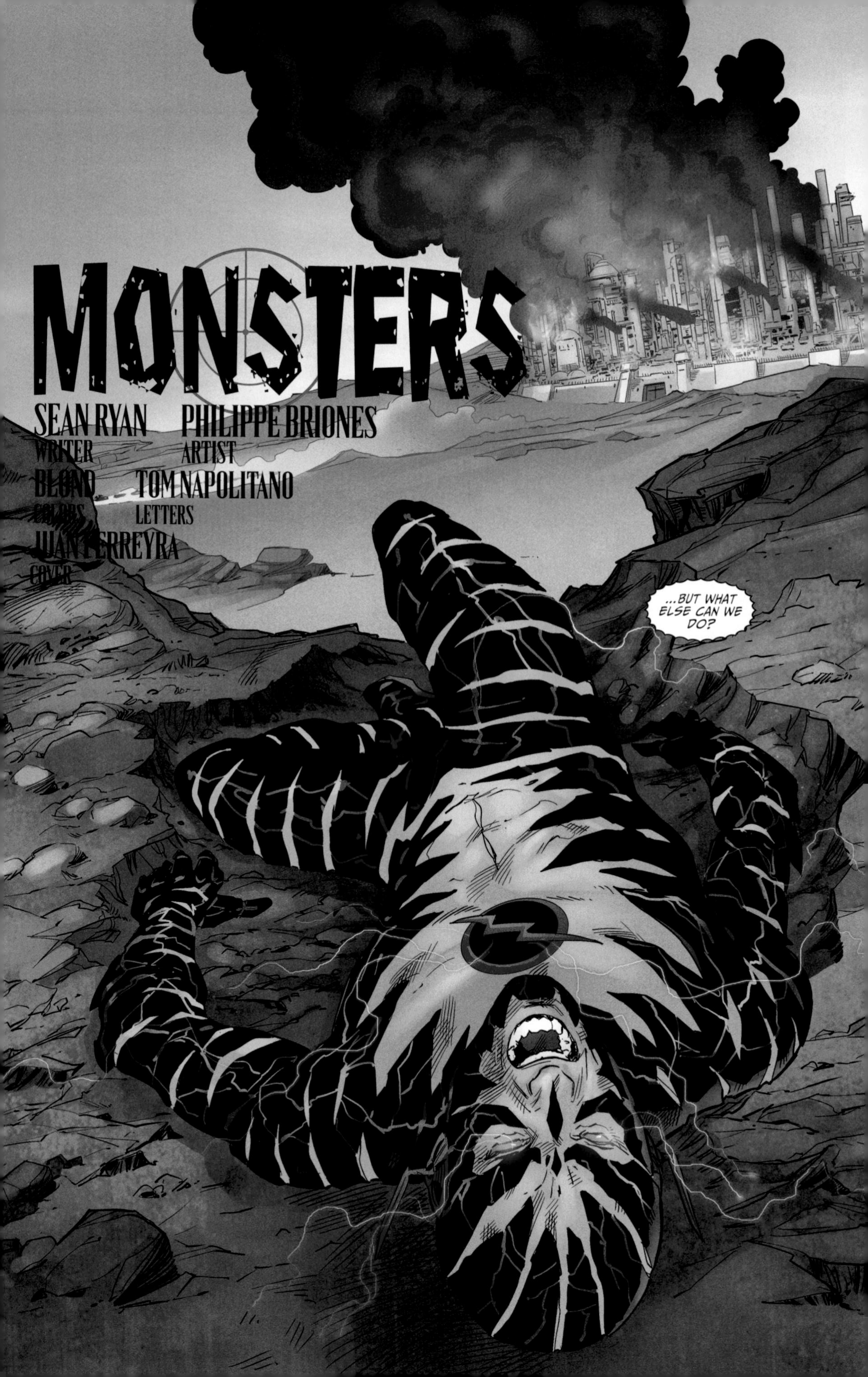
MONSTERS
SEAN RYAN WRITER
PHILIPPE BRIONES ARTIST
BLOND COLORS
TOM NAPOLITANO LETTERS
JUAN FERREYRA COVER
...BUT WHAT ELSE CAN WE DO?

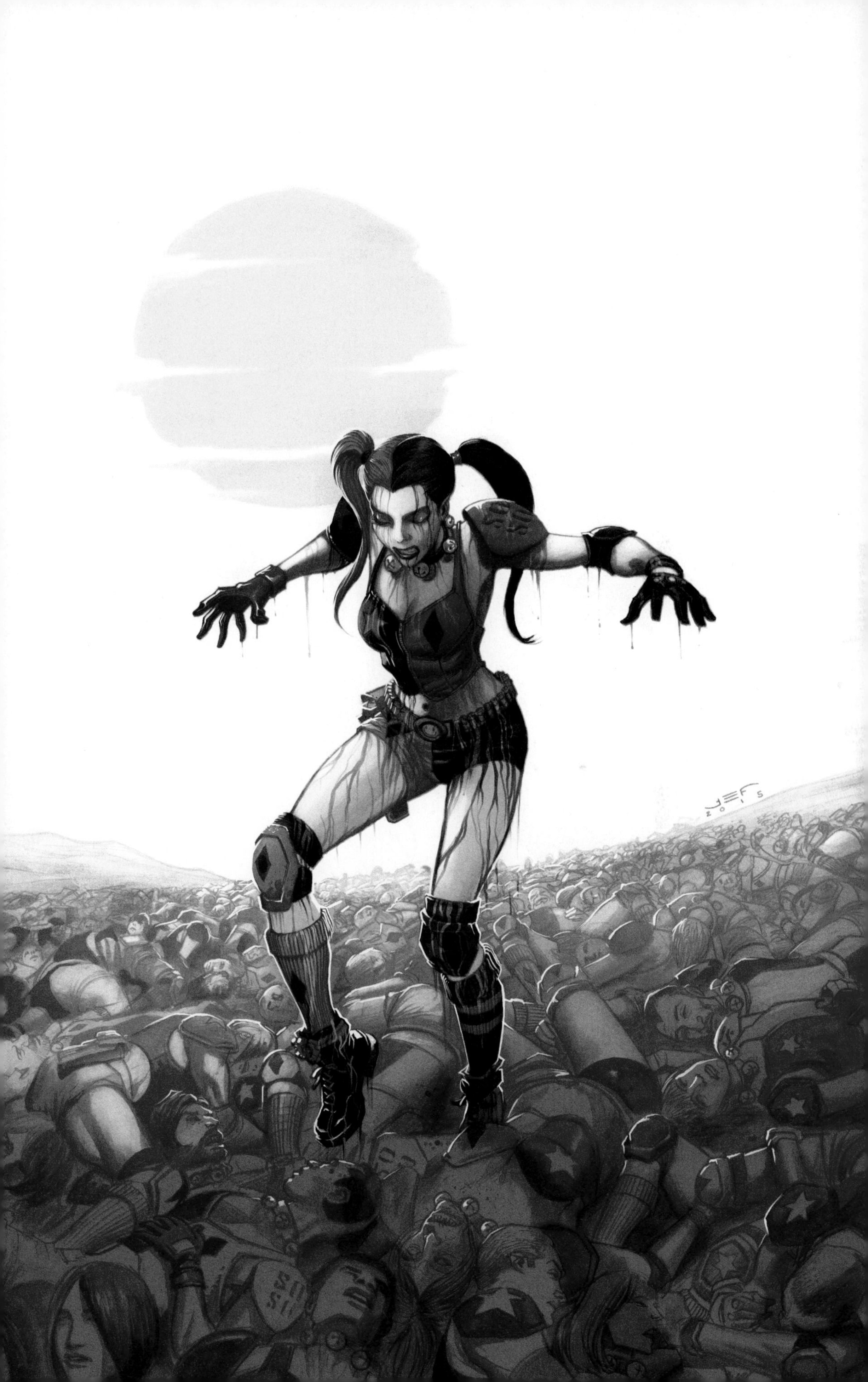

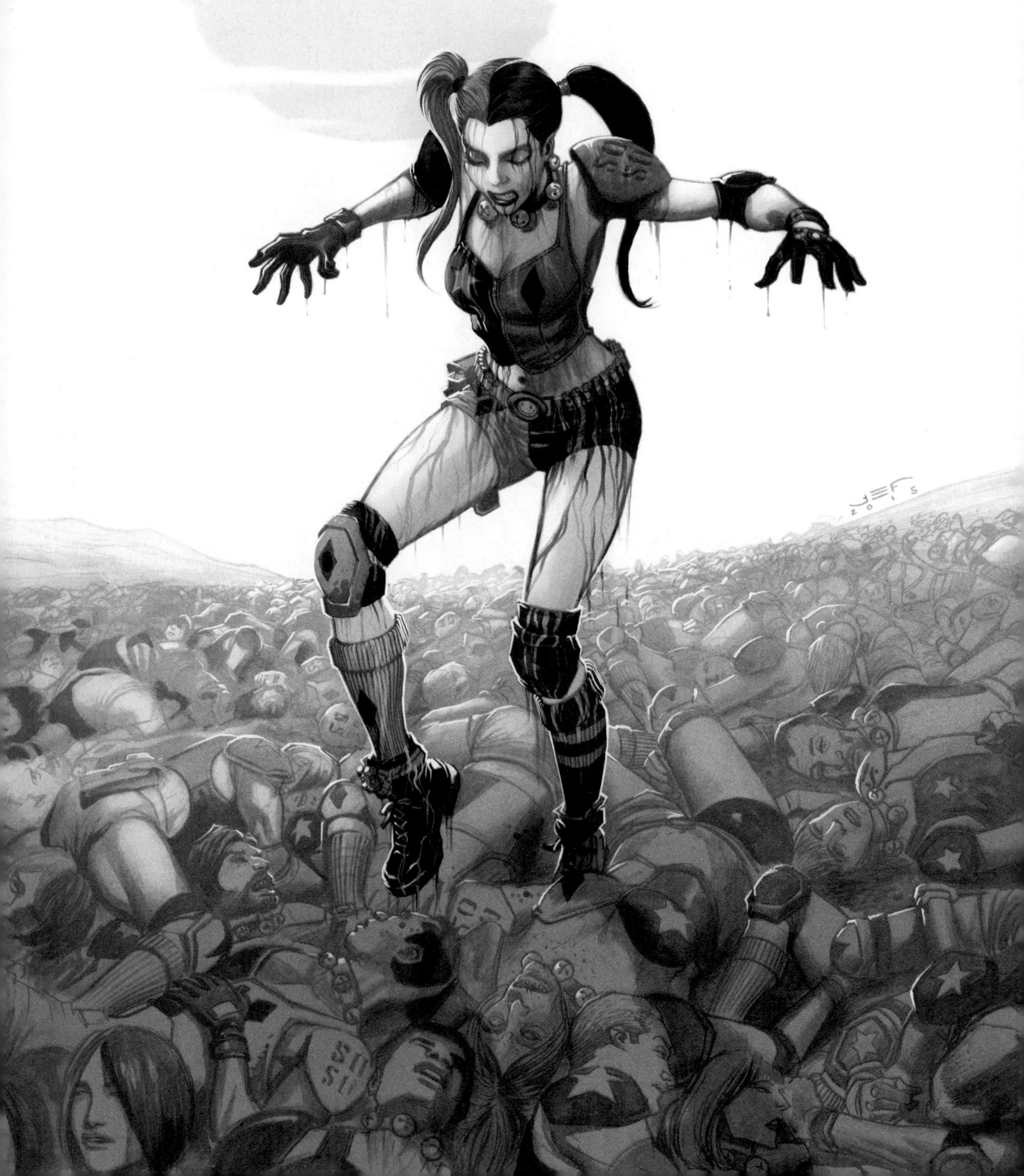

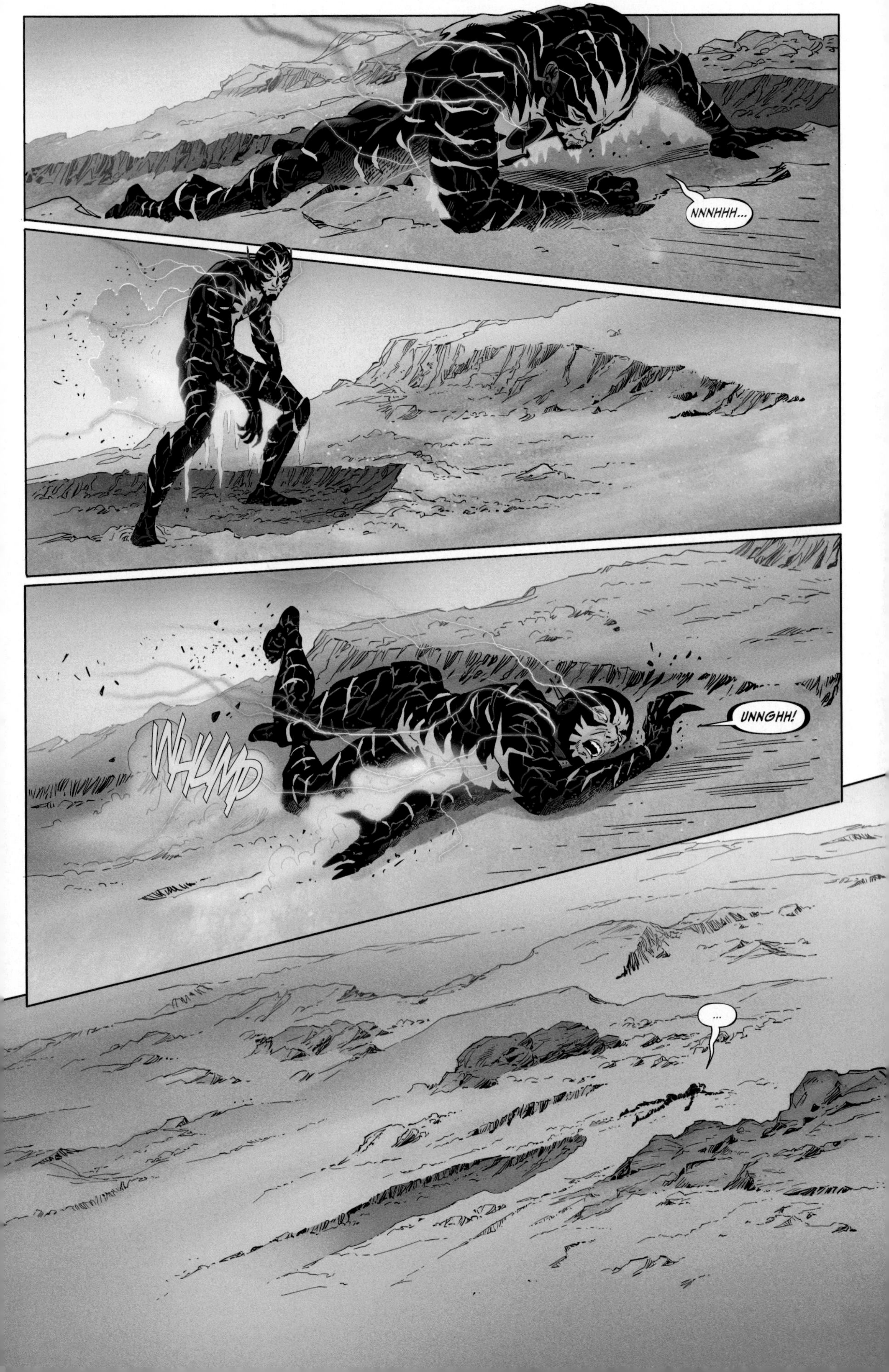
NNNHHH...
WHUMP
UNNGHH!
...

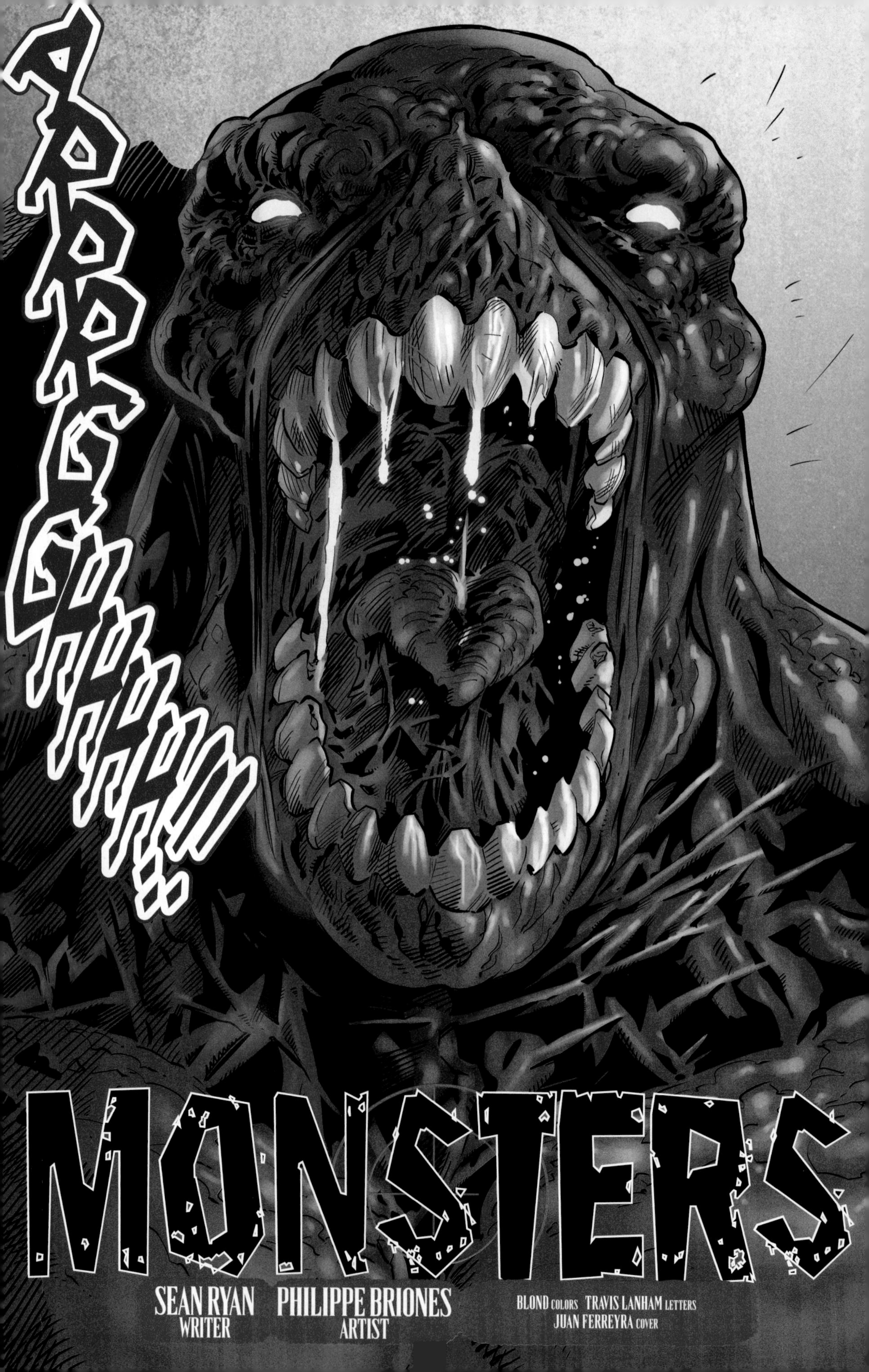
ARRRGGHHHH!!
MONSTERS
SEAN RYAN WRITER
PHILIPPE BRIONES ARTIST
BLOND COLORS TRAVIS LANHAM LETTERS
JUAN FERREYRA COVER

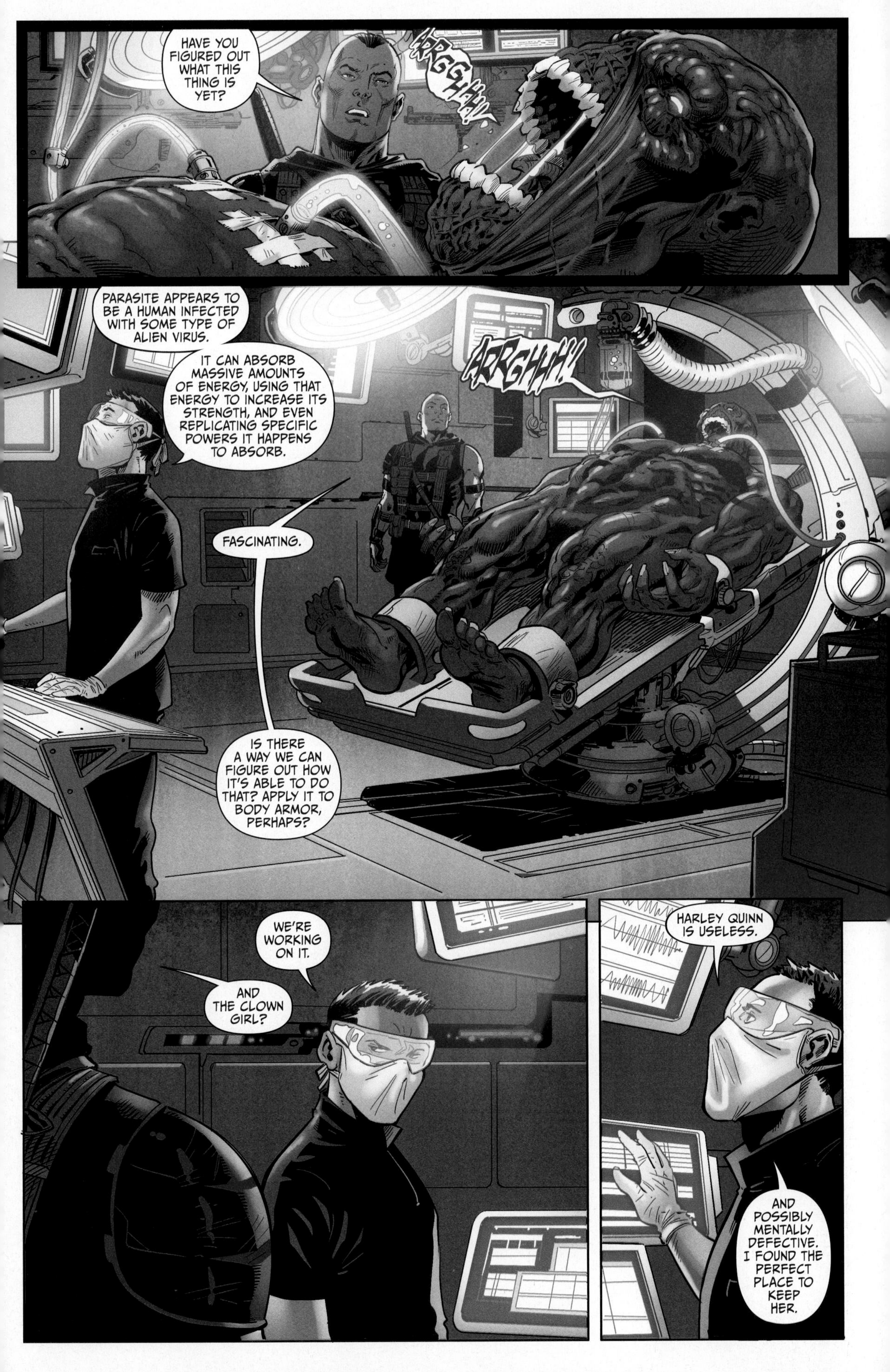
HAVE YOU FIGURED OUT WHAT THIS THING IS YET?
ARRGGHHH!
PARASITE APPEARS TO BE A HUMAN INFECTED WITH SOME TYPE OF ALIEN VIRUS.
IT CAN ABSORB MASSIVE AMOUNTS OF ENERGY, USING THAT ENERGY TO INCREASE ITS STRENGTH, AND EVEN REPLICATING SPECIFIC POWERS IT HAPPENS TO ABSORB.
ARRGHHH!
FASCINATING.
IS THERE A WAY WE CAN FIGURE OUT HOW IT'S ABLE TO DO THAT? APPLY IT TO BODY ARMOR, PERHAPS?
WE'RE WORKING ON IT.
AND THE CLOWN GIRL?
HARLEY QUINN IS USELESS.
AND POSSIBLY MENTALLY DEFECTIVE. I FOUND THE PERFECT PLACE TO KEEP HER.

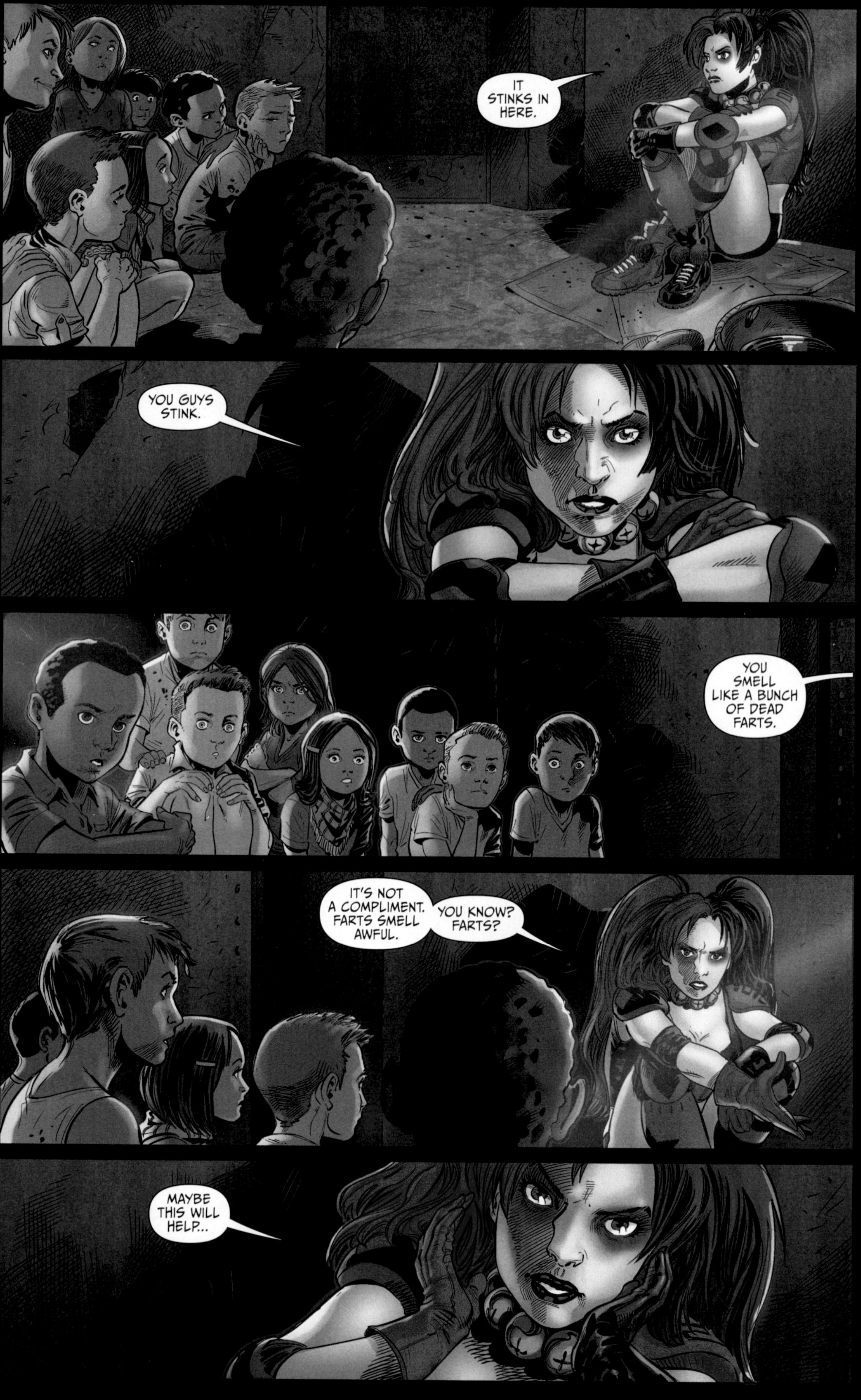
IT STINKS IN HERE.
YOU GUYS STINK.
YOU SMELL LIKE A BUNCH OF DEAD FARTS.
IT'S NOT A COMPLIMENT. FARTS SMELL AWFUL.
YOU KNOW? FARTS?
MAYBE THIS WILL HELP...

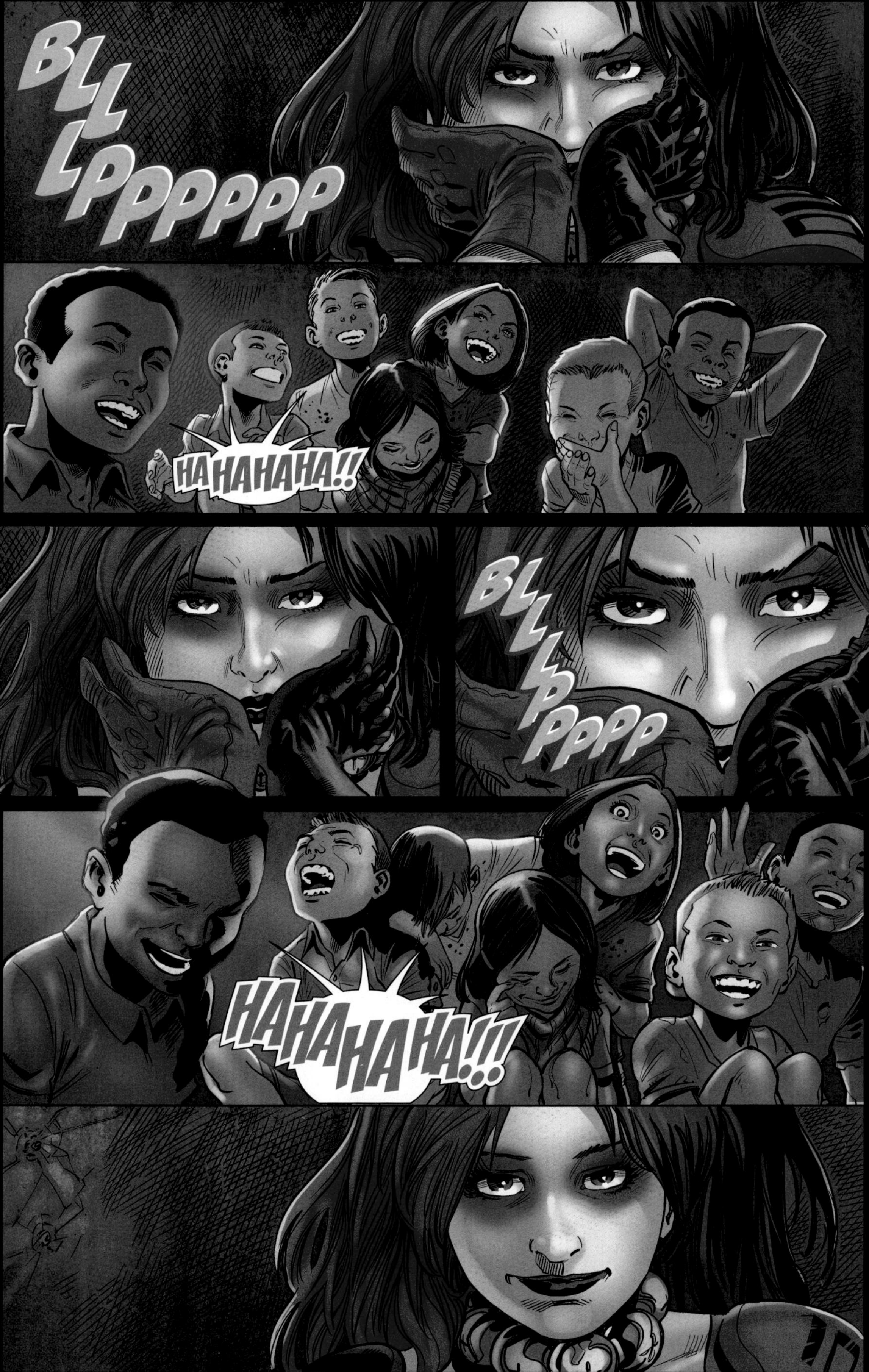
BLLLPPPPPP
HAHAHAHA!!
BLLLPPPP
HAHAHAHA!!!

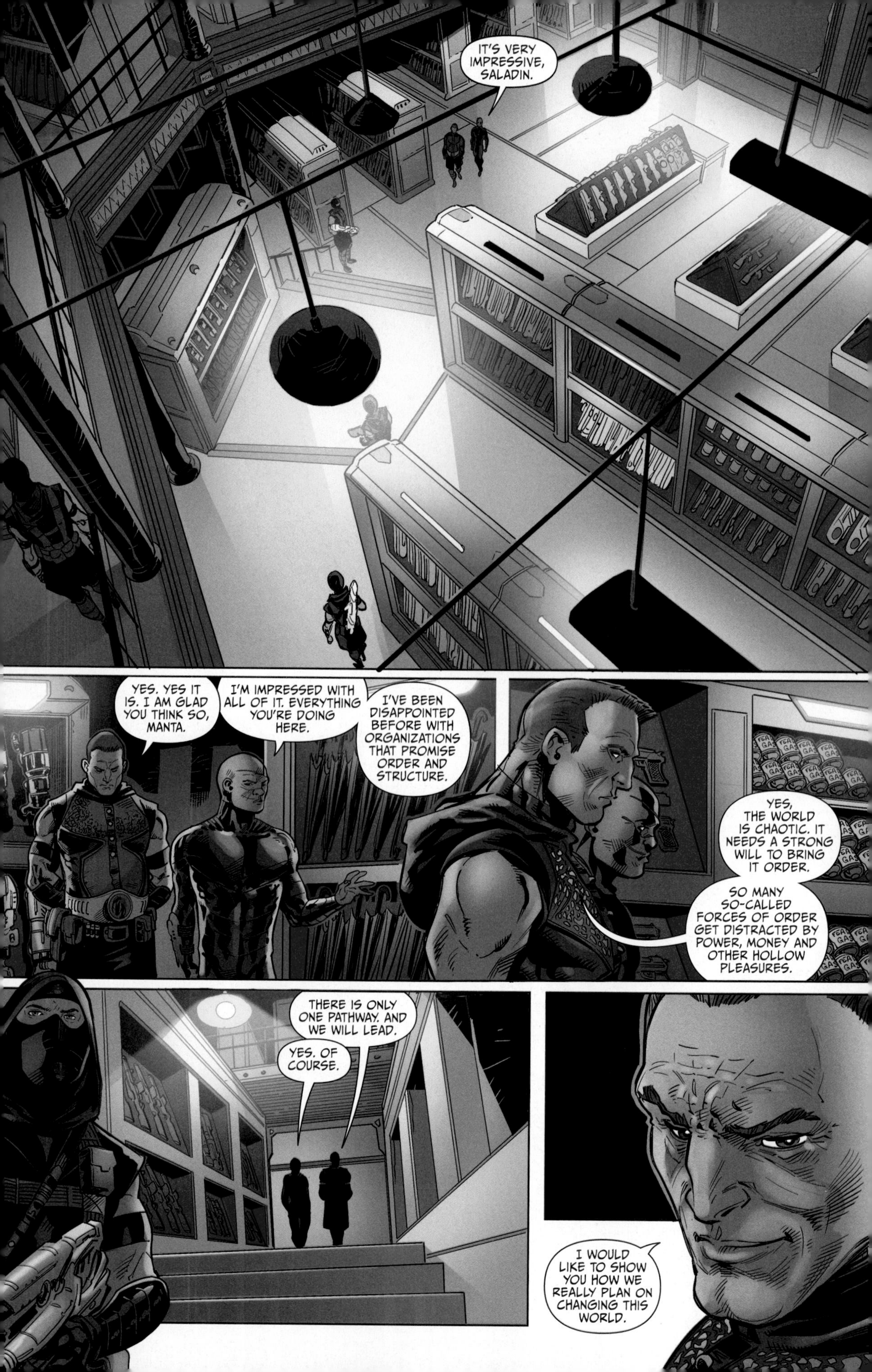
IT'S VERY IMPRESSIVE, SALADIN.
YES. YES IT IS. I AM GLAD YOU THINK SO, MANTA.
I'M IMPRESSED WITH ALL OF IT. EVERYTHING YOU'RE DOING HERE.
I'VE BEEN DISAPPOINTED BEFORE WITH ORGANIZATIONS THAT PROMISE ORDER AND STRUCTURE.
YES, THE WORLD IS CHAOTIC. IT NEEDS A STRONG WILL TO BRING IT ORDER.
SO MANY SO-CALLED FORCES OF ORDER GET DISTRACTED BY POWER, MONEY AND OTHER HOLLOW PLEASURES.
THERE IS ONLY ONE PATHWAY. AND WE WILL LEAD.
YES. OF COURSE.
I WOULD LIKE TO SHOW YOU HOW WE REALLY PLAN ON CHANGING THIS WORLD.

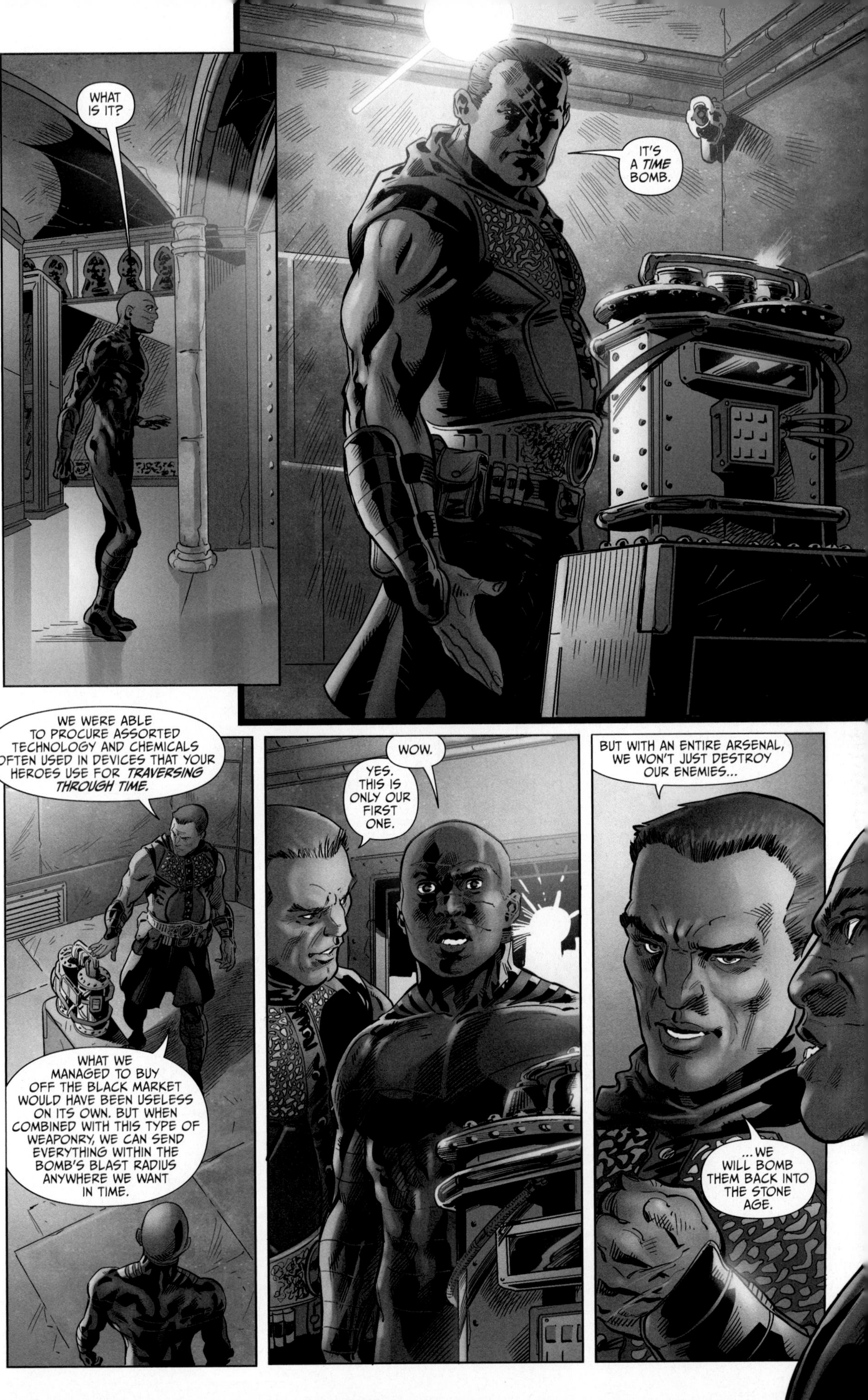
WHAT IS IT?
IT'S A *TIME* BOMB.
WE WERE ABLE TO PROCURE ASSORTED TECHNOLOGY AND CHEMICALS OFTEN USED IN DEVICES THAT YOUR HEROES USE FOR *TRAVERSING THROUGH TIME.*
WHAT WE MANAGED TO BUY OFF THE BLACK MARKET WOULD HAVE BEEN USELESS ON ITS OWN. BUT WHEN COMBINED WITH THIS TYPE OF WEAPONRY, WE CAN SEND EVERYTHING WITHIN THE BOMB'S BLAST RADIUS ANYWHERE WE WANT IN TIME.
WOW.
YES. THIS IS ONLY OUR FIRST ONE.
BUT WITH AN ENTIRE ARSENAL, WE WON'T JUST DESTROY OUR ENEMIES...
...WE WILL BOMB THEM BACK INTO THE STONE AGE.

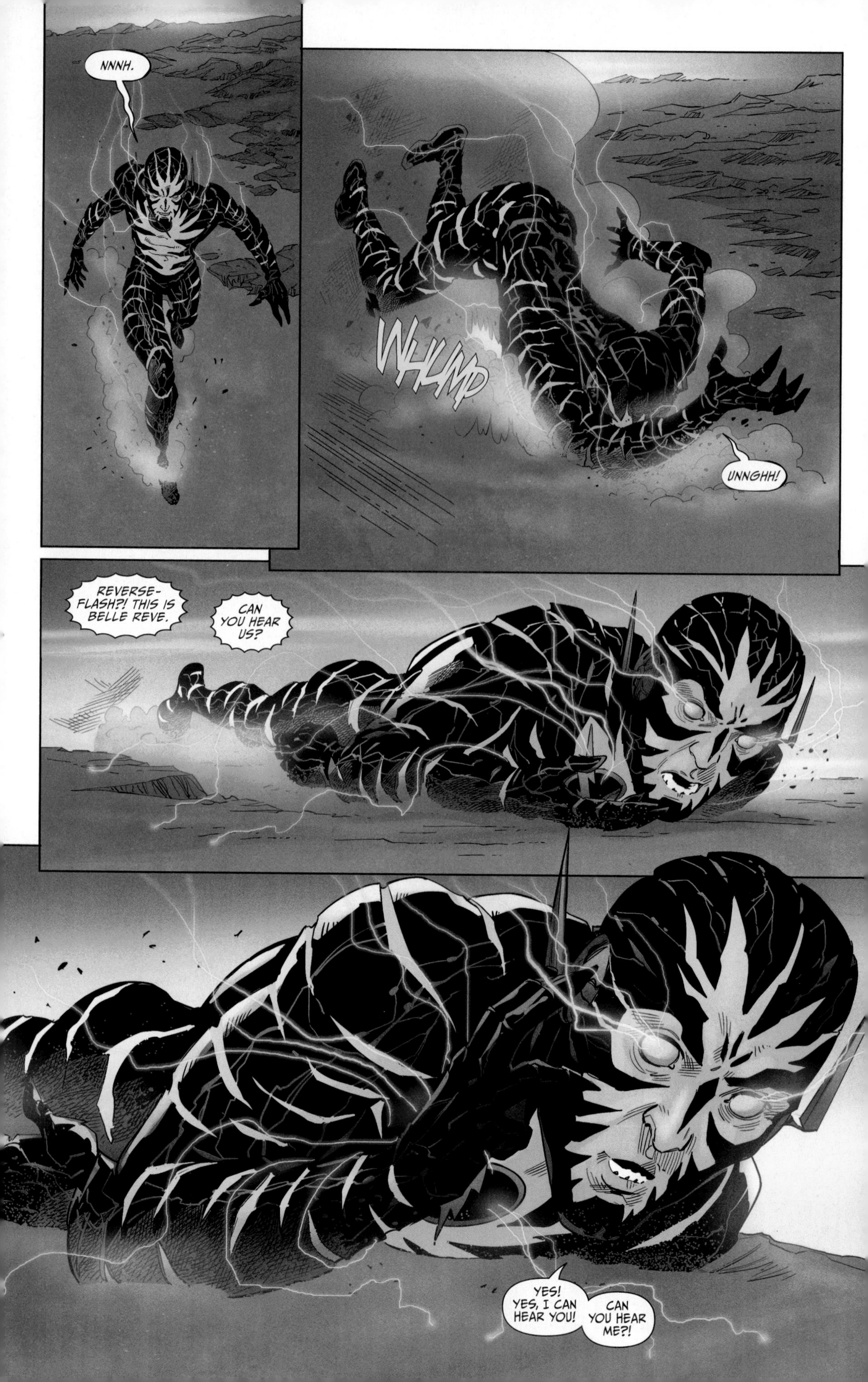
NNNH.
WHUMP
UNNGHH!
REVERSE-FLASH?! THIS IS BELLE REVE.
CAN YOU HEAR US?
YES! YES, I CAN HEAR YOU!
CAN YOU HEAR ME?!

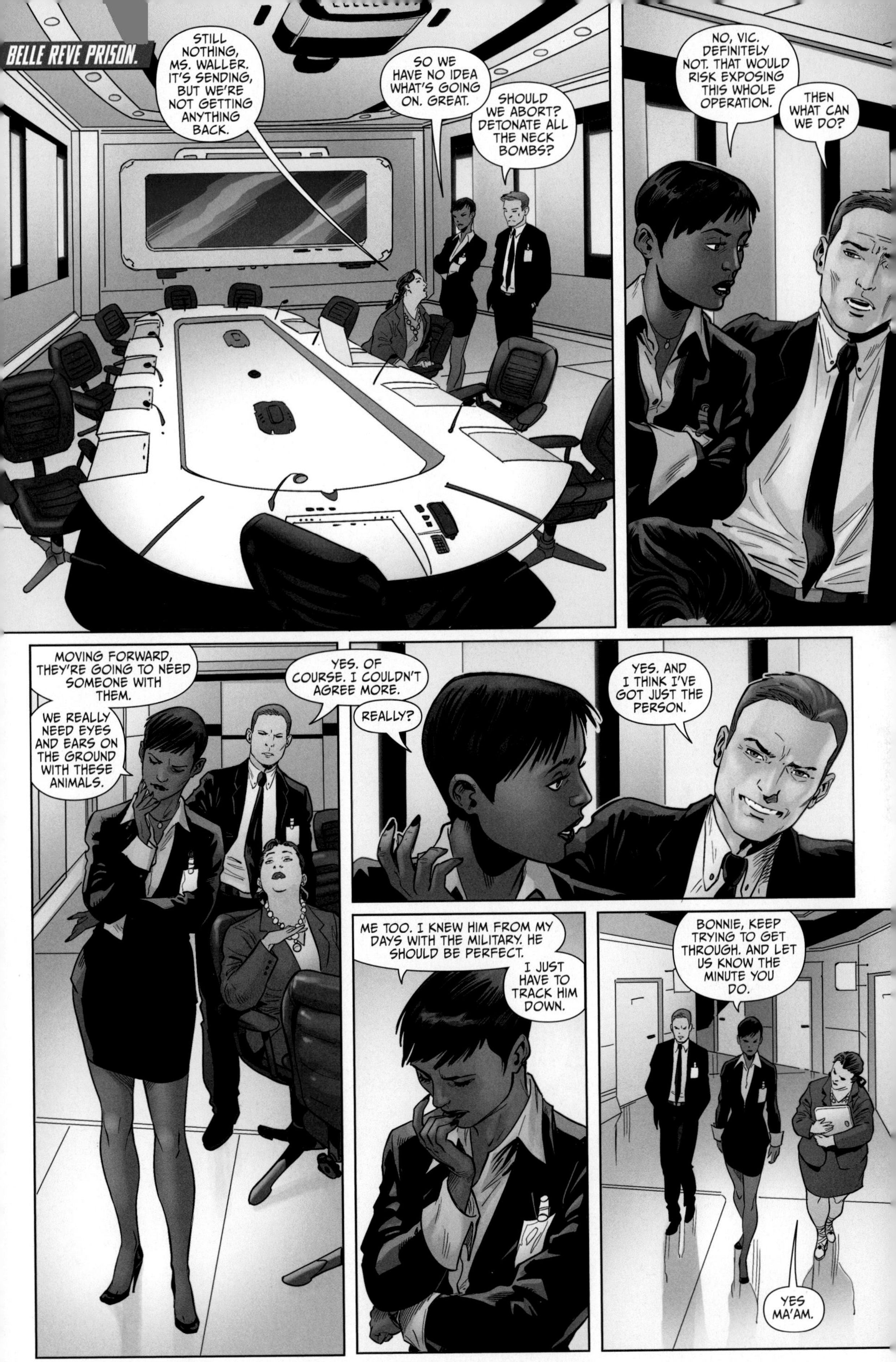
BELLE REVE PRISON.
STILL NOTHING, MS. WALLER. IT'S SENDING, BUT WE'RE NOT GETTING ANYTHING BACK.
SO WE HAVE NO IDEA WHAT'S GOING ON. GREAT.
SHOULD WE ABORT? DETONATE ALL THE NECK BOMBS?
NO, VIC. DEFINITELY NOT. THAT WOULD RISK EXPOSING THIS WHOLE OPERATION.
THEN WHAT CAN WE DO?
MOVING FORWARD, THEY'RE GOING TO NEED SOMEONE WITH THEM.
WE REALLY NEED EYES AND EARS ON THE GROUND WITH THESE ANIMALS.
YES. OF COURSE. I COULDN'T AGREE MORE.
REALLY?
YES. AND I THINK I'VE GOT JUST THE PERSON.
ME TOO. I KNEW HIM FROM MY DAYS WITH THE MILITARY. HE SHOULD BE PERFECT.
I JUST HAVE TO TRACK HIM DOWN.
BONNIE, KEEP TRYING TO GET THROUGH. AND LET US KNOW THE MINUTE YOU DO.
YES MA'AM.

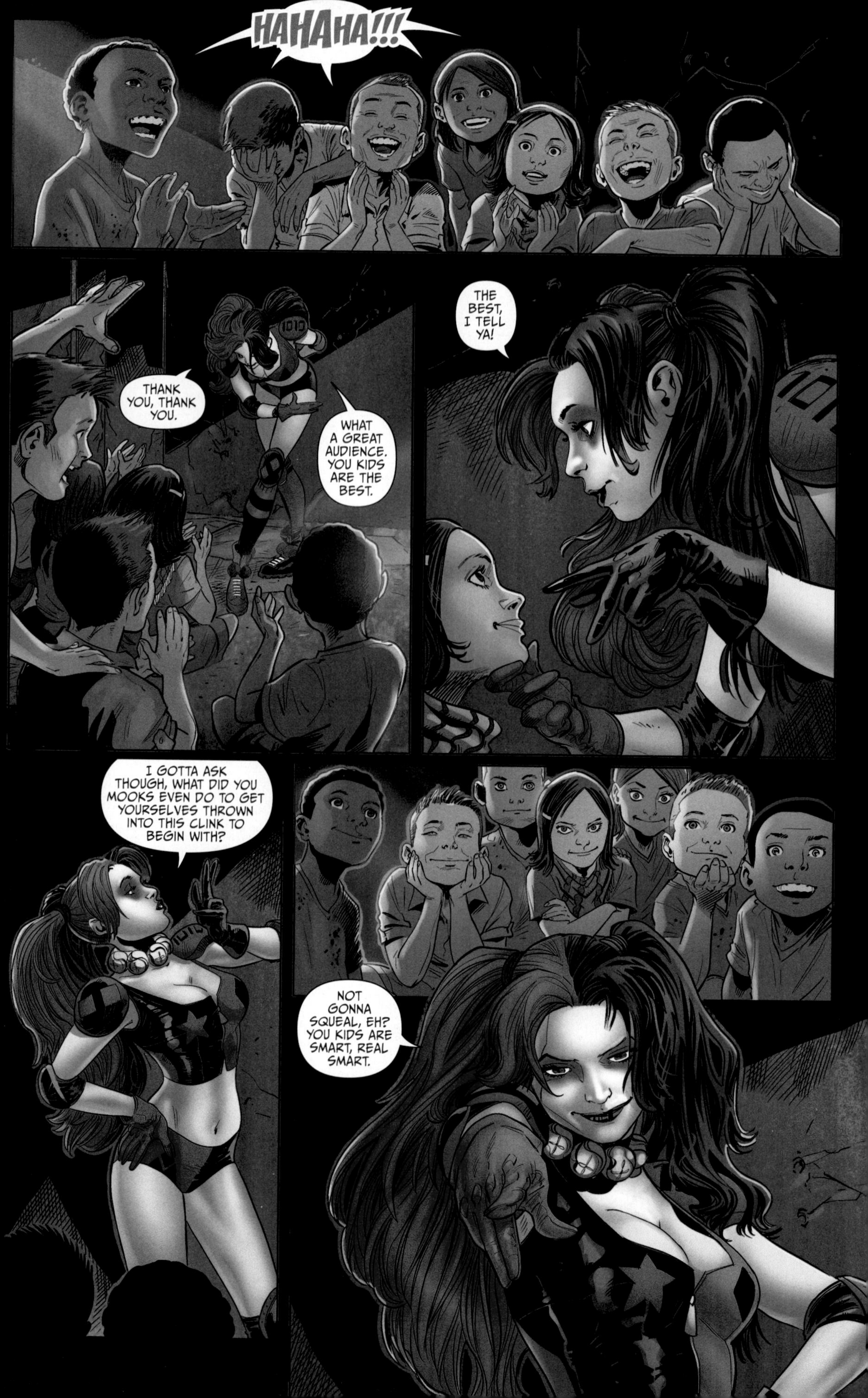
HAHAHA!!!
THANK YOU, THANK YOU.
WHAT A GREAT AUDIENCE. YOU KIDS ARE THE BEST.
THE BEST, I TELL YA!
I GOTTA ASK THOUGH, WHAT DID YOU MOOKS EVEN DO TO GET YOURSELVES THROWN INTO THIS CLINK TO BEGIN WITH?
NOT GONNA SQUEAL, EH? YOU KIDS ARE SMART, REAL SMART.

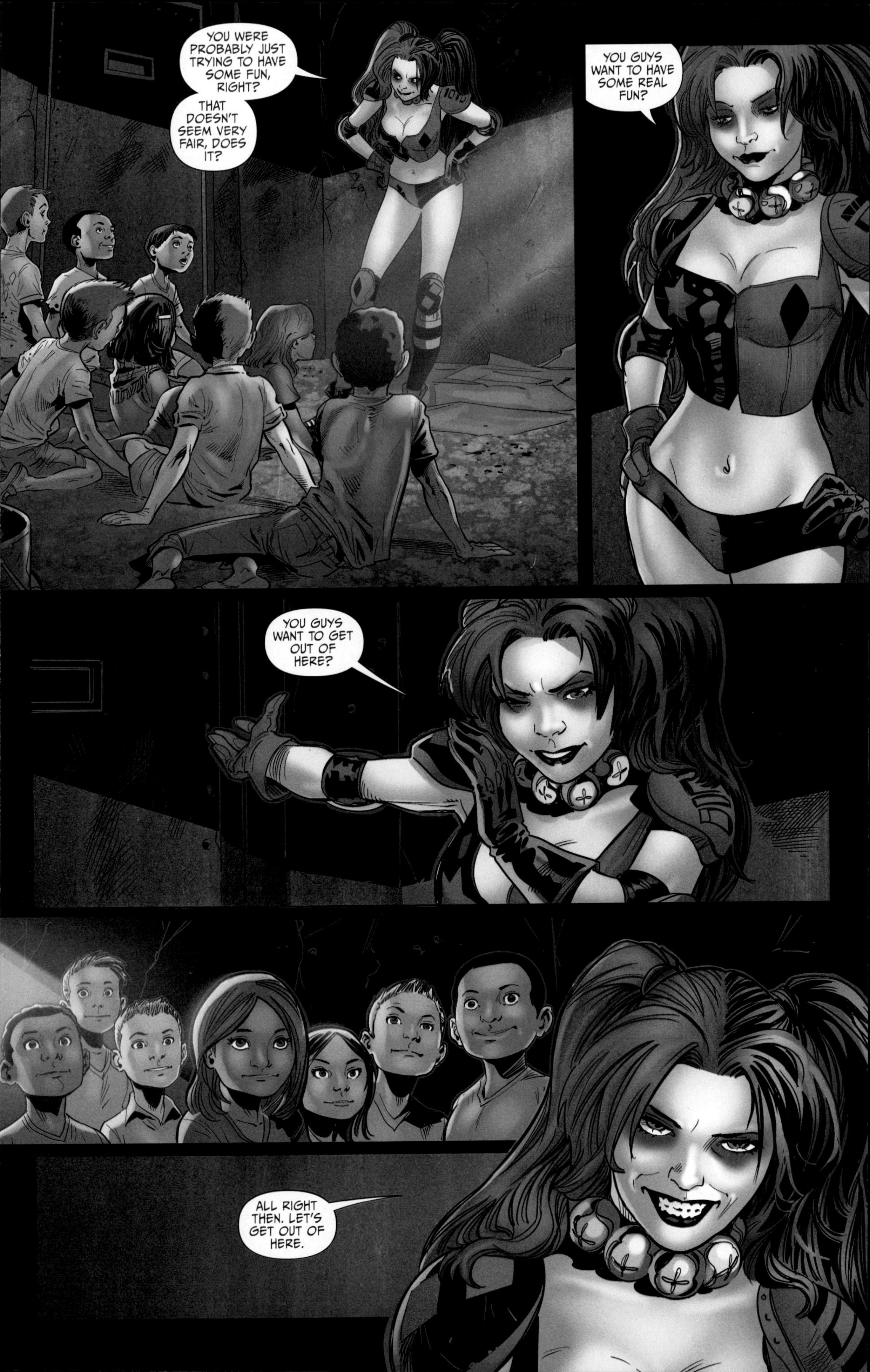
YOU WERE PROBABLY JUST TRYING TO HAVE SOME FUN, RIGHT?
THAT DOESN'T SEEM VERY FAIR, DOES IT?
YOU GUYS WANT TO HAVE SOME REAL FUN?
YOU GUYS WANT TO GET OUT OF HERE?
ALL RIGHT THEN. LET'S GET OUT OF HERE.

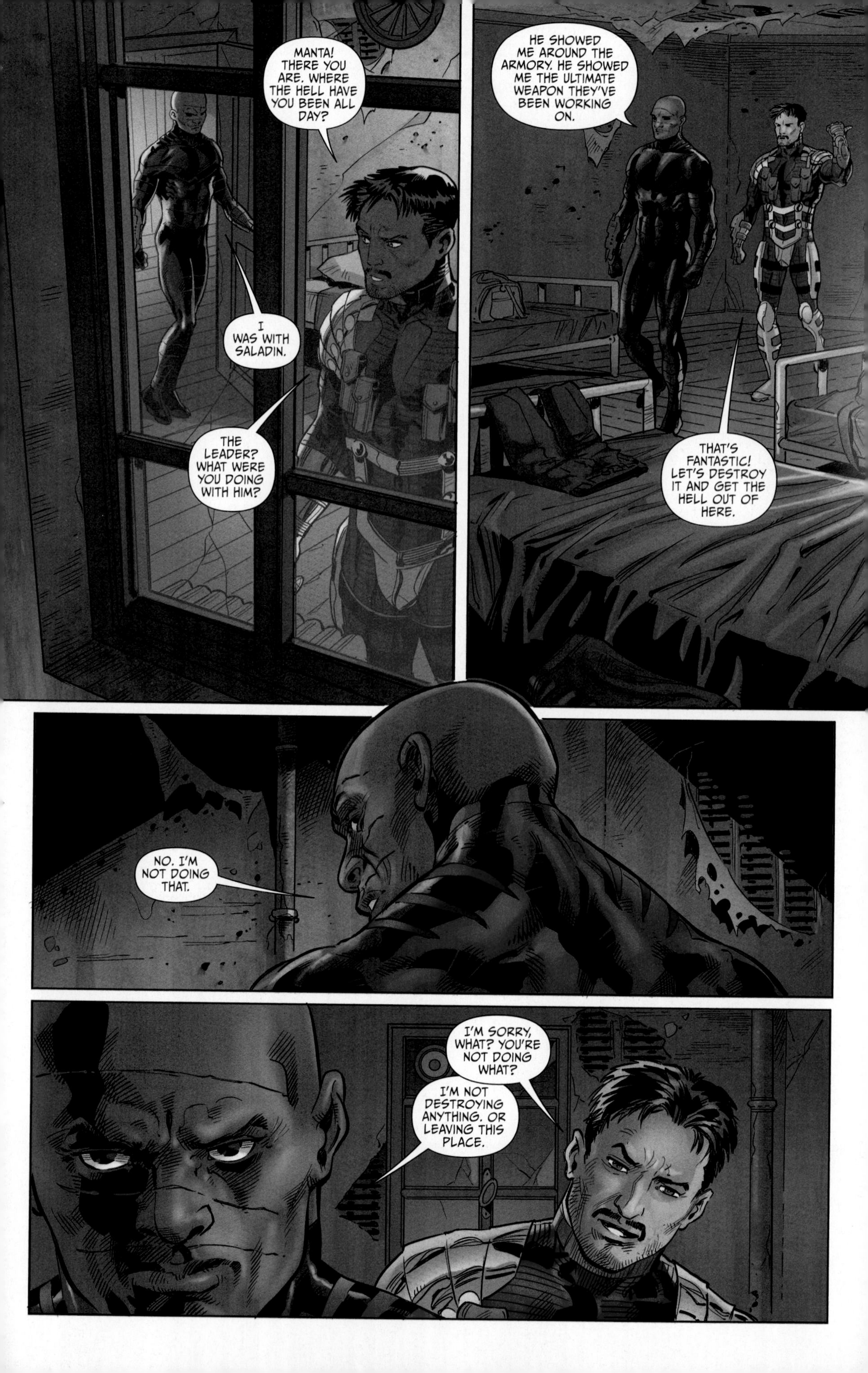
MANTA! THERE YOU ARE. WHERE THE HELL HAVE YOU BEEN ALL DAY?
I WAS WITH SALADIN.
THE LEADER? WHAT WERE YOU DOING WITH HIM?
HE SHOWED ME AROUND THE ARMORY. HE SHOWED ME THE ULTIMATE WEAPON THEY'VE BEEN WORKING ON.
THAT'S FANTASTIC! LET'S DESTROY IT AND GET THE HELL OUT OF HERE.
NO. I'M NOT DOING THAT.
I'M SORRY, WHAT? YOU'RE NOT DOING WHAT?
I'M NOT DESTROYING ANYTHING. OR LEAVING THIS PLACE.

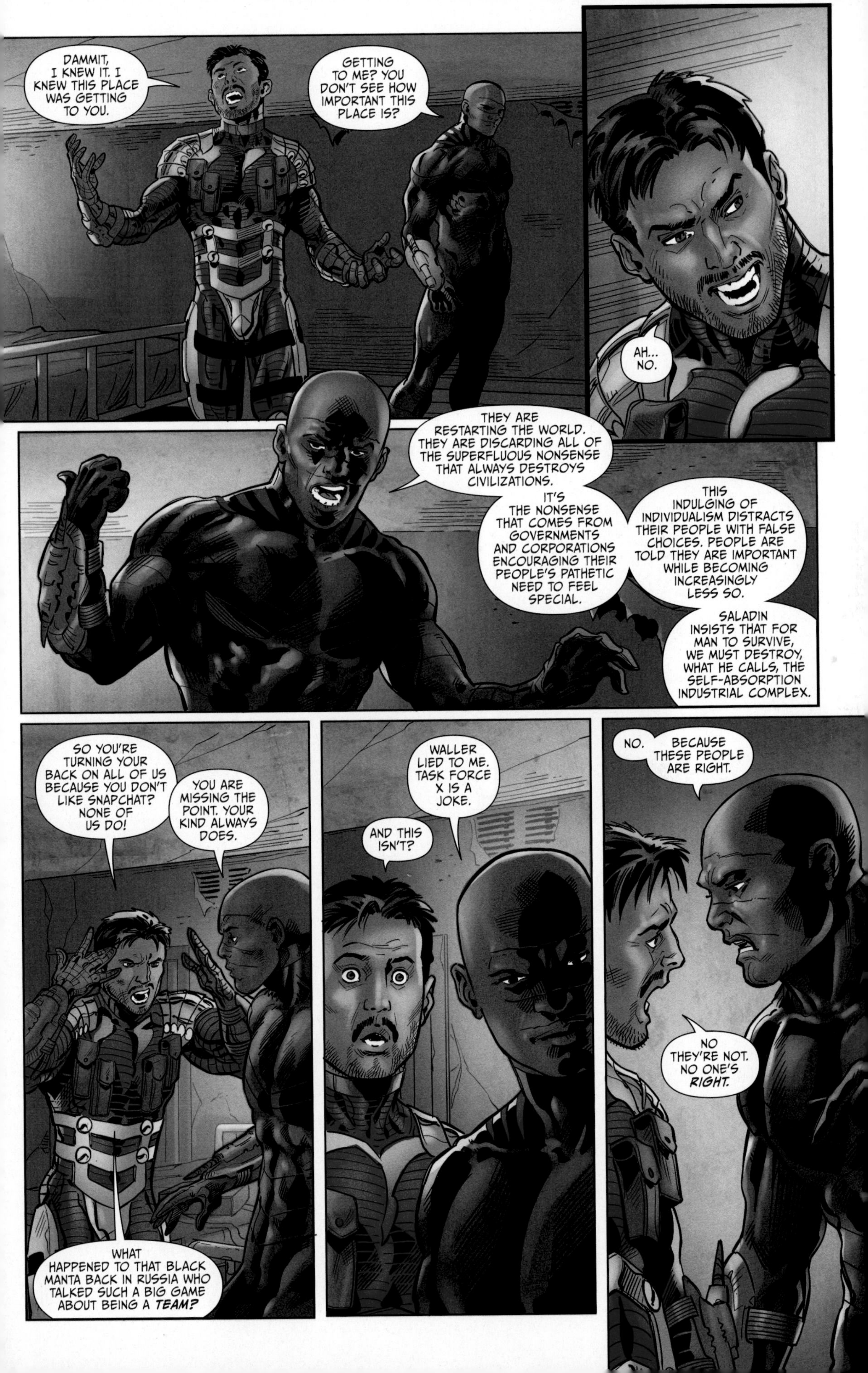
DAMMIT, I KNEW IT. I KNEW THIS PLACE WAS GETTING TO YOU.
GETTING TO ME? YOU DON'T SEE HOW IMPORTANT THIS PLACE IS?
AH... NO.
THEY ARE RESTARTING THE WORLD. THEY ARE DISCARDING ALL OF THE SUPERFLUOUS NONSENSE THAT ALWAYS DESTROYS CIVILIZATIONS.
IT'S THE NONSENSE THAT COMES FROM GOVERNMENTS AND CORPORATIONS ENCOURAGING THEIR PEOPLE'S PATHETIC NEED TO FEEL SPECIAL.
THIS INDULGING OF INDIVIDUALISM DISTRACTS THEIR PEOPLE WITH FALSE CHOICES. PEOPLE ARE TOLD THEY ARE IMPORTANT WHILE BECOMING INCREASINGLY LESS SO.
SALADIN INSISTS THAT FOR MAN TO SURVIVE, WE MUST DESTROY, WHAT HE CALLS, THE SELF-ABSORPTION INDUSTRIAL COMPLEX.
SO YOU'RE TURNING YOUR BACK ON ALL OF US BECAUSE YOU DON'T LIKE SNAPCHAT? NONE OF US DO!
YOU ARE MISSING THE POINT. YOUR KIND ALWAYS DOES.
WHAT HAPPENED TO THAT BLACK MANTA BACK IN RUSSIA WHO TALKED SUCH A BIG GAME ABOUT BEING A *TEAM?*
WALLER LIED TO ME. TASK FORCE X IS A JOKE.
AND THIS ISN'T?
NO.
BECAUSE THESE PEOPLE ARE RIGHT.
NO THEY'RE NOT. NO ONE'S *RIGHT.*

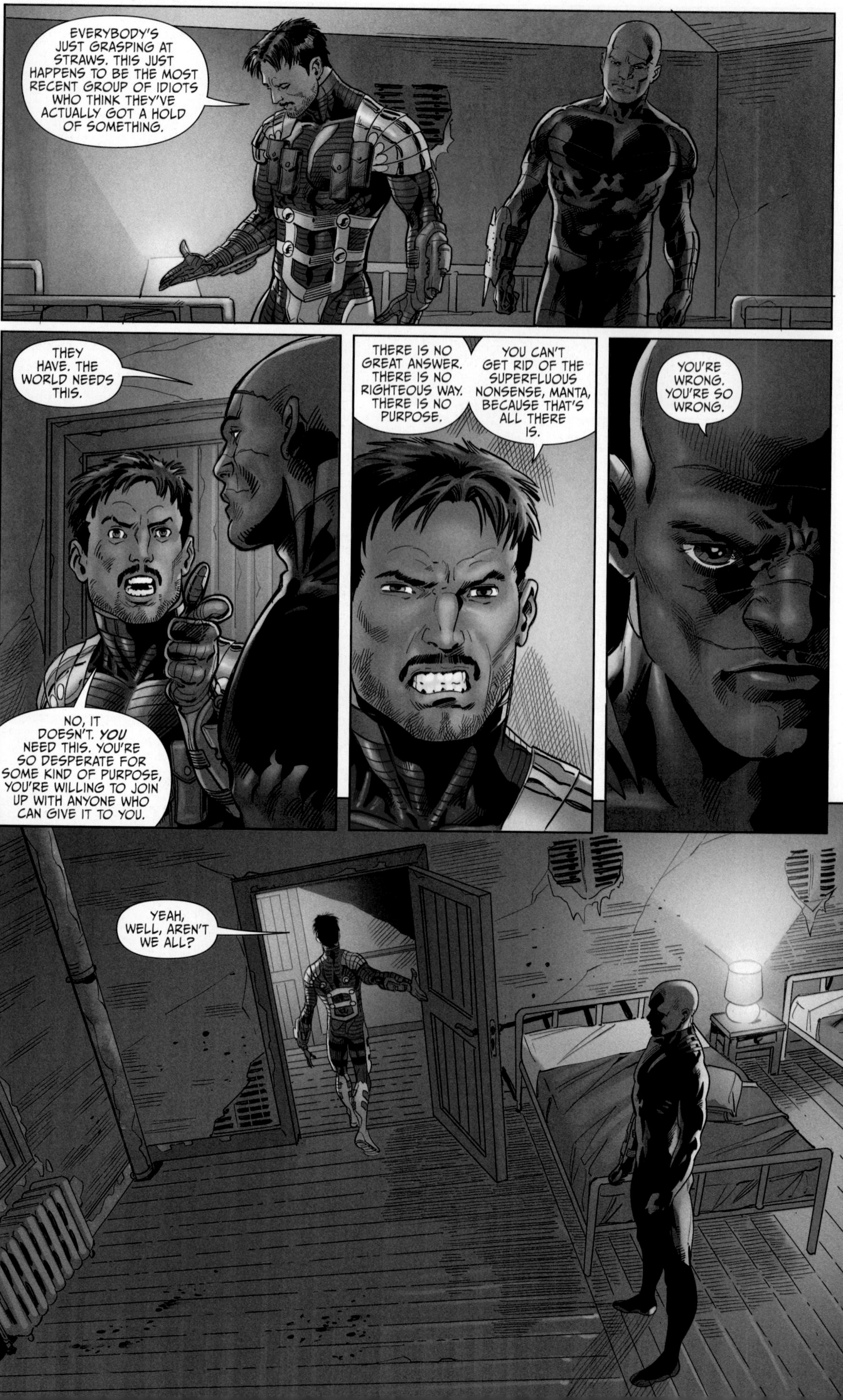
EVERYBODY'S JUST GRASPING AT STRAWS. THIS JUST HAPPENS TO BE THE MOST RECENT GROUP OF IDIOTS WHO THINK THEY'VE ACTUALLY GOT A HOLD OF SOMETHING.
THEY HAVE. THE WORLD NEEDS THIS.
NO, IT DOESN'T. *YOU* NEED THIS. YOU'RE SO DESPERATE FOR SOME KIND OF PURPOSE, YOU'RE WILLING TO JOIN UP WITH ANYONE WHO CAN GIVE IT TO YOU.
THERE IS NO GREAT ANSWER. THERE IS NO RIGHTEOUS WAY. THERE IS NO PURPOSE.
YOU CAN'T GET RID OF THE SUPERFLUOUS NONSENSE, MANTA, BECAUSE THAT'S ALL THERE IS.
YOU'RE WRONG. YOU'RE SO WRONG.
YEAH, WELL, AREN'T WE ALL?

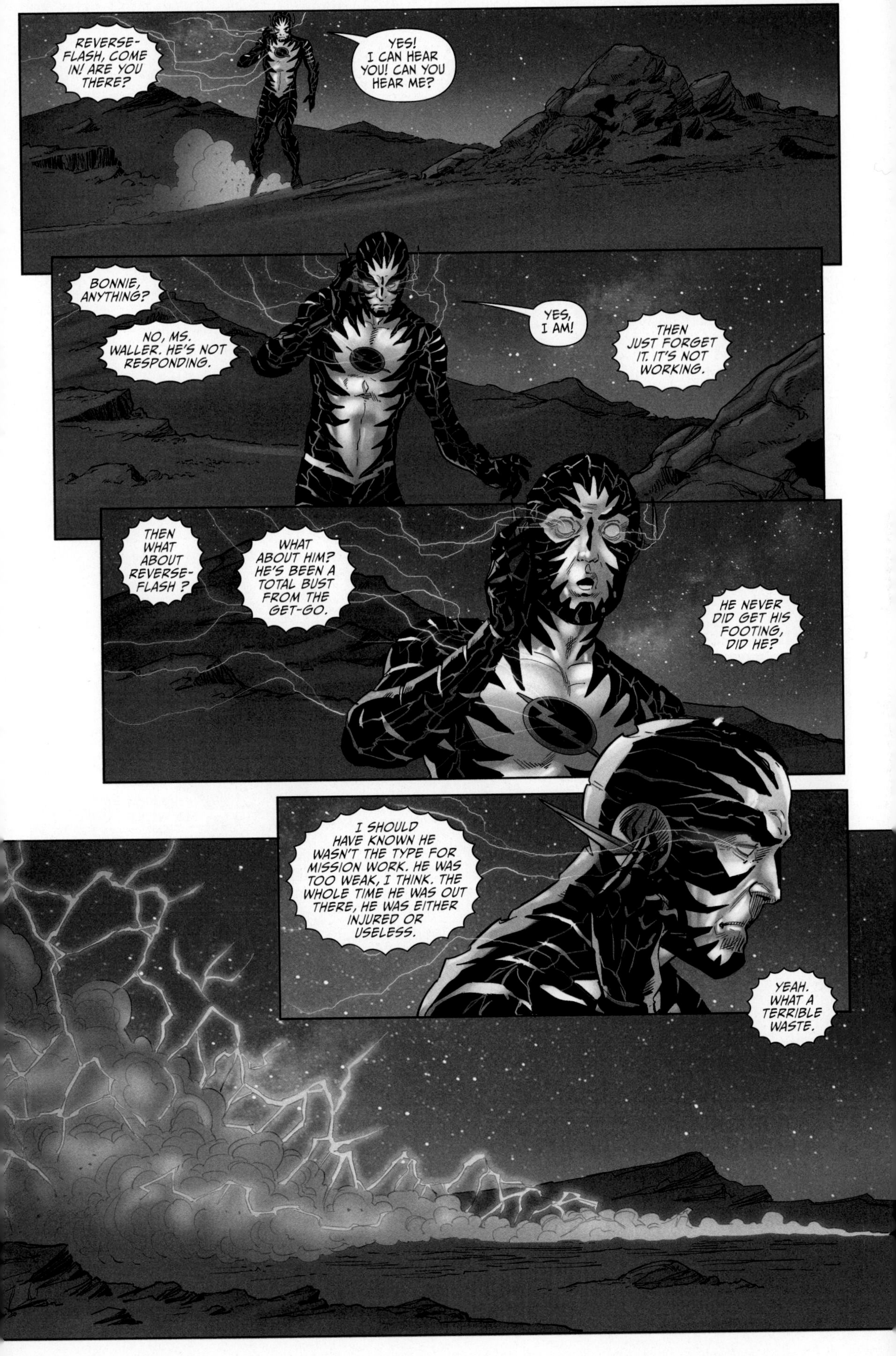
REVERSE-FLASH, COME IN! ARE YOU THERE?
YES! I CAN HEAR YOU! CAN YOU HEAR ME?
BONNIE, ANYTHING?
NO, MS. WALLER. HE'S NOT RESPONDING.
YES, I AM!
THEN JUST FORGET IT. IT'S NOT WORKING.
THEN WHAT ABOUT REVERSE-FLASH?
WHAT ABOUT HIM? HE'S BEEN A TOTAL BUST FROM THE GET-GO.
HE NEVER DID GET HIS FOOTING, DID HE?
I SHOULD HAVE KNOWN HE WASN'T THE TYPE FOR MISSION WORK. HE WAS TOO WEAK, I THINK. THE WHOLE TIME HE WAS OUT THERE, HE WAS EITHER INJURED OR USELESS.
YEAH. WHAT A TERRIBLE WASTE.

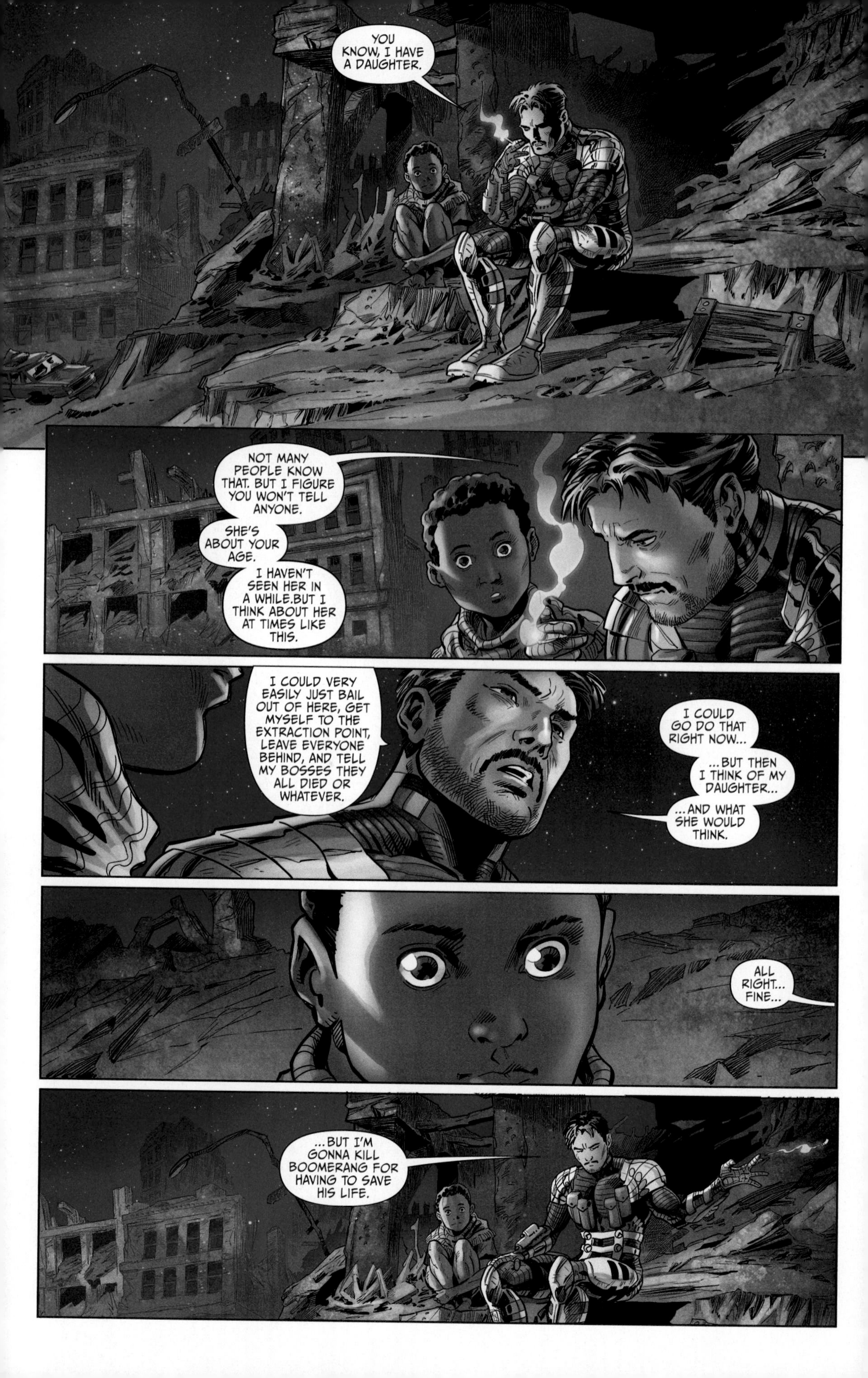

YOU KNOW, I HAVE A DAUGHTER.
NOT MANY PEOPLE KNOW THAT. BUT I FIGURE YOU WON'T TELL ANYONE.
SHE'S ABOUT YOUR AGE.
I HAVEN'T SEEN HER IN A WHILE.BUT I THINK ABOUT HER AT TIMES LIKE THIS.
I COULD VERY EASILY JUST BAIL OUT OF HERE, GET MYSELF TO THE EXTRACTION POINT, LEAVE EVERYONE BEHIND, AND TELL MY BOSSES THEY ALL DIED OR WHATEVER.
I COULD GO DO THAT RIGHT NOW...
...BUT THEN I THINK OF MY DAUGHTER...
...AND WHAT SHE WOULD THINK.
ALL RIGHT... FINE...
...BUT I'M GONNA KILL BOOMERANG FOR HAVING TO SAVE HIS LIFE.

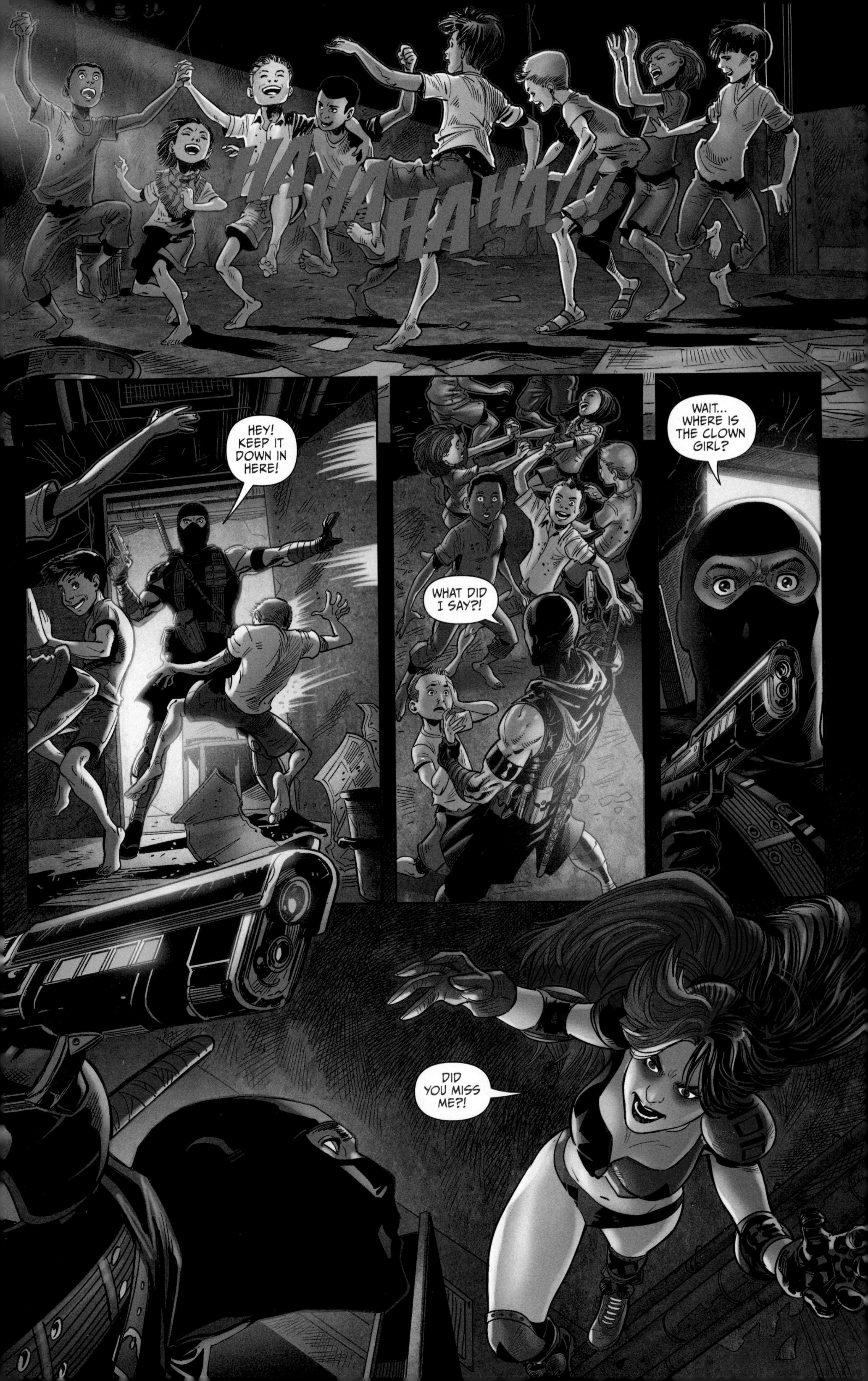
HA HA HA HA HA!!!
HEY! KEEP IT DOWN IN HERE!
WHAT DID I SAY?!
WAIT... WHERE IS THE CLOWN GIRL?
DID YOU MISS ME?!

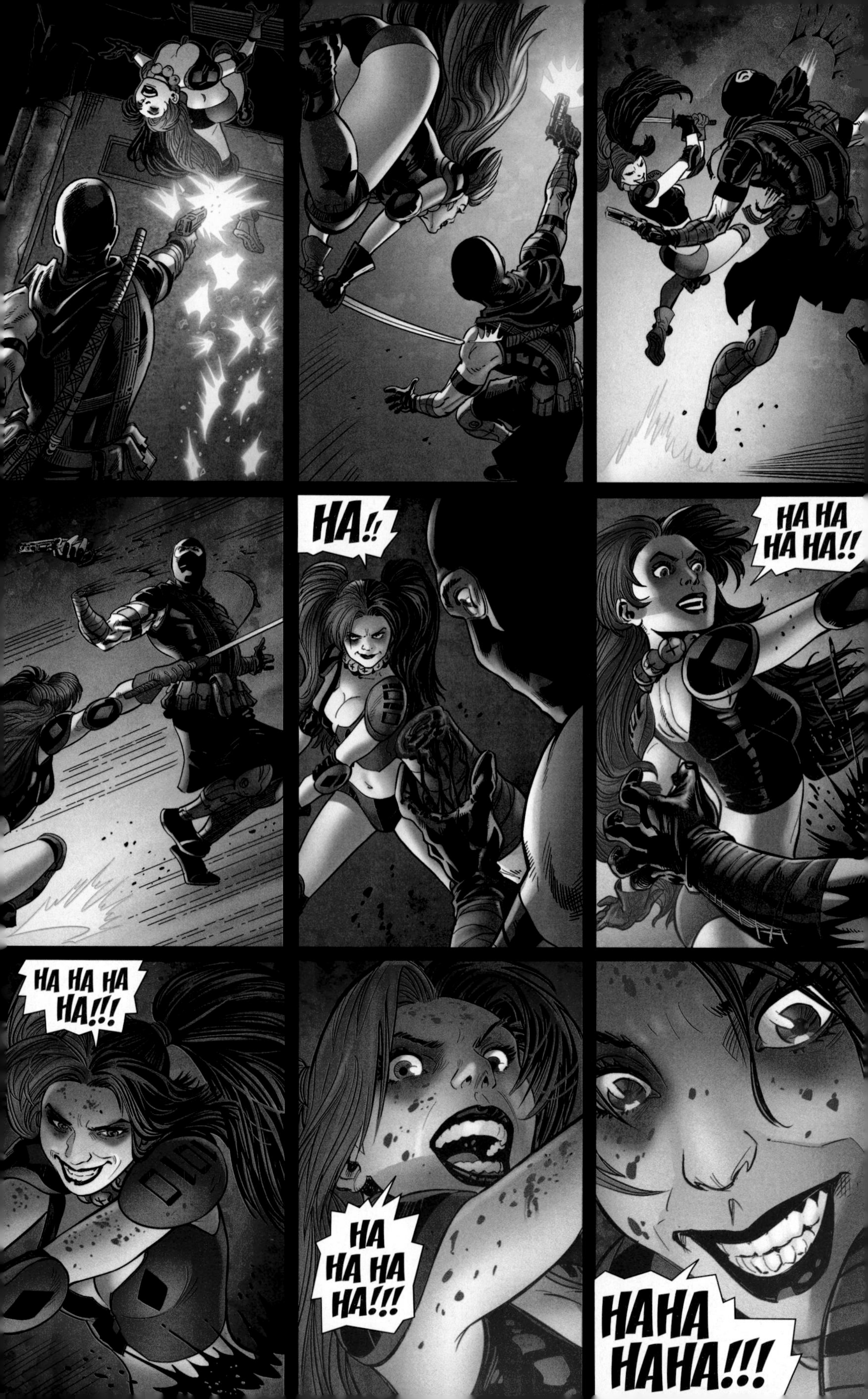
HA!!
HA HA HA HA!!
HA HA HA HA!!!
HA HA HA HA!!!
HAHA HAHA!!!

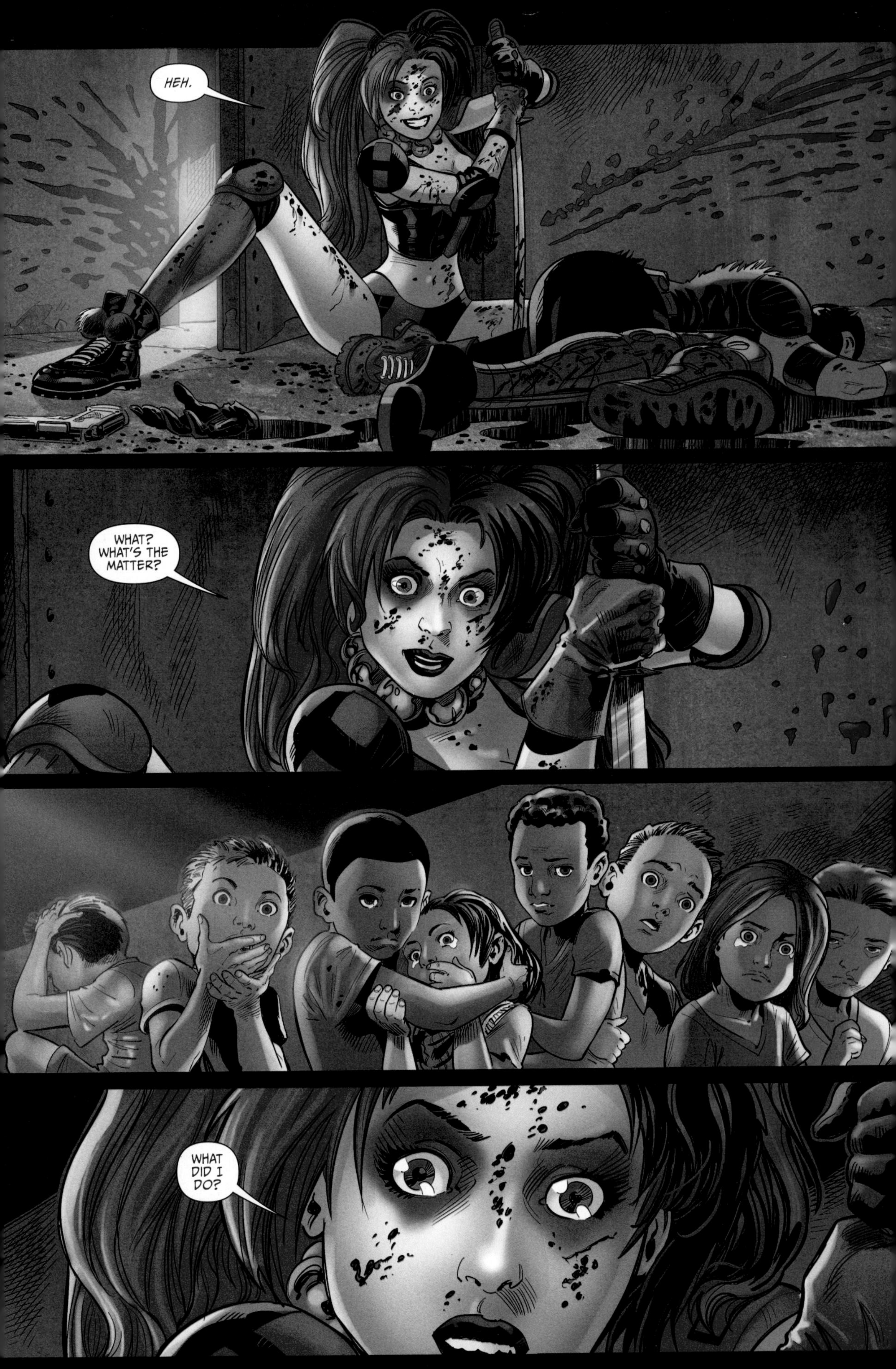
HEH.
WHAT? WHAT'S THE MATTER?
WHAT DID I DO?

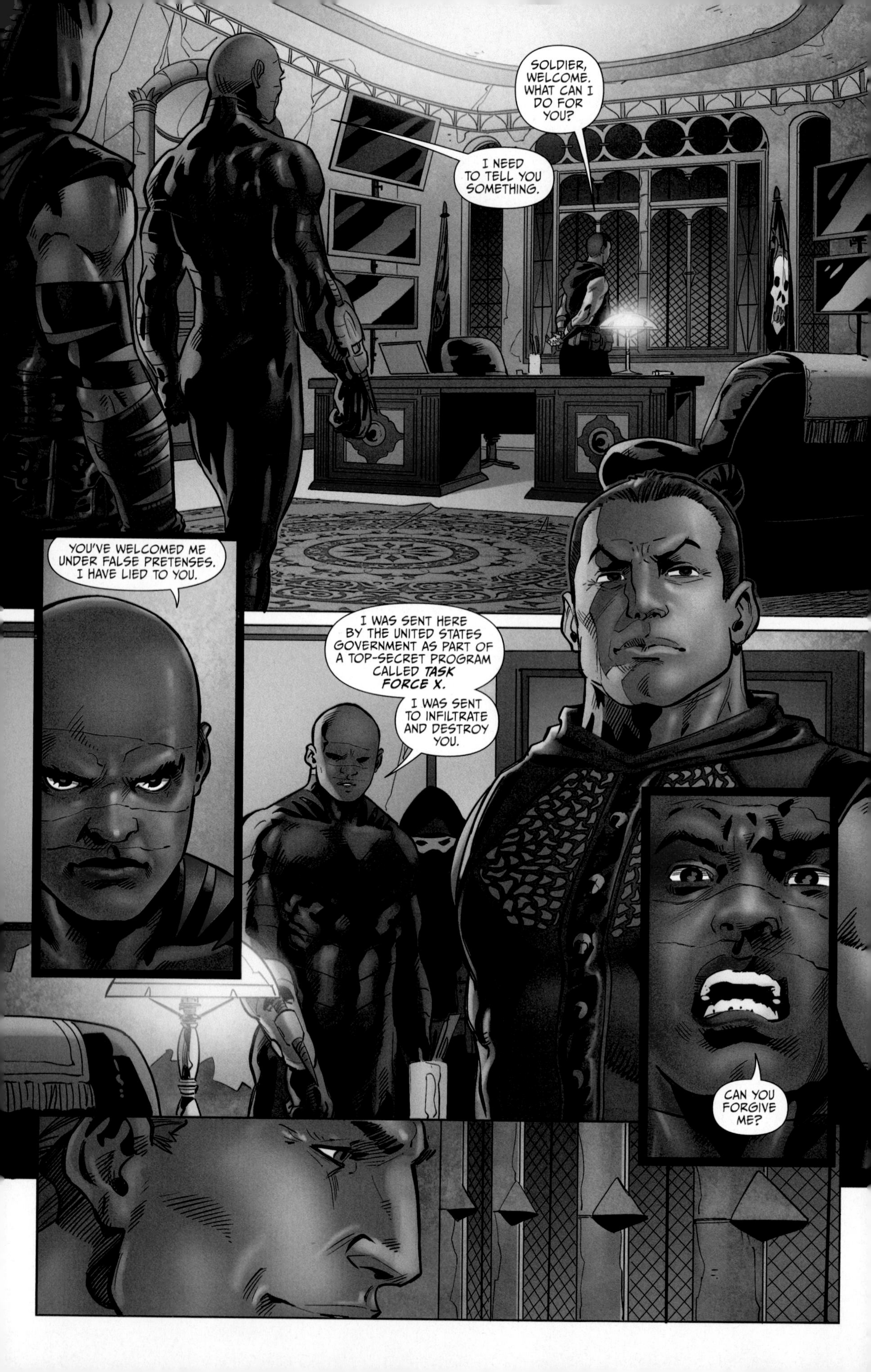

SOLDIER, WELCOME. WHAT CAN I DO FOR YOU?
I NEED TO TELL YOU SOMETHING.
YOU'VE WELCOMED ME UNDER FALSE PRETENSES. I HAVE LIED TO YOU.
I WAS SENT HERE BY THE UNITED STATES GOVERNMENT AS PART OF A TOP-SECRET PROGRAM CALLED TASK FORCE X.
I WAS SENT TO INFILTRATE AND DESTROY YOU.
CAN YOU FORGIVE ME?

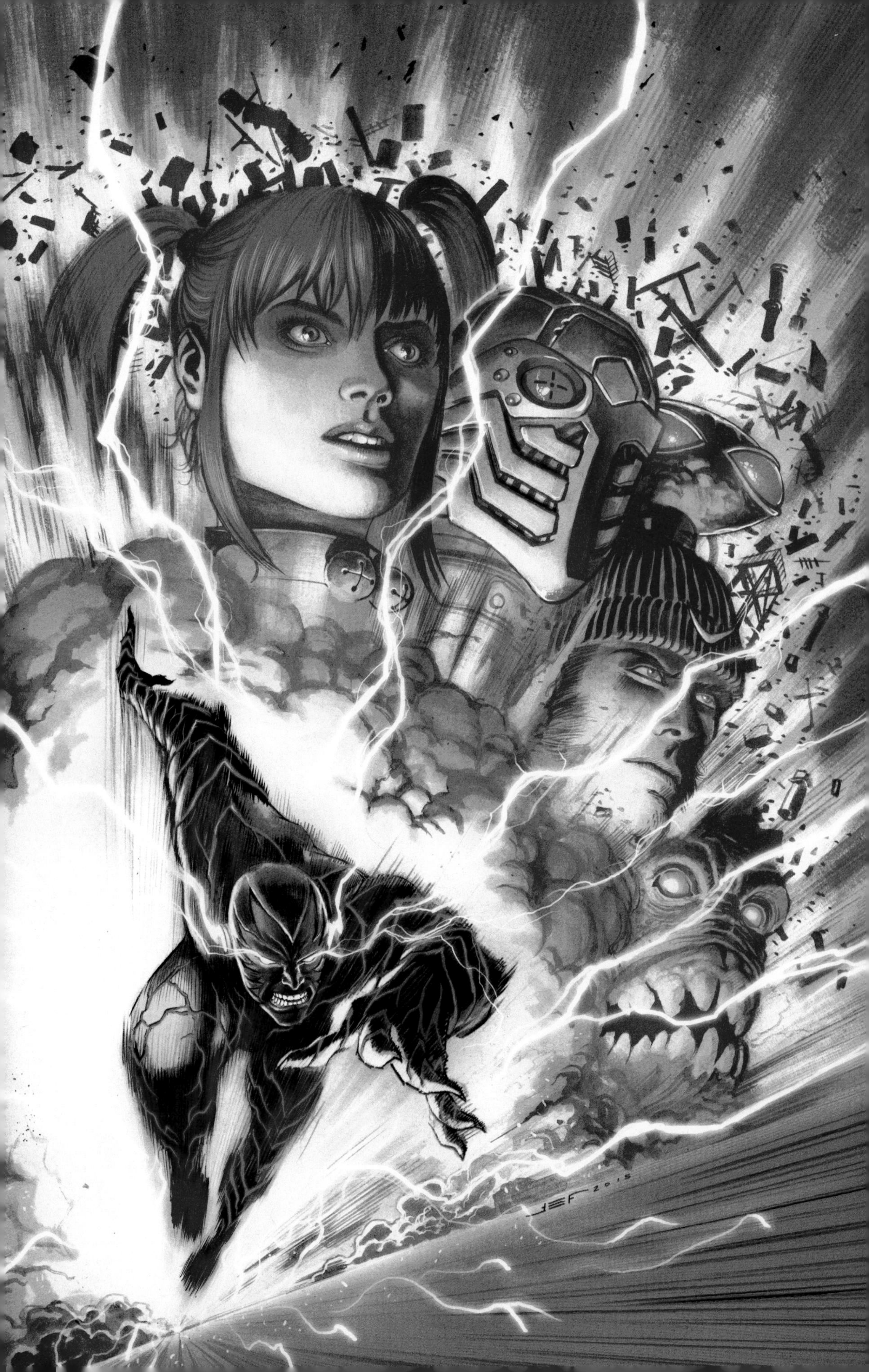

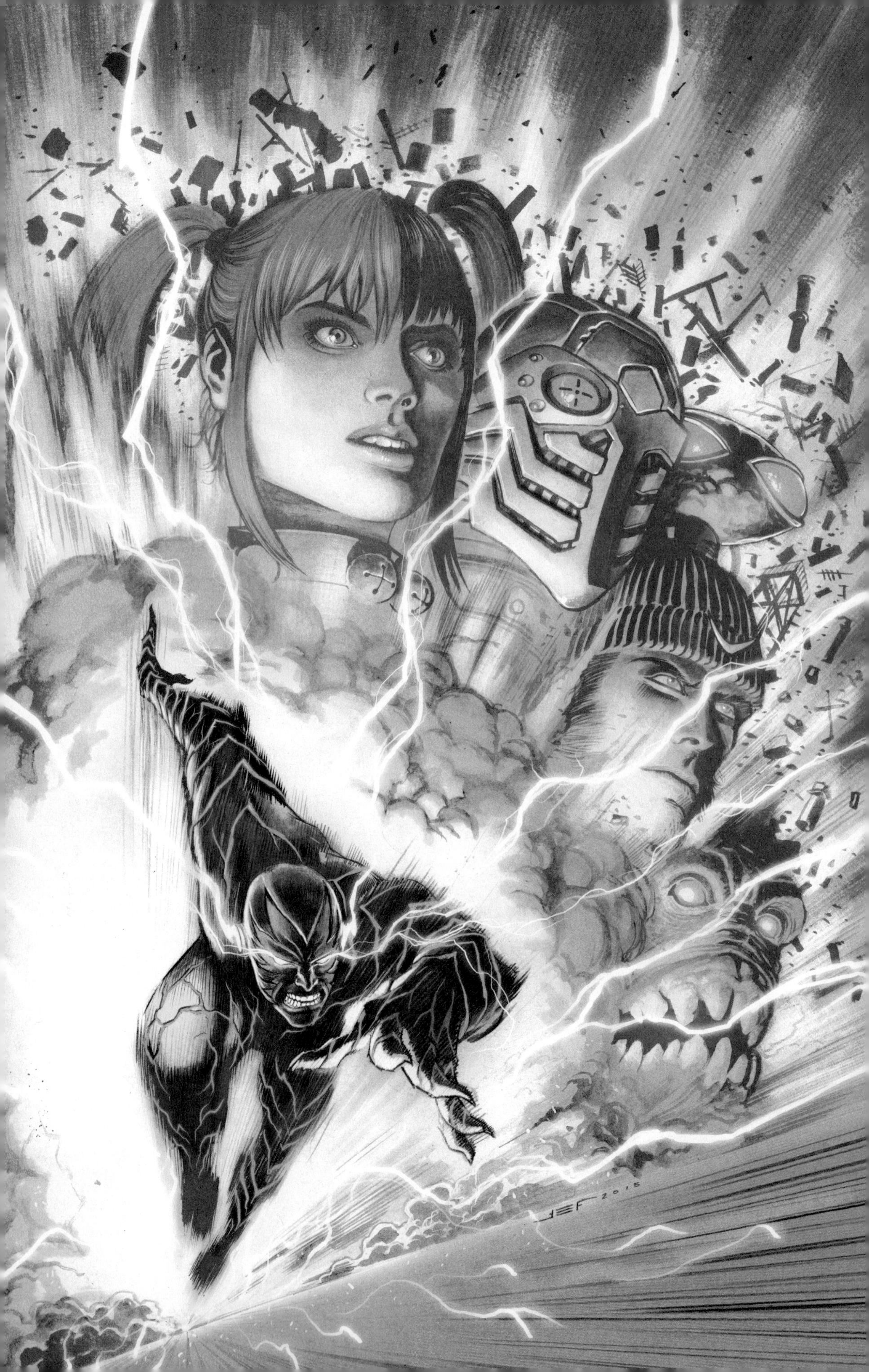

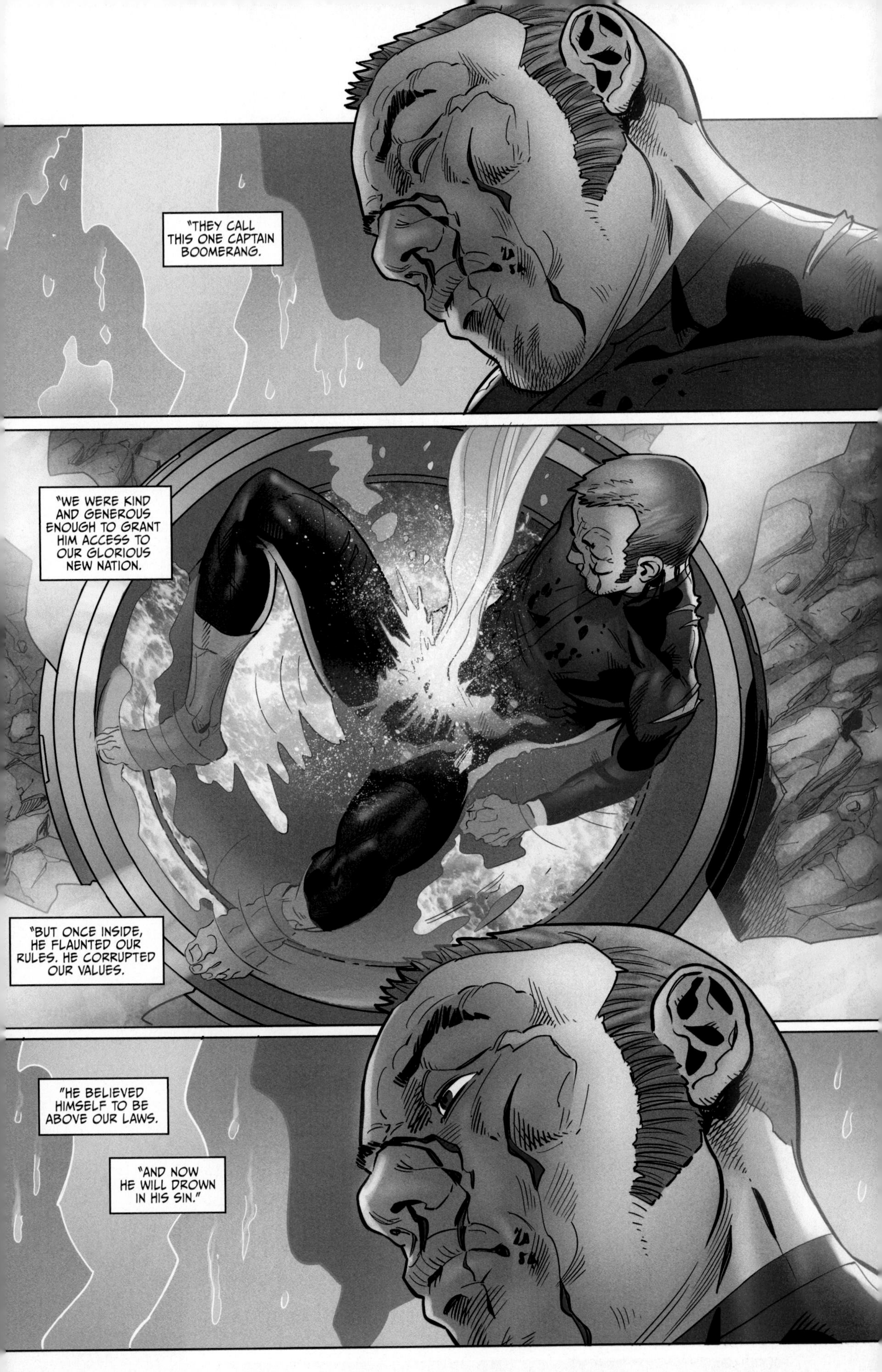
"THEY CALL THIS ONE CAPTAIN BOOMERANG.
"WE WERE KIND AND GENEROUS ENOUGH TO GRANT HIM ACCESS TO OUR GLORIOUS NEW NATION.
"BUT ONCE INSIDE, HE FLAUNTED OUR RULES. HE CORRUPTED OUR VALUES.
"HE BELIEVED HIMSELF TO BE ABOVE OUR LAWS.
"AND NOW HE WILL DROWN IN HIS SIN."

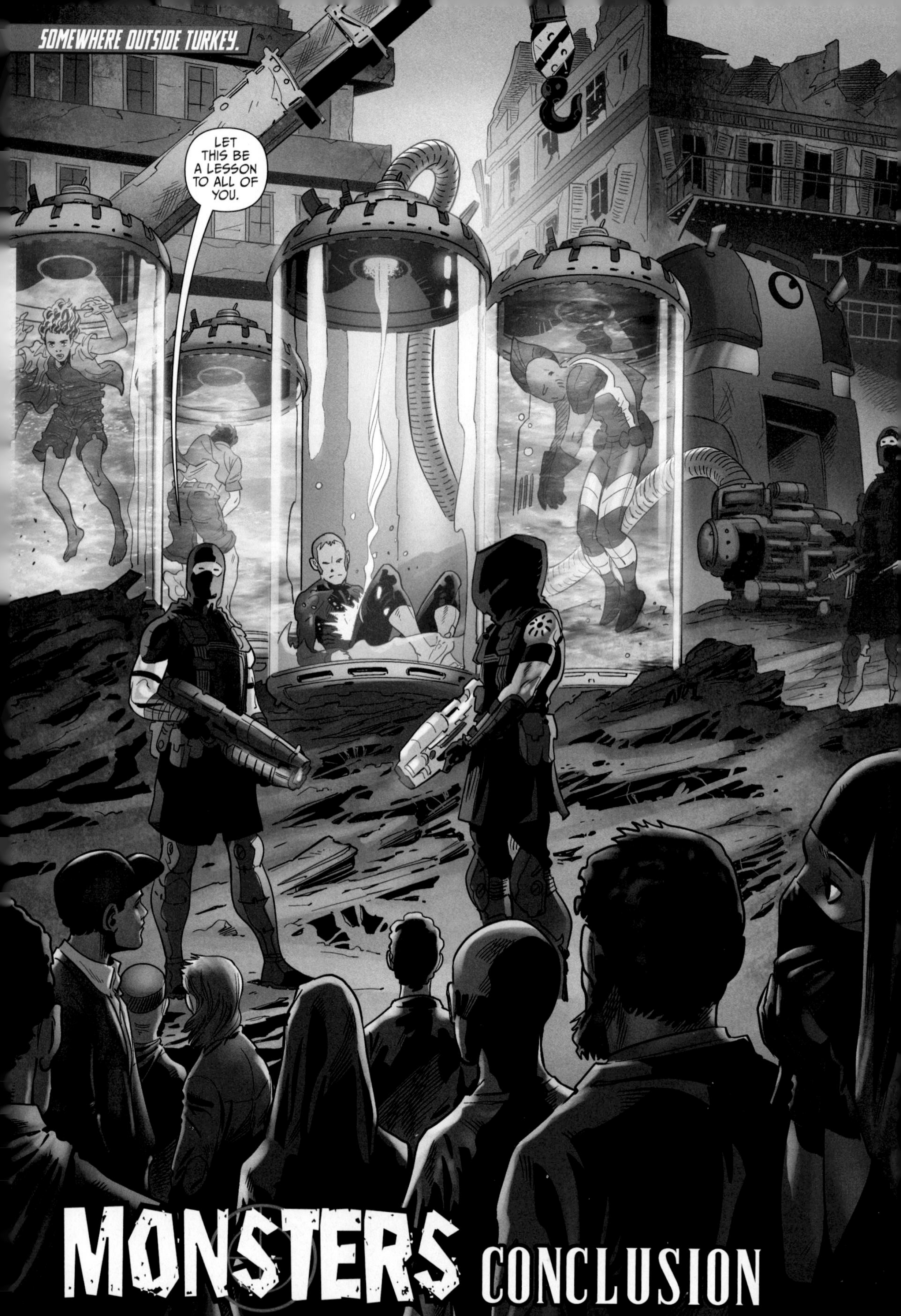
SOMEWHERE OUTSIDE TURKEY.
LET THIS BE A LESSON TO ALL OF YOU.

MONSTERS CONCLUSION

SEAN RYAN WRITER
PHILIPPE BRIONES ARTIST
BLOND COLORS
TRAVIS LANHAM LETTERS
JUAN FERREYRA COVER

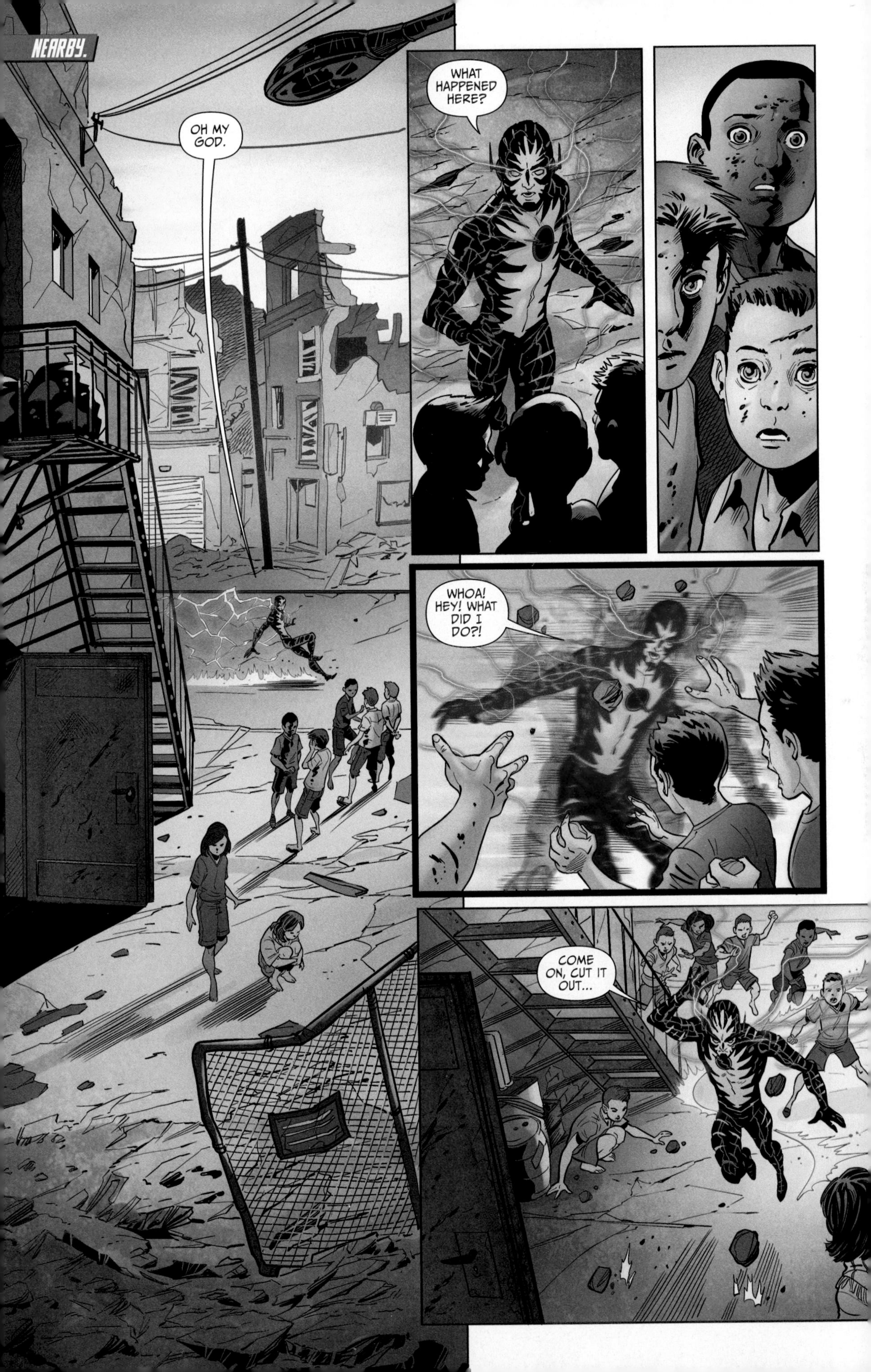
NEARBY.
OH MY GOD.
WHAT HAPPENED HERE?
WHOA! HEY! WHAT DID I DO?!
COME ON, CUT IT OUT...

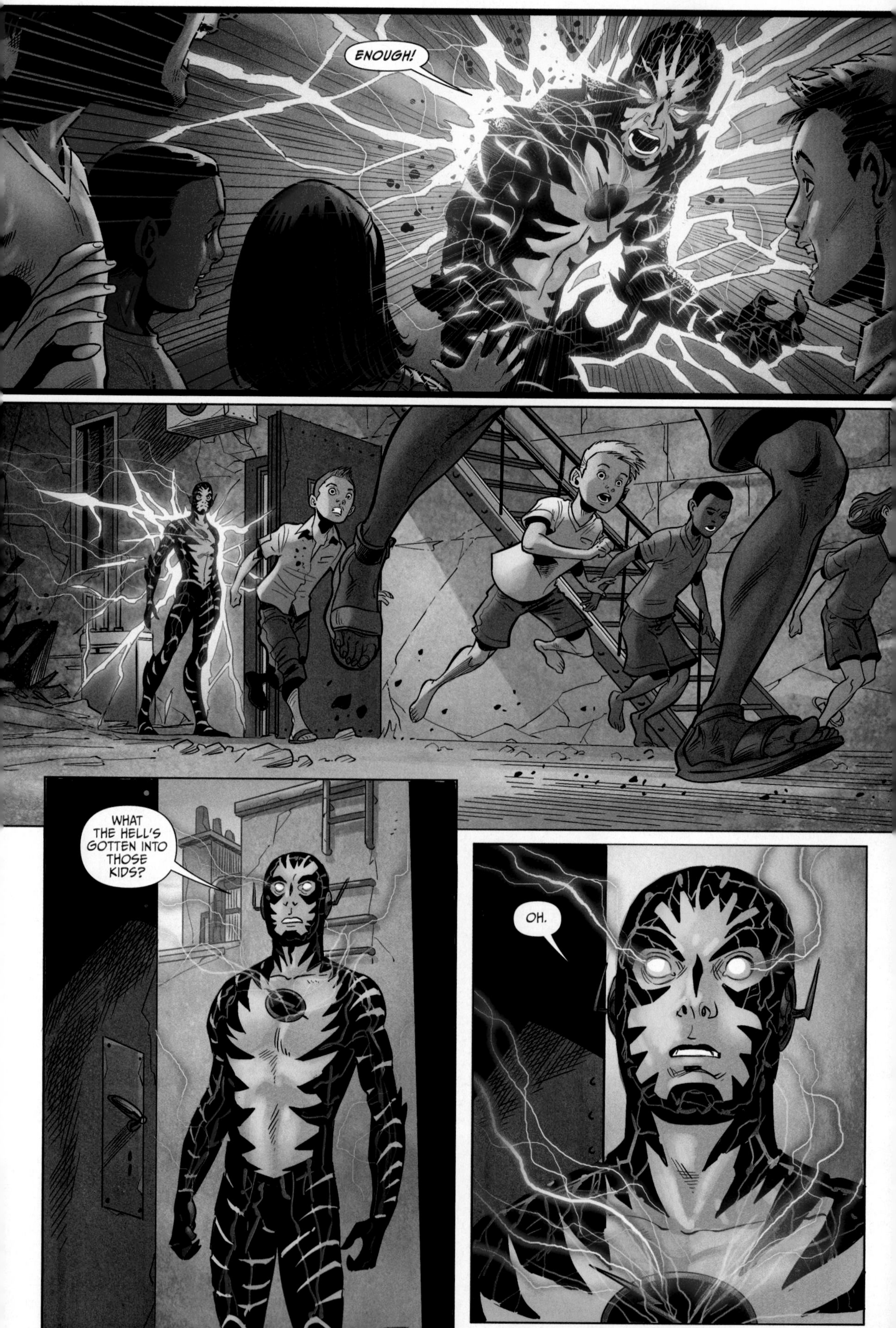
ENOUGH!
WHAT THE HELL'S GOTTEN INTO THOSE KIDS?
OH.

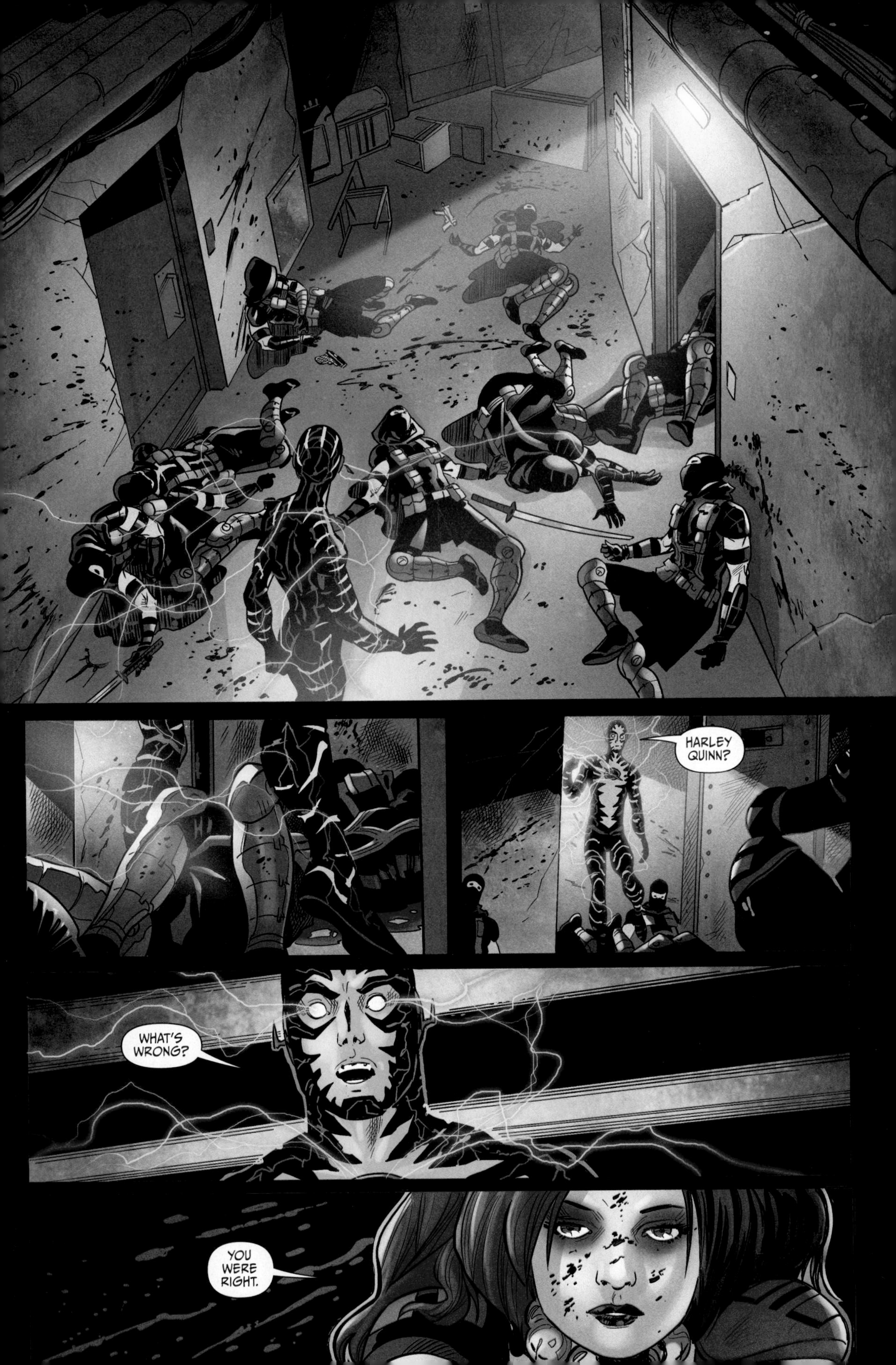
HARLEY QUINN?
WHAT'S WRONG?
YOU WERE RIGHT.

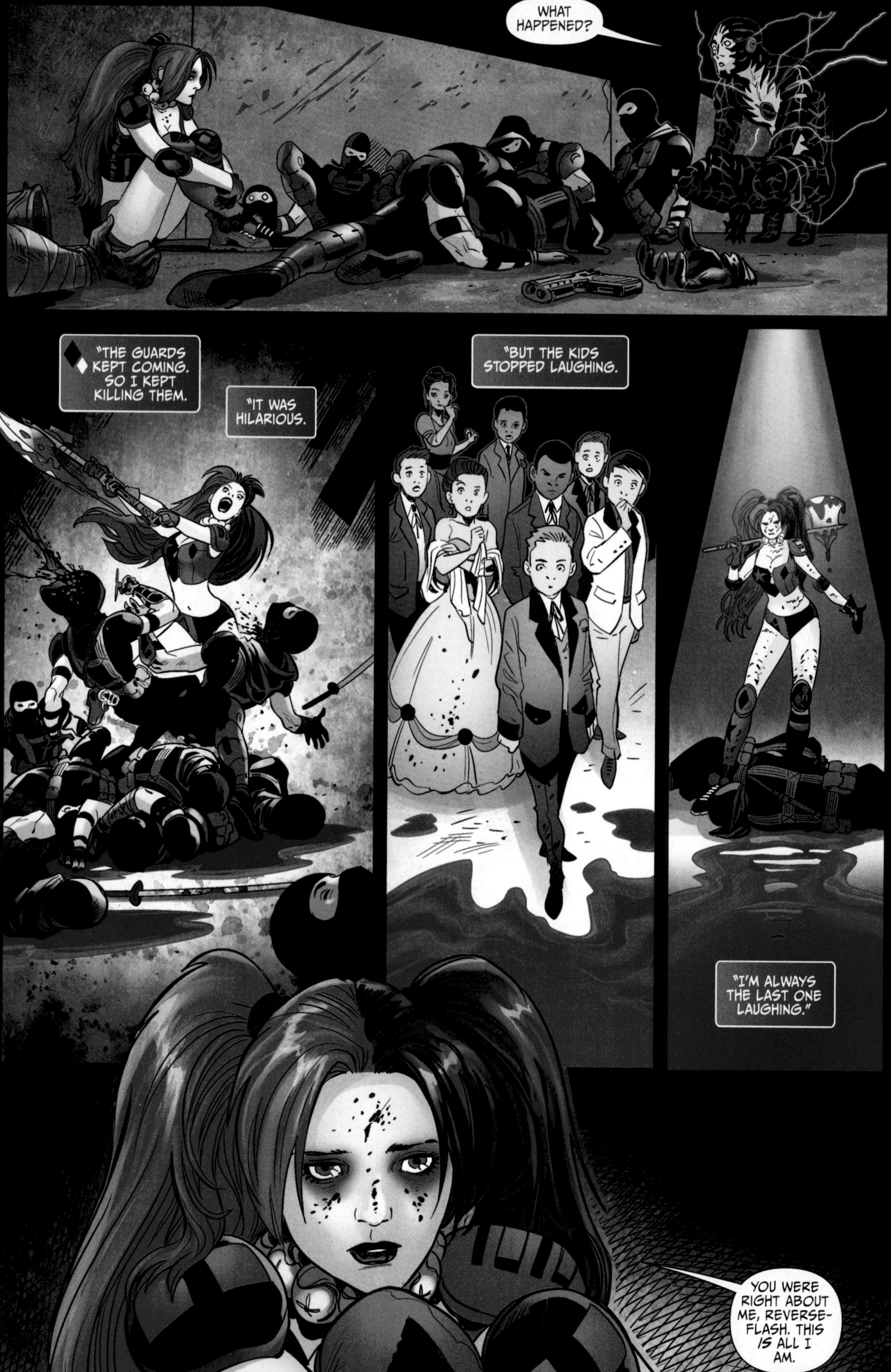

WHAT HAPPENED?
"THE GUARDS KEPT COMING. SO I KEPT KILLING THEM.
"IT WAS HILARIOUS.
"BUT THE KIDS STOPPED LAUGHING.
"I'M ALWAYS THE LAST ONE LAUGHING."
YOU WERE RIGHT ABOUT ME, REVERSE-FLASH. THIS *IS* ALL I AM.

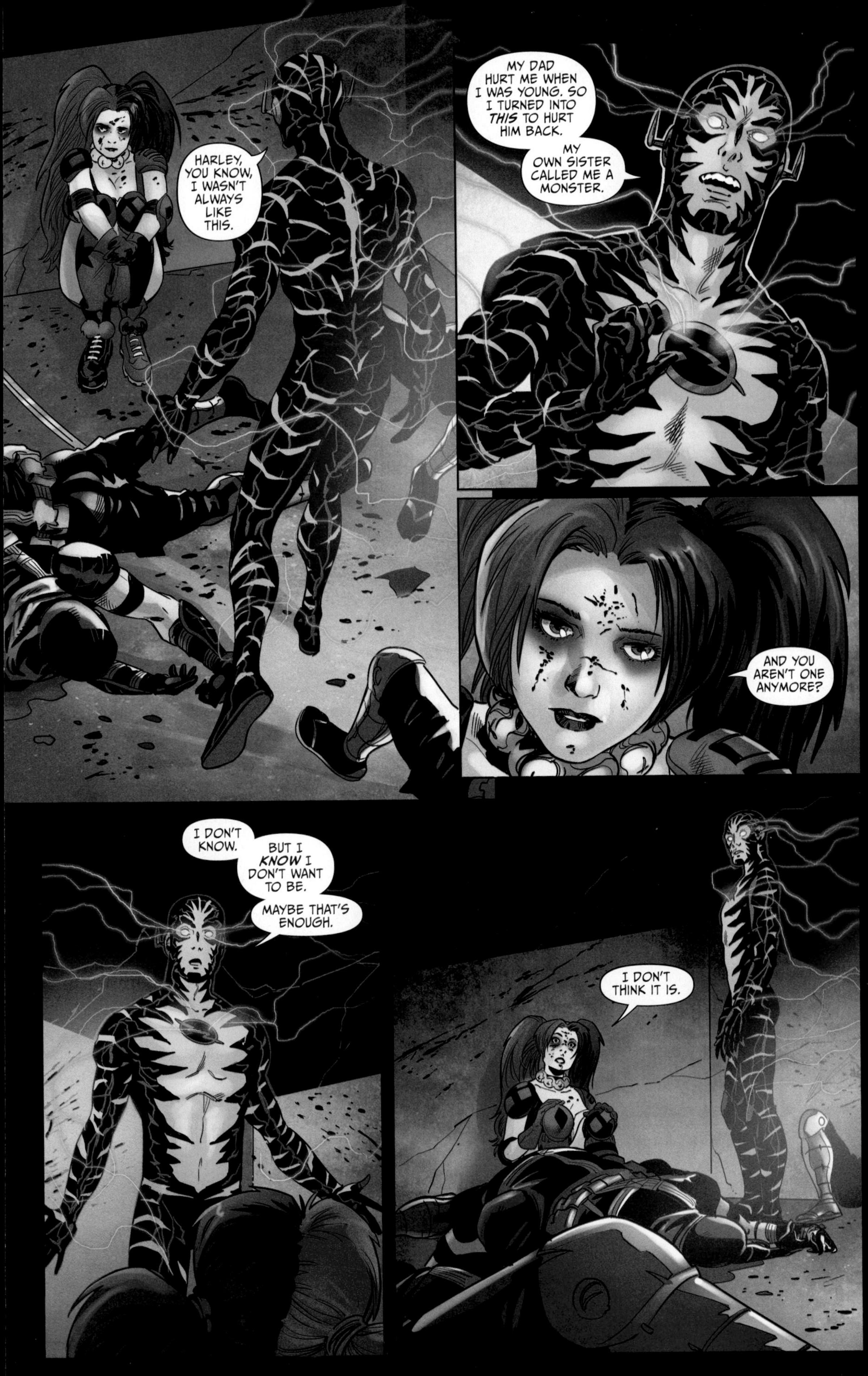
HARLEY, YOU KNOW, I WASN'T ALWAYS LIKE THIS.
MY DAD HURT ME WHEN I WAS YOUNG. SO I TURNED INTO *THIS* TO HURT HIM BACK.
MY OWN SISTER CALLED ME A MONSTER.
AND YOU AREN'T ONE ANYMORE?
I DON'T KNOW.
BUT I *KNOW* I DON'T WANT TO BE.
MAYBE THAT'S ENOUGH.
I DON'T THINK IT IS.

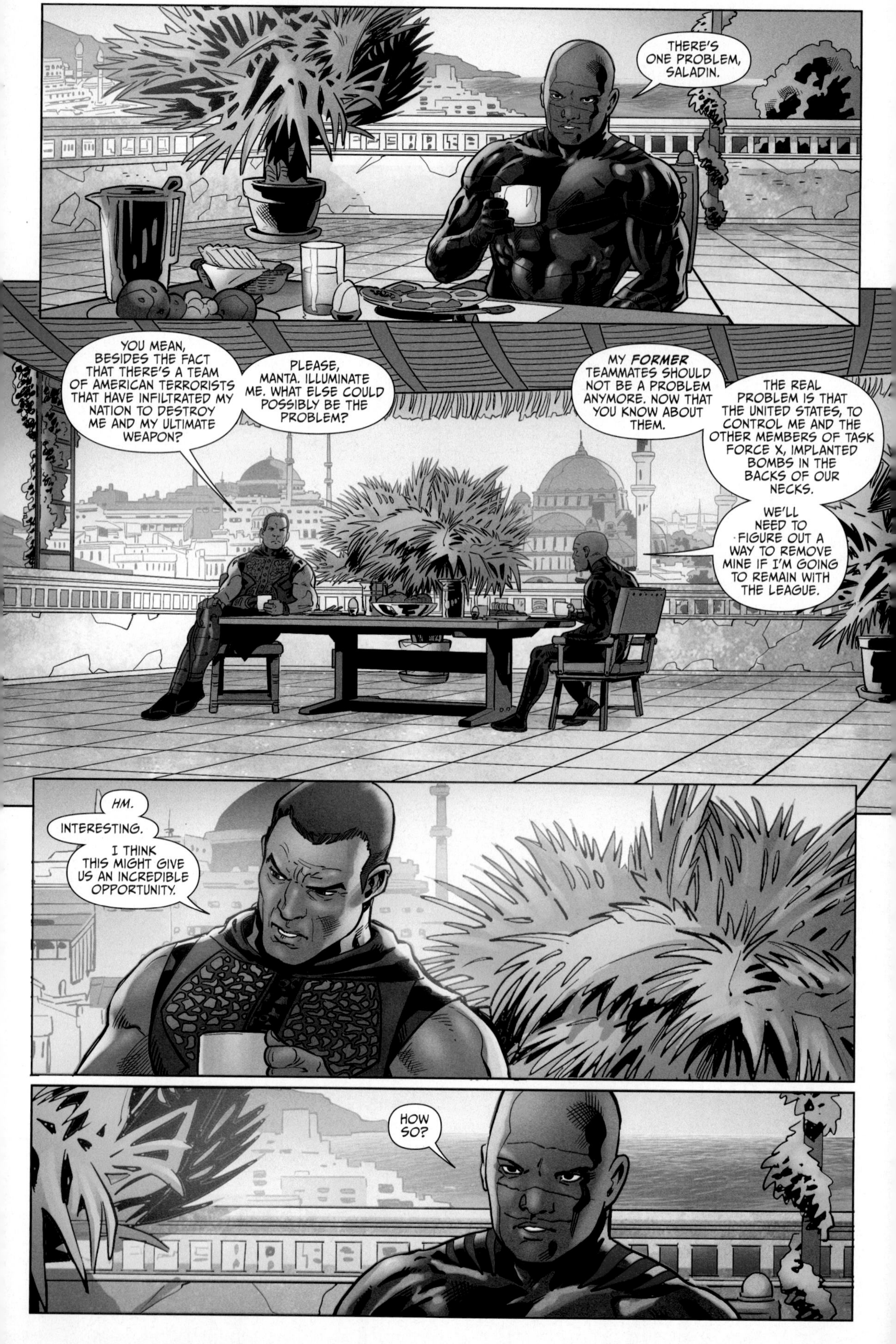
THERE'S ONE PROBLEM, SALADIN.
YOU MEAN, BESIDES THE FACT THAT THERE'S A TEAM OF AMERICAN TERRORISTS THAT HAVE INFILTRATED MY NATION TO DESTROY ME AND MY ULTIMATE WEAPON?
PLEASE, MANTA. ILLUMINATE ME. WHAT ELSE COULD POSSIBLY BE THE PROBLEM?
MY FORMER TEAMMATES SHOULD NOT BE A PROBLEM ANYMORE. NOW THAT YOU KNOW ABOUT THEM.
THE REAL PROBLEM IS THAT THE UNITED STATES, TO CONTROL ME AND THE OTHER MEMBERS OF TASK FORCE X, IMPLANTED BOMBS IN THE BACKS OF OUR NECKS.
WE'LL NEED TO FIGURE OUT A WAY TO REMOVE MINE IF I'M GOING TO REMAIN WITH THE LEAGUE.
HM.
INTERESTING.
I THINK THIS MIGHT GIVE US AN INCREDIBLE OPPORTUNITY.
HOW SO?

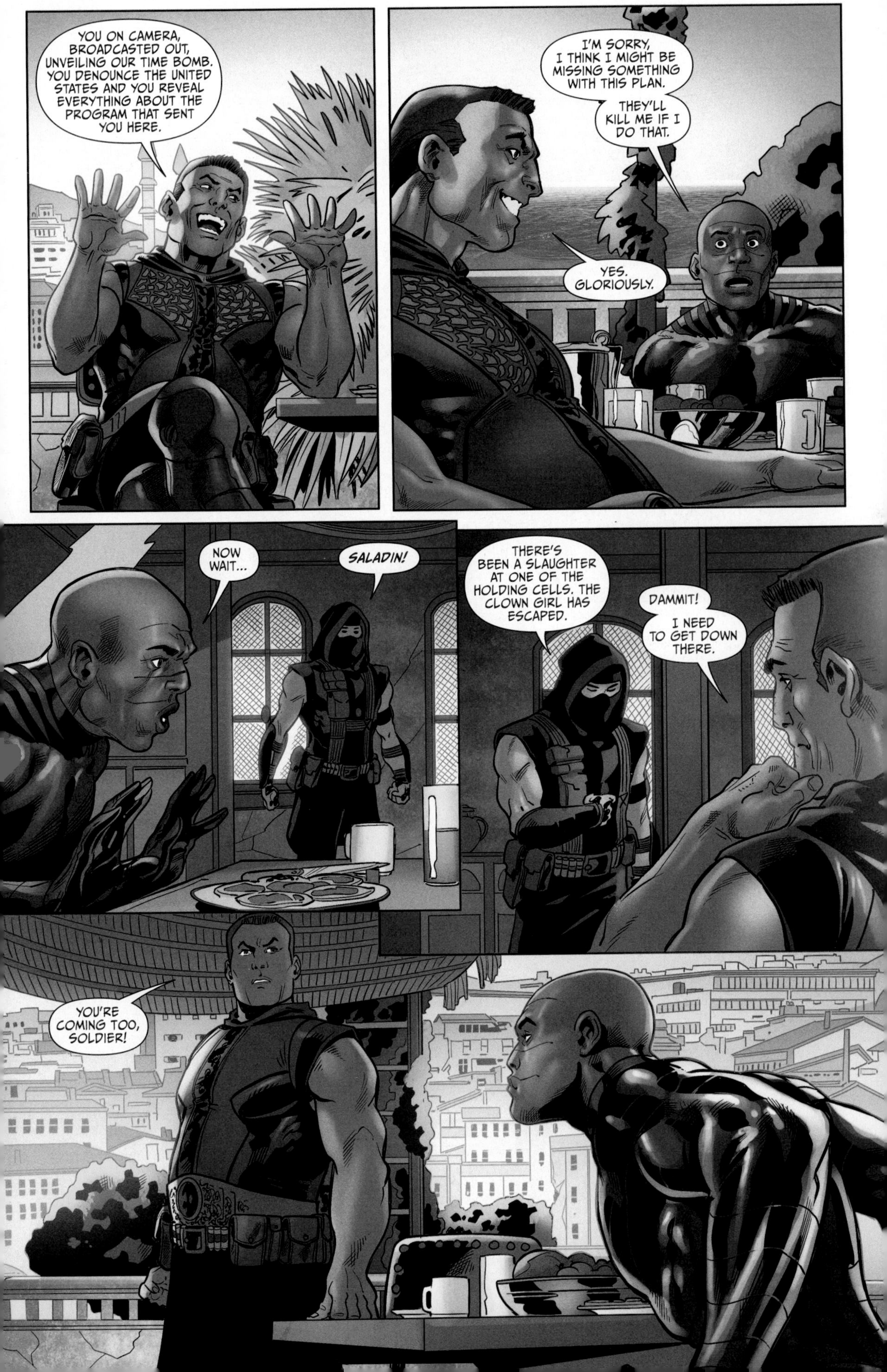
YOU ON CAMERA, BROADCASTED OUT, UNVEILING OUR TIME BOMB. YOU DENOUNCE THE UNITED STATES AND YOU REVEAL EVERYTHING ABOUT THE PROGRAM THAT SENT YOU HERE.
I'M SORRY, I THINK I MIGHT BE MISSING SOMETHING WITH THIS PLAN.
THEY'LL KILL ME IF I DO THAT.
YES. GLORIOUSLY.
NOW WAIT...
SALADIN!
THERE'S BEEN A SLAUGHTER AT ONE OF THE HOLDING CELLS. THE CLOWN GIRL HAS ESCAPED.
DAMMIT!
I NEED TO GET DOWN THERE.
YOU'RE COMING TOO, SOLDIER!

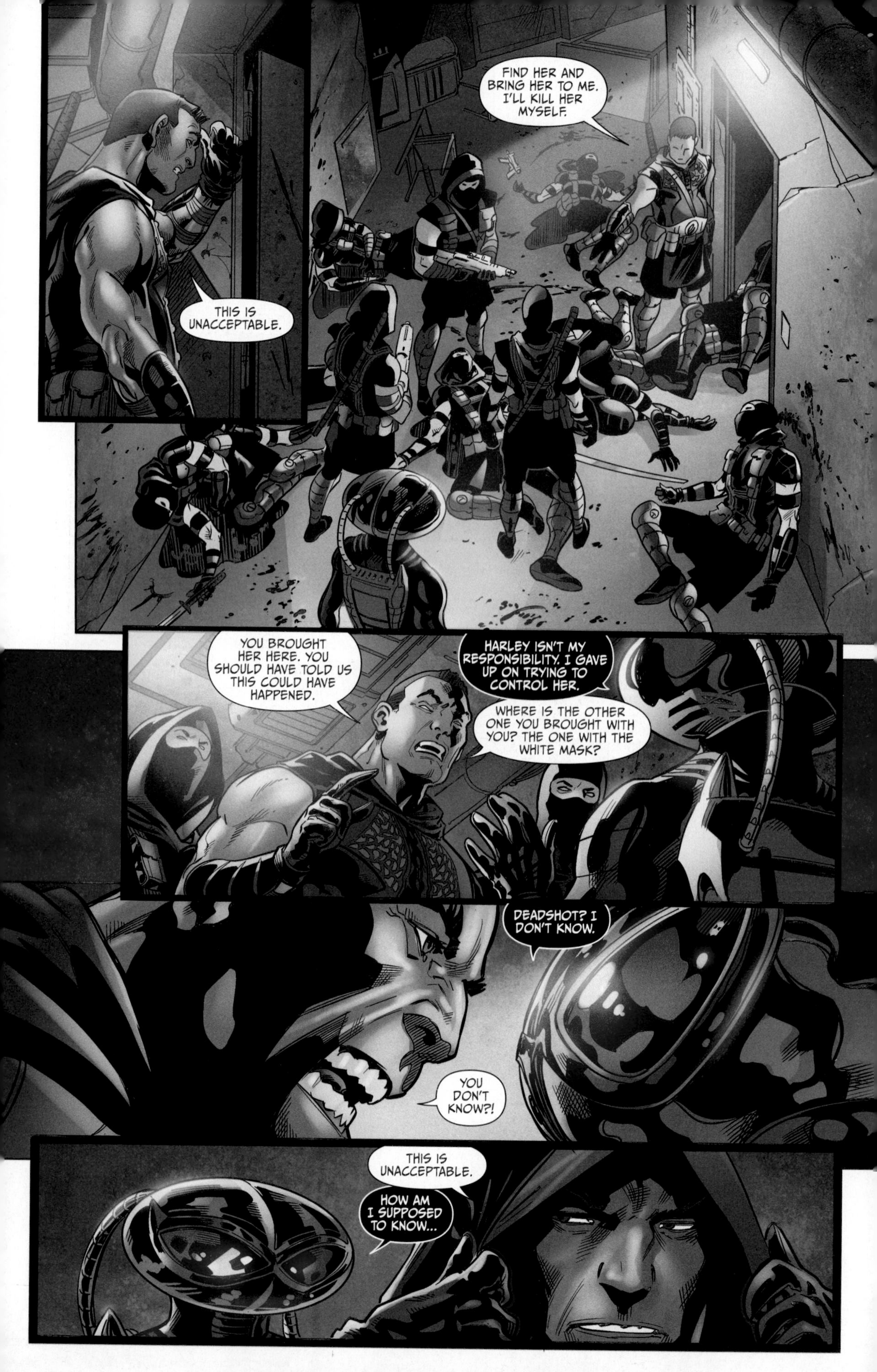
FIND HER AND BRING HER TO ME. I'LL KILL HER MYSELF.
THIS IS UNACCEPTABLE.
YOU BROUGHT HER HERE. YOU SHOULD HAVE TOLD US THIS COULD HAVE HAPPENED.
HARLEY ISN'T MY RESPONSIBILITY. I GAVE UP ON TRYING TO CONTROL HER.
WHERE IS THE OTHER ONE YOU BROUGHT WITH YOU? THE ONE WITH THE WHITE MASK?
DEADSHOT? I DON'T KNOW.
YOU DON'T KNOW?!
THIS IS UNACCEPTABLE.
HOW AM I SUPPOSED TO KNOW...

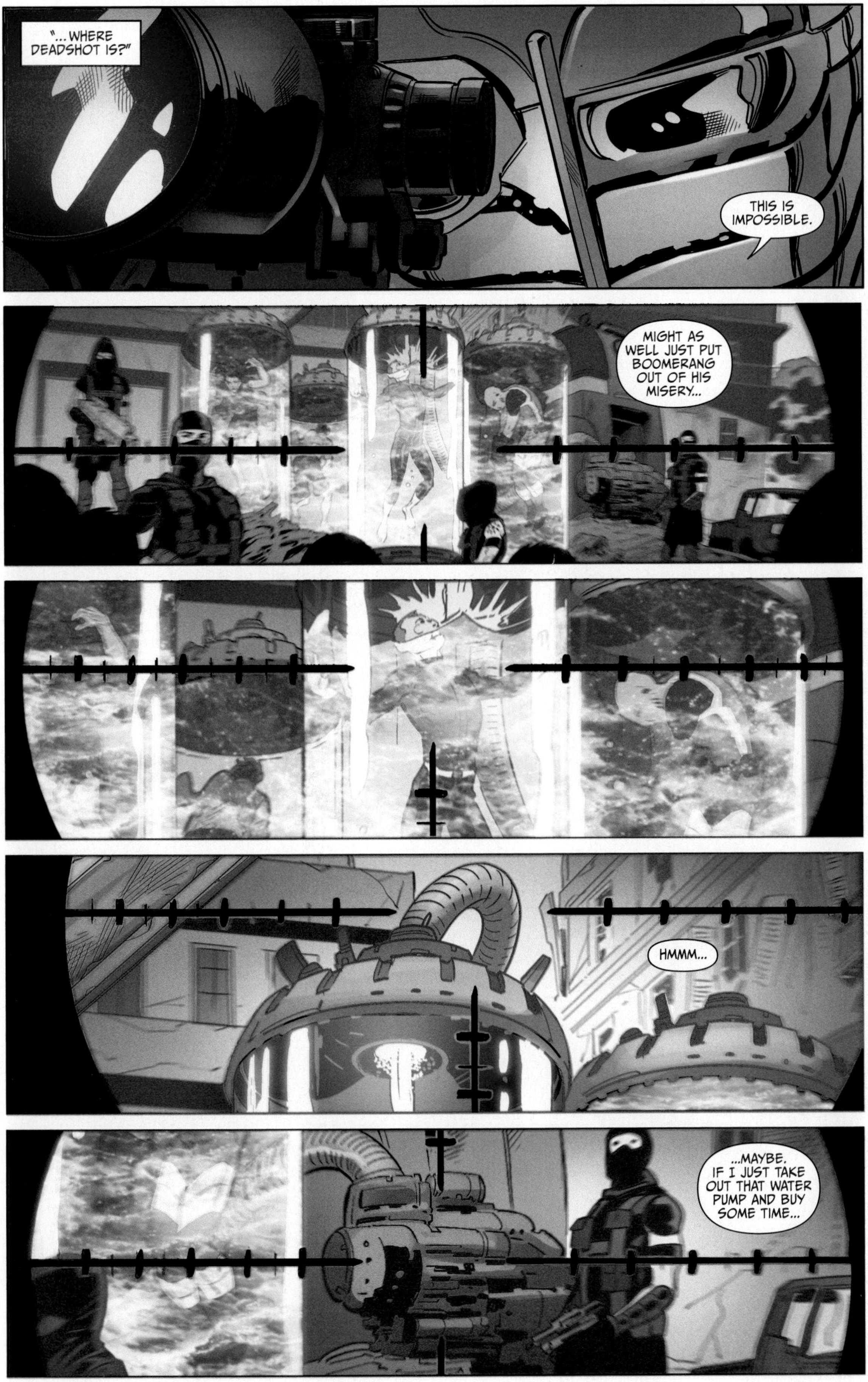
"...WHERE DEADSHOT IS?"
THIS IS IMPOSSIBLE.
MIGHT AS WELL JUST PUT BOOMERANG OUT OF HIS MISERY...
HMMM...
...MAYBE. IF I JUST TAKE OUT THAT WATER PUMP AND BUY SOME TIME...

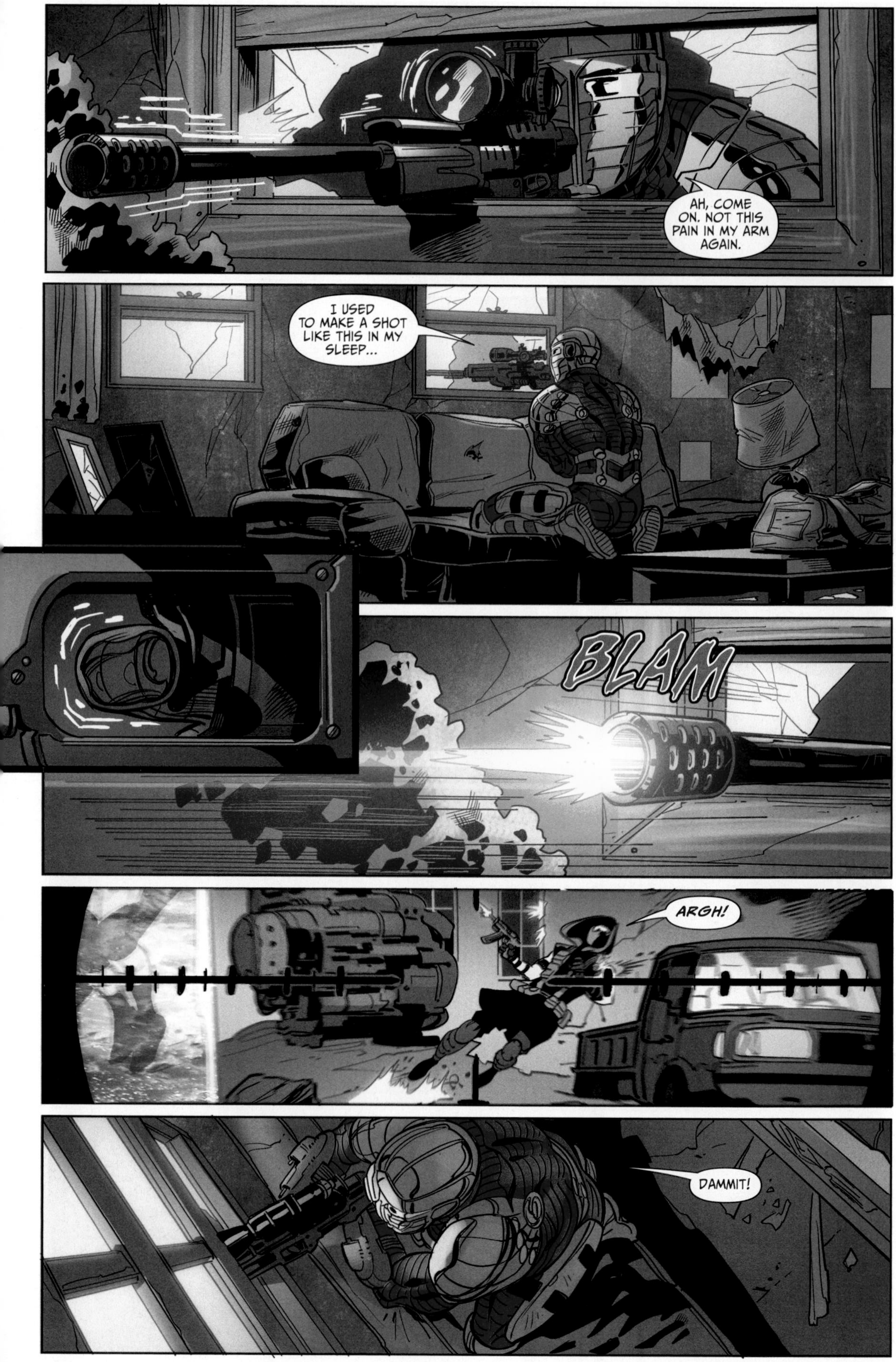
AH, COME ON. NOT THIS PAIN IN MY ARM AGAIN.
I USED TO MAKE A SHOT LIKE THIS IN MY SLEEP...
BLAM
ARGH!
DAMMIT!

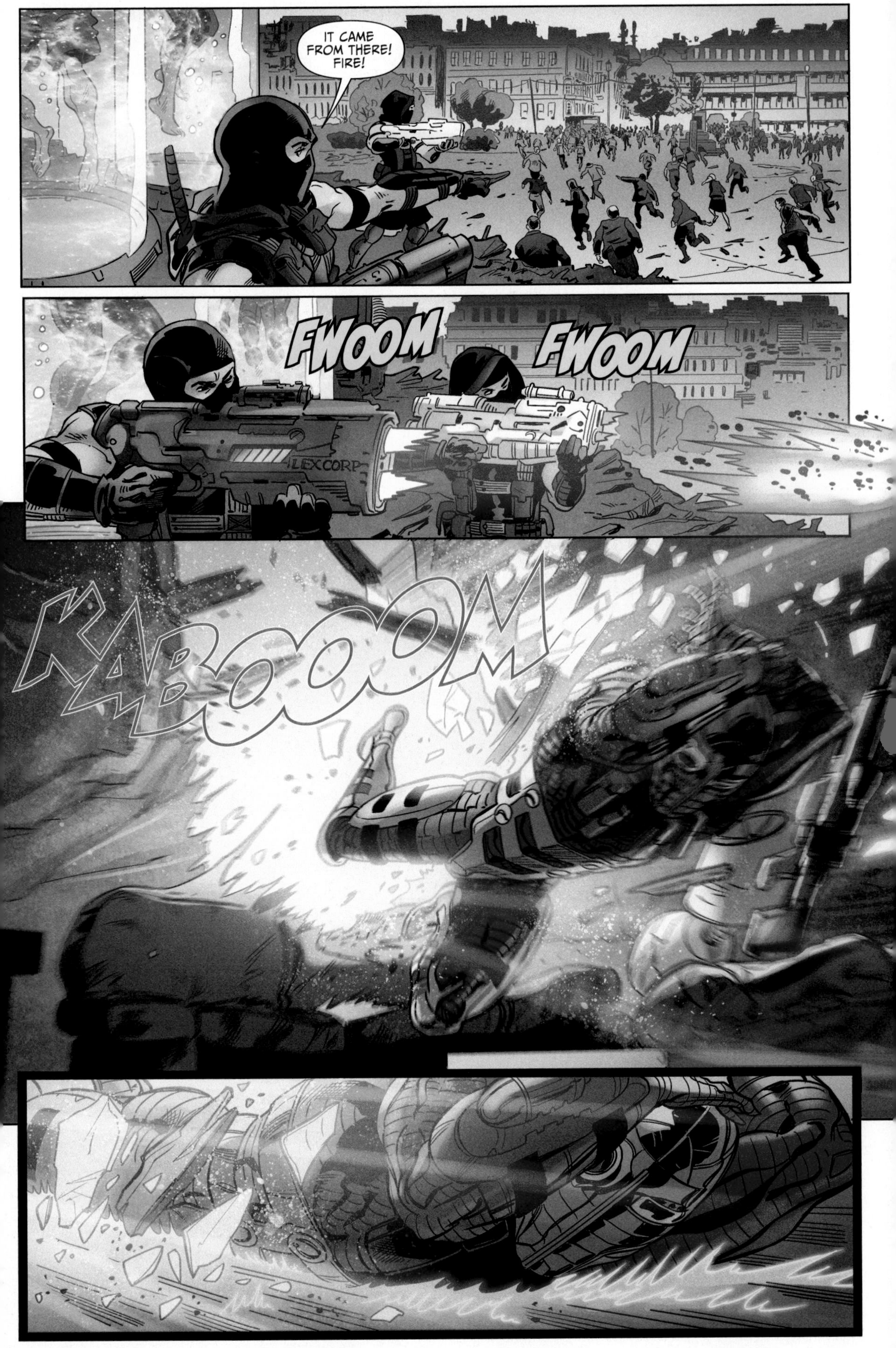
IT CAME FROM THERE! FIRE!
FWOOM
FWOOM
LEXCORP
KABOOOM

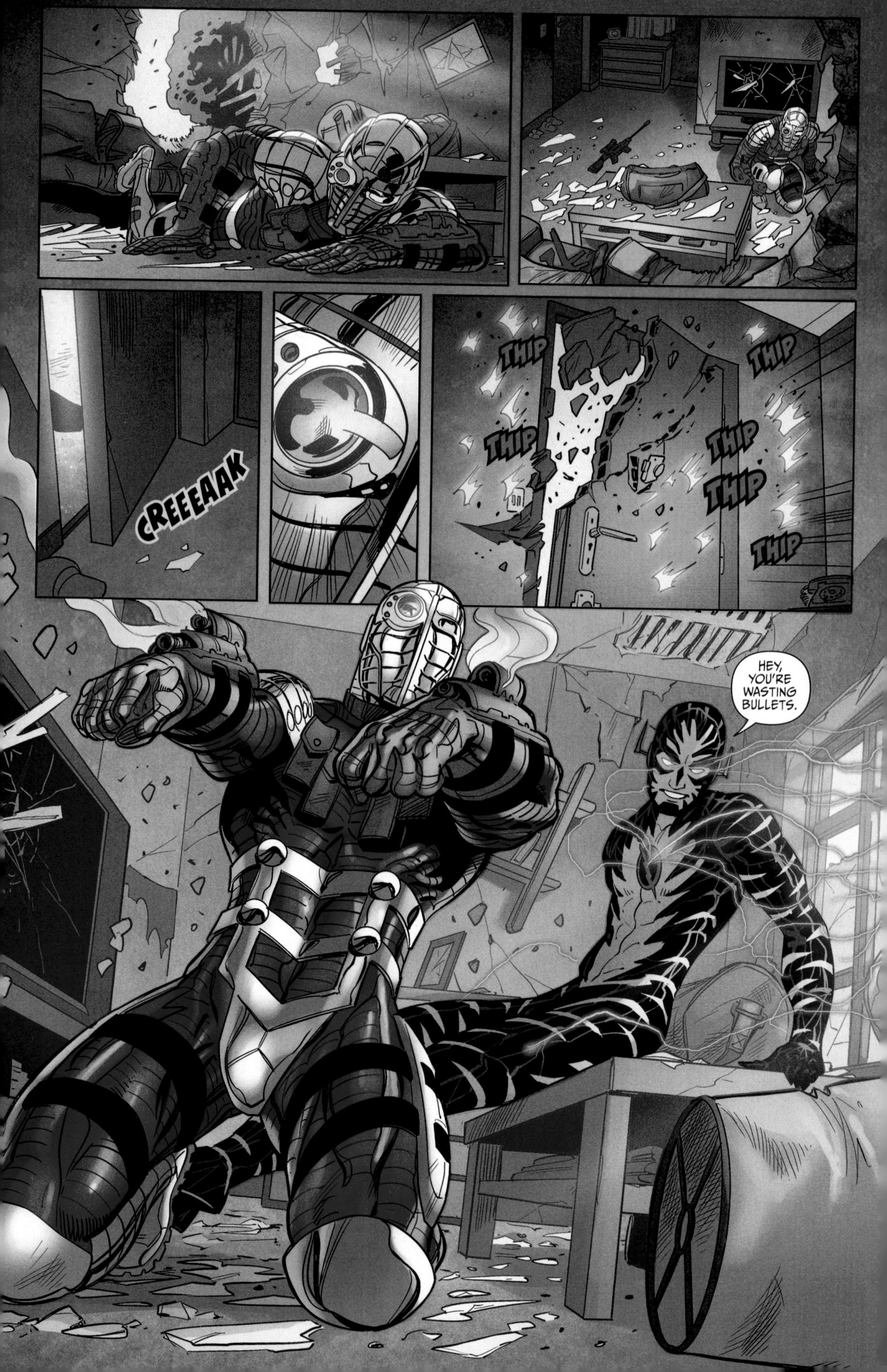
CREEEAAK
THIP
THIP
THIP
THIP
THIP
THIP
HEY, YOU'RE WASTING BULLETS.

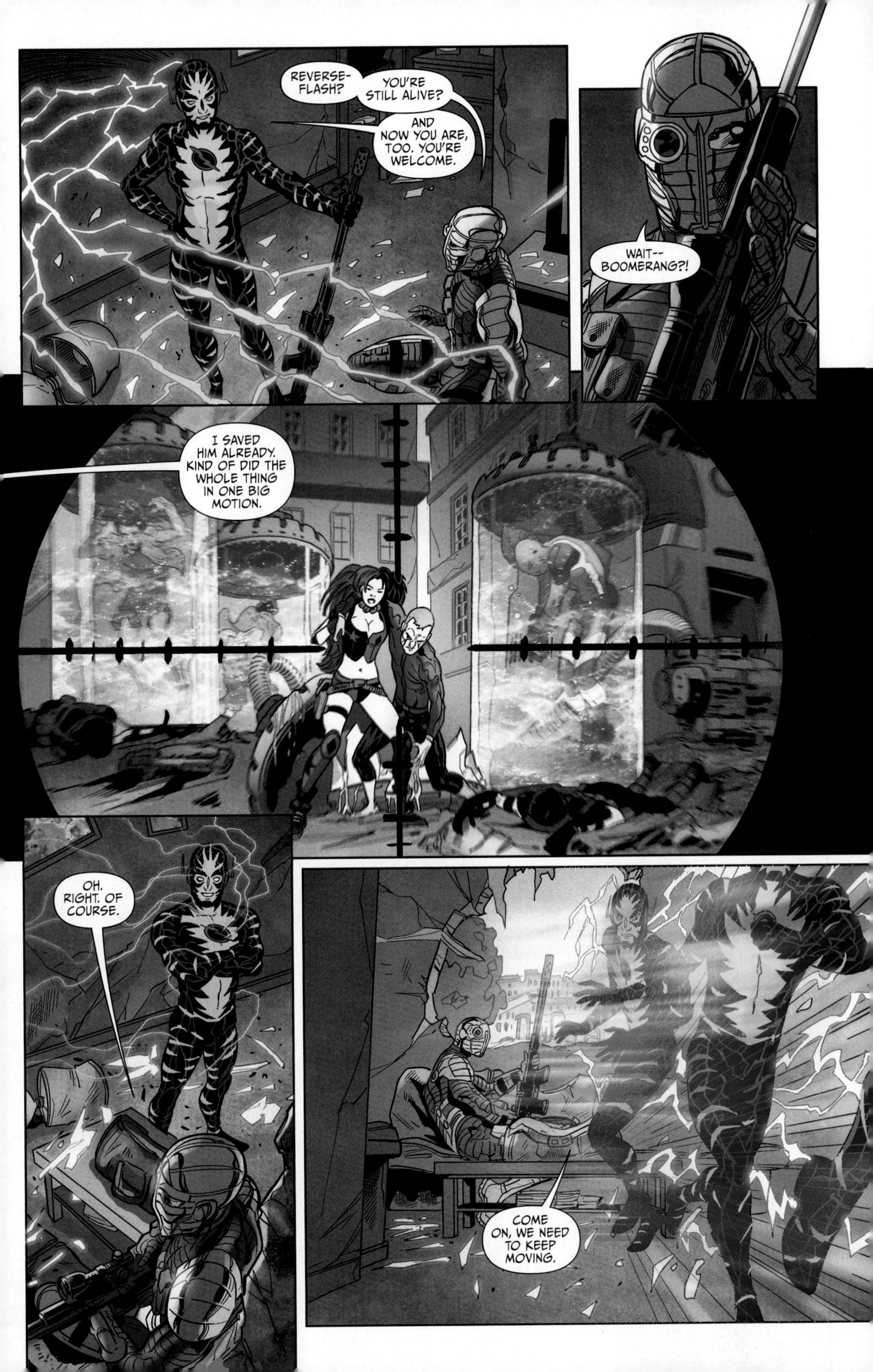
REVERSE-FLASH?
YOU'RE STILL ALIVE?
AND NOW YOU ARE, TOO. YOU'RE WELCOME.
WAIT-- BOOMERANG?!
I SAVED HIM ALREADY. KIND OF DID THE WHOLE THING IN ONE BIG MOTION.
OH. RIGHT. OF COURSE.
COME ON, WE NEED TO KEEP MOVING.

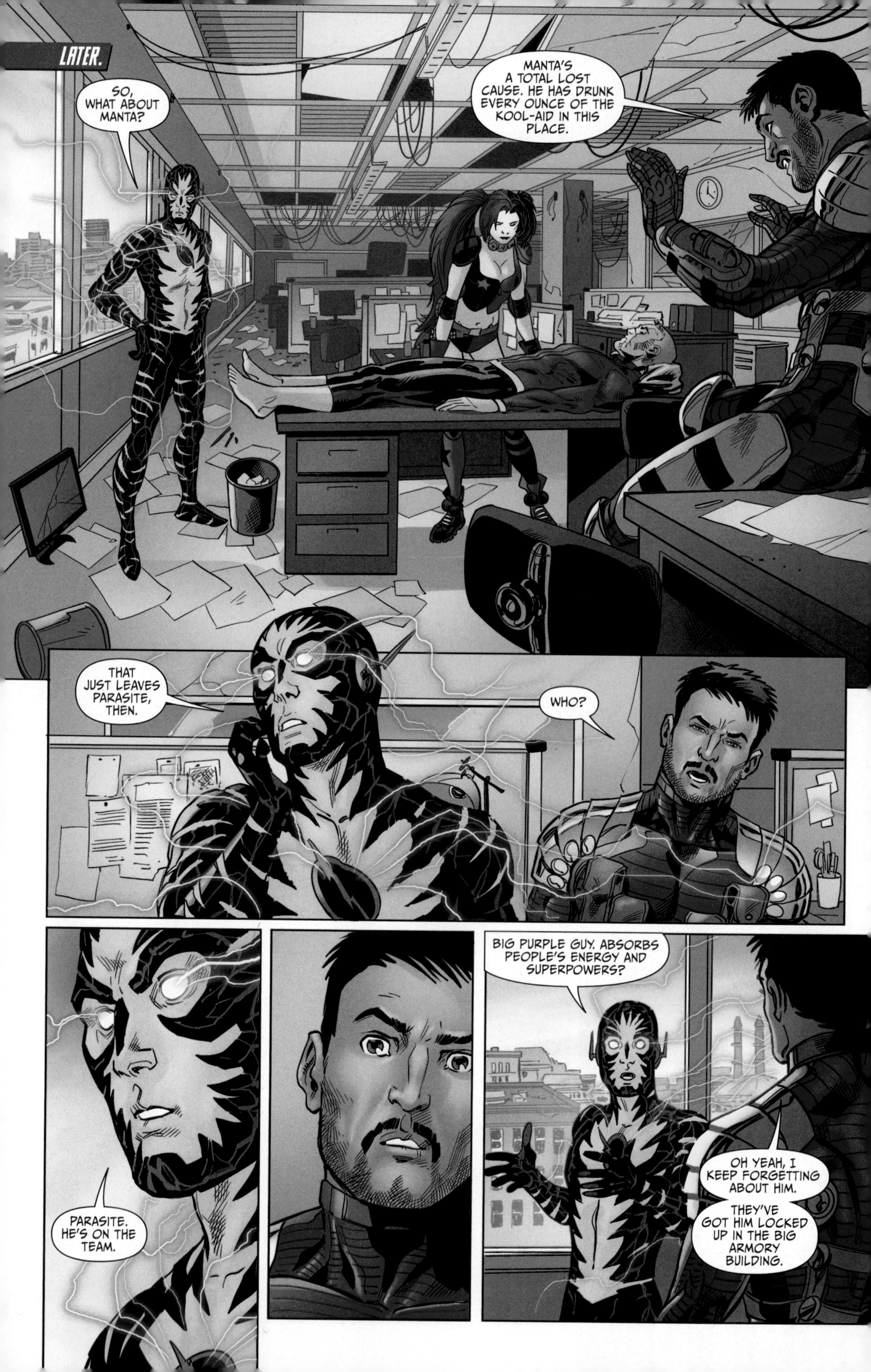
LATER.
SO, WHAT ABOUT MANTA?
MANTA'S A TOTAL LOST CAUSE. HE HAS DRUNK EVERY OUNCE OF THE KOOL-AID IN THIS PLACE.
THAT JUST LEAVES PARASITE, THEN.
WHO?
PARASITE. HE'S ON THE TEAM.
BIG PURPLE GUY. ABSORBS PEOPLE'S ENERGY AND SUPERPOWERS?
OH YEAH, I KEEP FORGETTING ABOUT HIM.
THEY'VE GOT HIM LOCKED UP IN THE BIG ARMORY BUILDING.

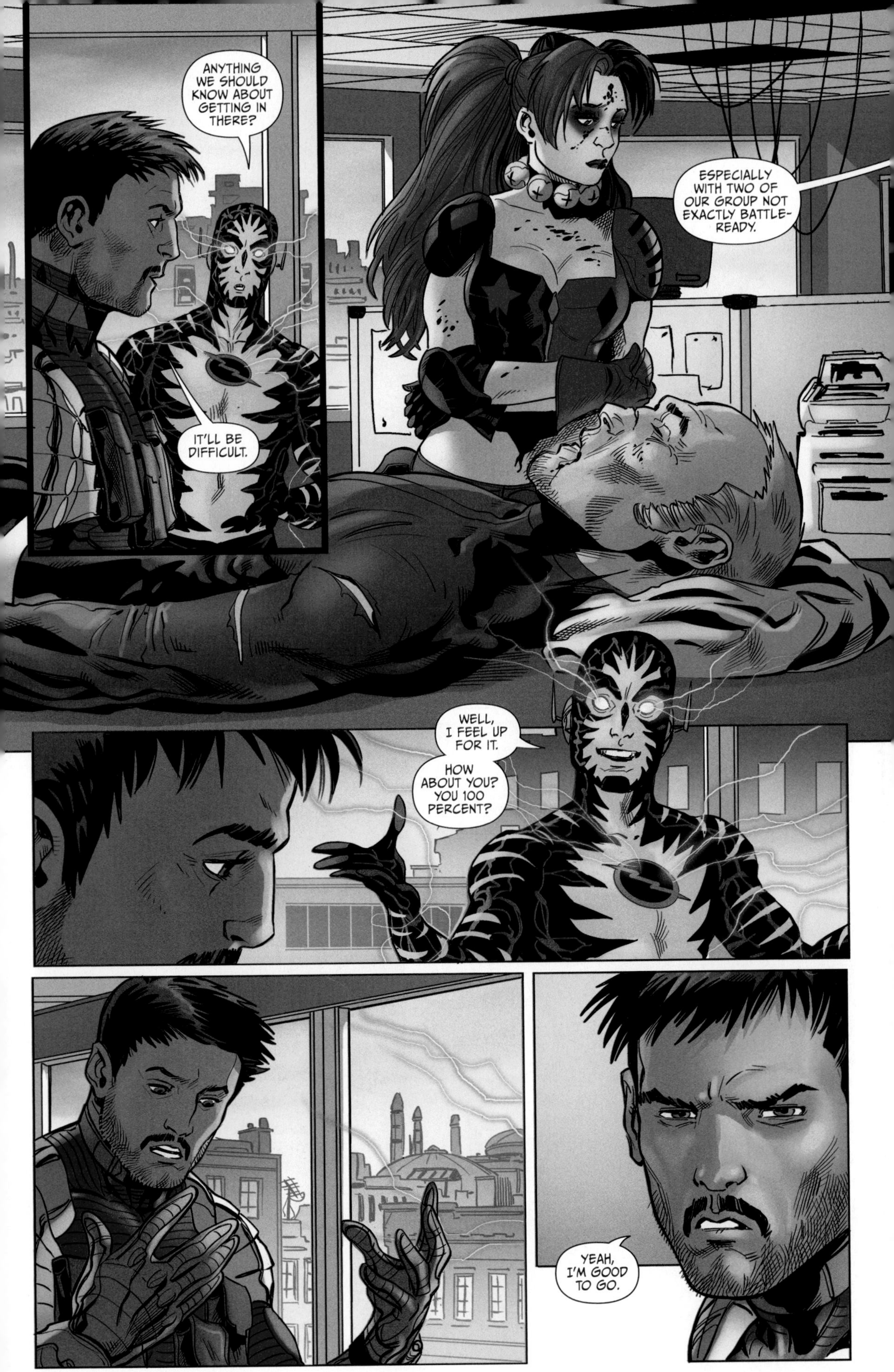
ANYTHING WE SHOULD KNOW ABOUT GETTING IN THERE?
IT'LL BE DIFFICULT.
ESPECIALLY WITH TWO OF OUR GROUP NOT EXACTLY BATTLE-READY.
WELL, I FEEL UP FOR IT.
HOW ABOUT YOU? YOU 100 PERCENT?
YEAH, I'M GOOD TO GO.

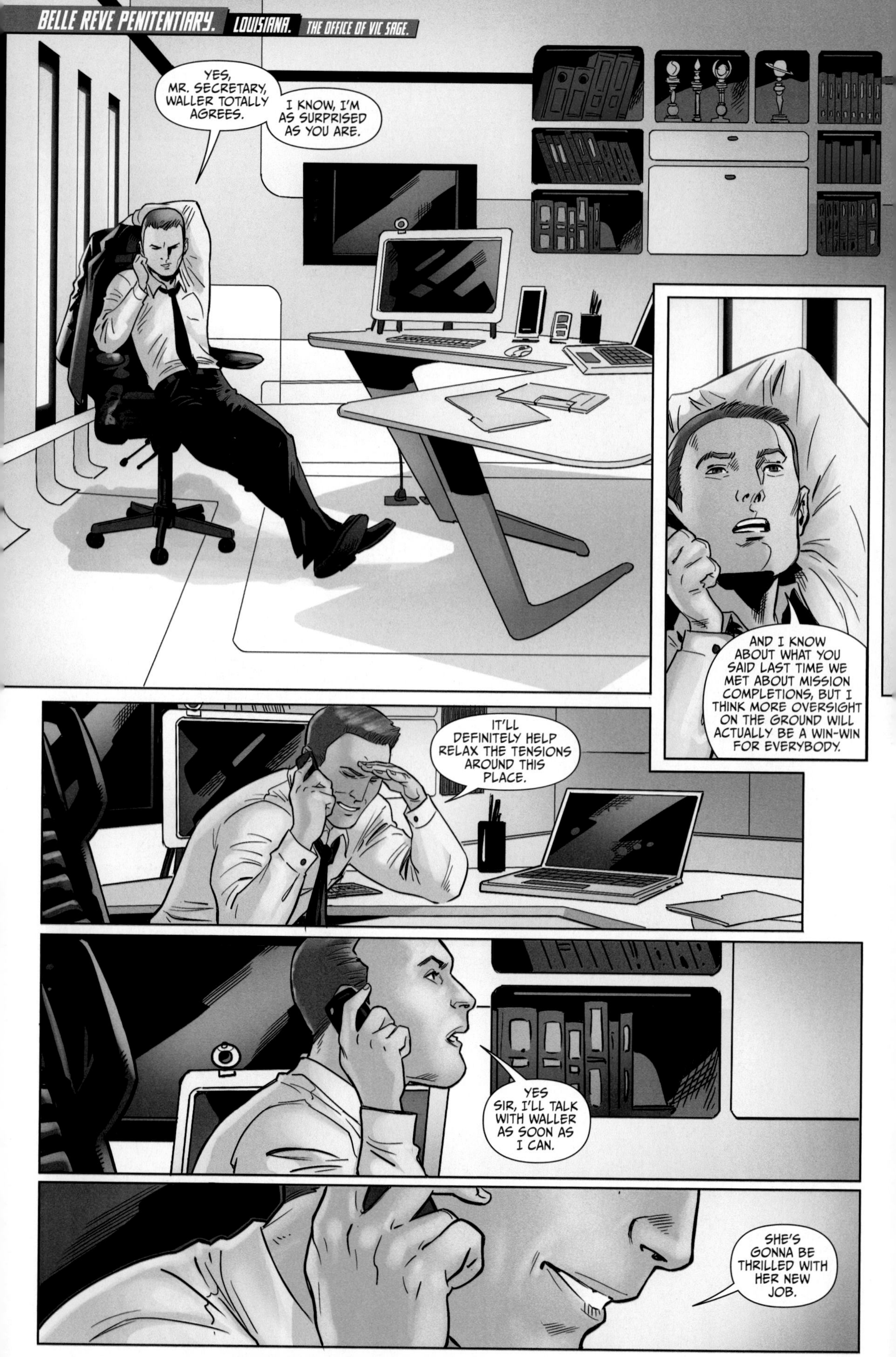
BELLE REVE PENITENTIARY. LOUISIANA. THE OFFICE OF VIC SAGE.
YES, MR. SECRETARY, WALLER TOTALLY AGREES.
I KNOW, I'M AS SURPRISED AS YOU ARE.
AND I KNOW ABOUT WHAT YOU SAID LAST TIME WE MET ABOUT MISSION COMPLETIONS, BUT I THINK MORE OVERSIGHT ON THE GROUND WILL ACTUALLY BE A WIN-WIN FOR EVERYBODY.
IT'LL DEFINITELY HELP RELAX THE TENSIONS AROUND THIS PLACE.
YES SIR, I'LL TALK WITH WALLER AS SOON AS I CAN.
SHE'S GONNA BE THRILLED WITH HER NEW JOB.

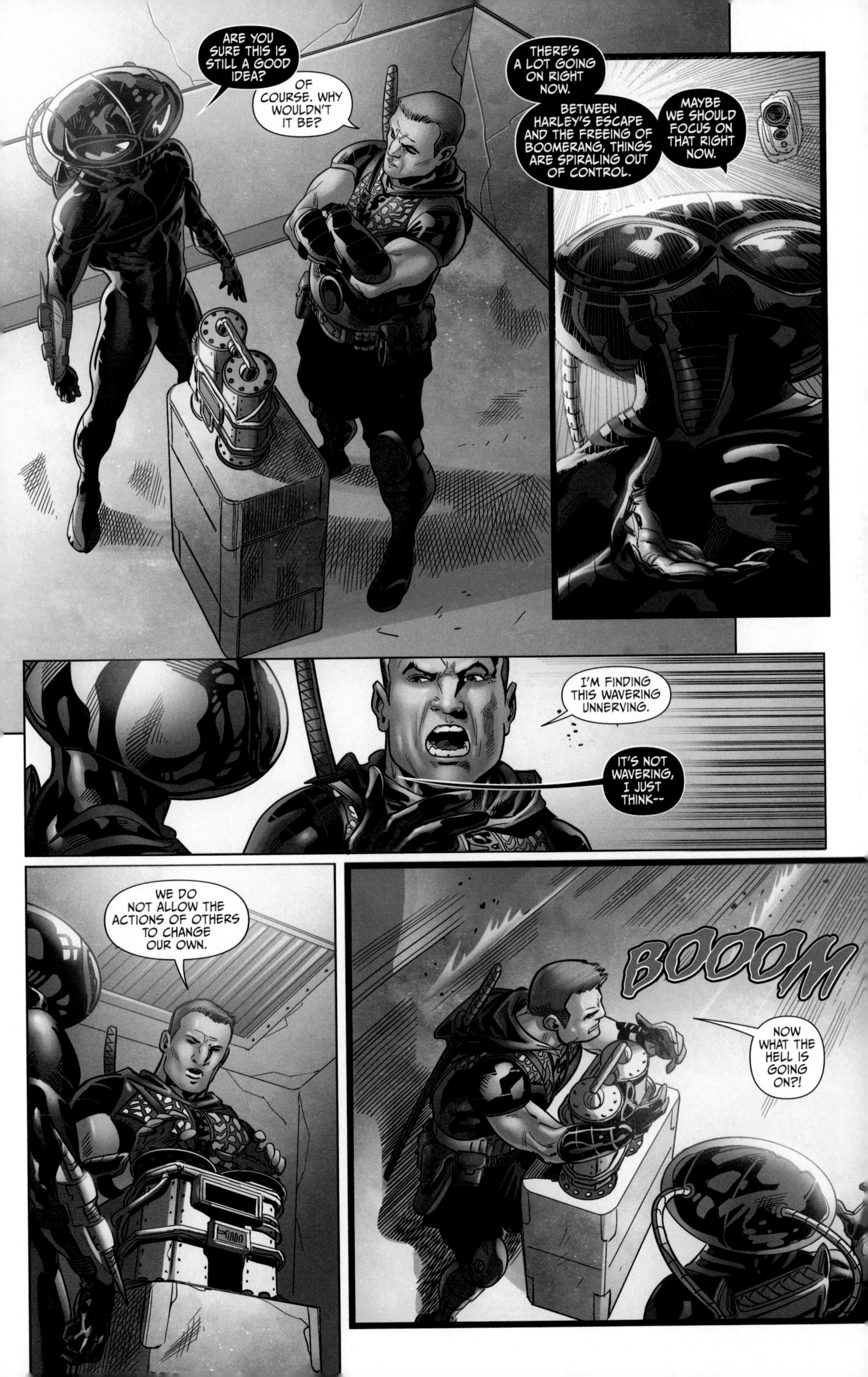

ARE YOU SURE THIS IS STILL A GOOD IDEA?
OF COURSE. WHY WOULDN'T IT BE?
THERE'S A LOT GOING ON RIGHT NOW.
BETWEEN HARLEY'S ESCAPE AND THE FREEING OF BOOMERANG, THINGS ARE SPIRALING OUT OF CONTROL.
MAYBE WE SHOULD FOCUS ON THAT RIGHT NOW.
I'M FINDING THIS WAVERING UNNERVING.
IT'S NOT WAVERING, I JUST THINK--
WE DO NOT ALLOW THE ACTIONS OF OTHERS TO CHANGE OUR OWN.
BOOOM
NOW WHAT THE HELL IS GOING ON?!

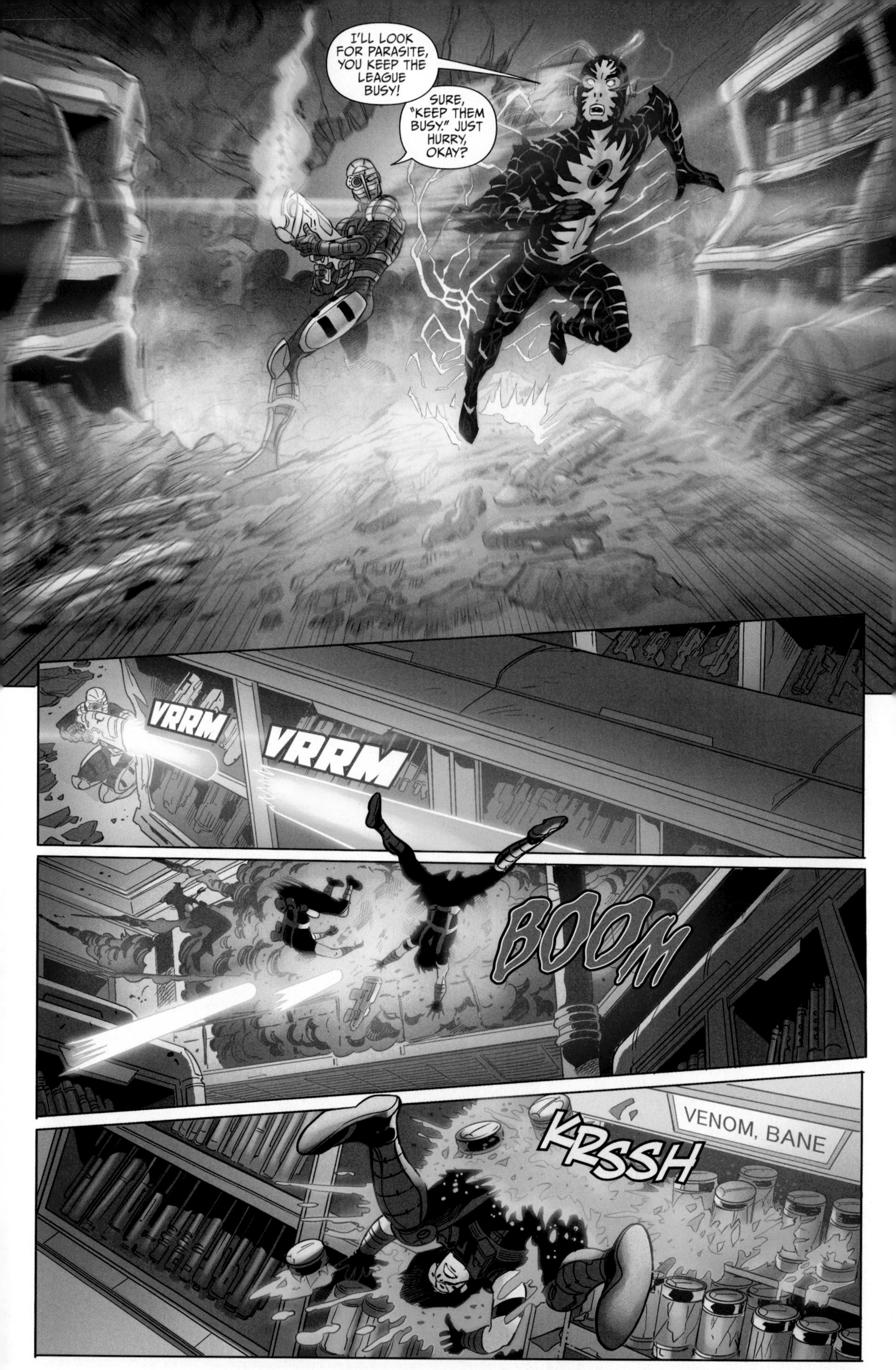
I'LL LOOK FOR PARASITE, YOU KEEP THE LEAGUE BUSY!
SURE, "KEEP THEM BUSY." JUST HURRY, OKAY?
VRRM
VRRM
BOOM
VENOM, BANE
KRSSH

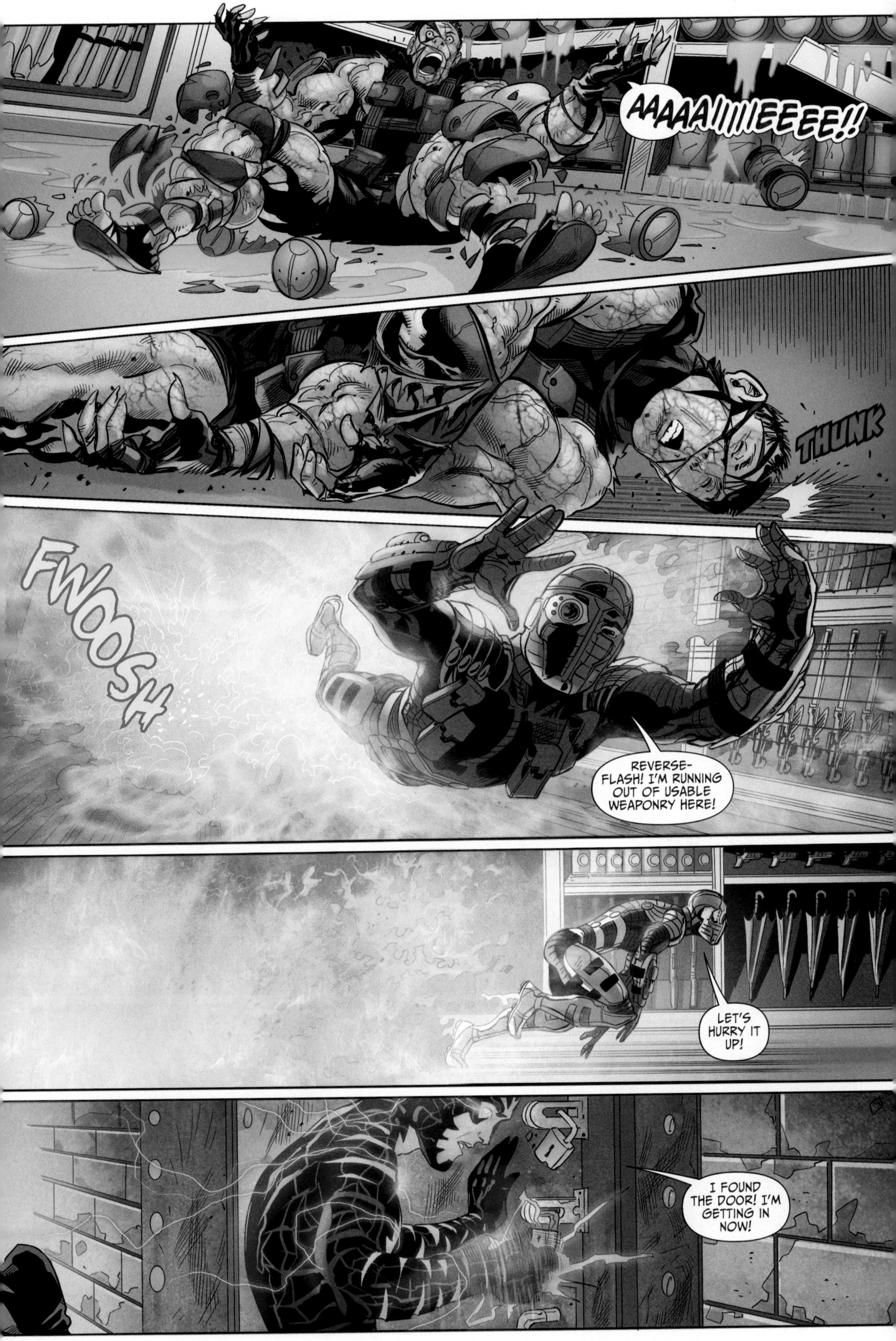
AAAAAIIIIIEEEEE!!
THUNK
FWOOSH
REVERSE-FLASH! I'M RUNNING OUT OF USABLE WEAPONRY HERE!
LET'S HURRY IT UP!
I FOUND THE DOOR! I'M GETTING IN NOW!

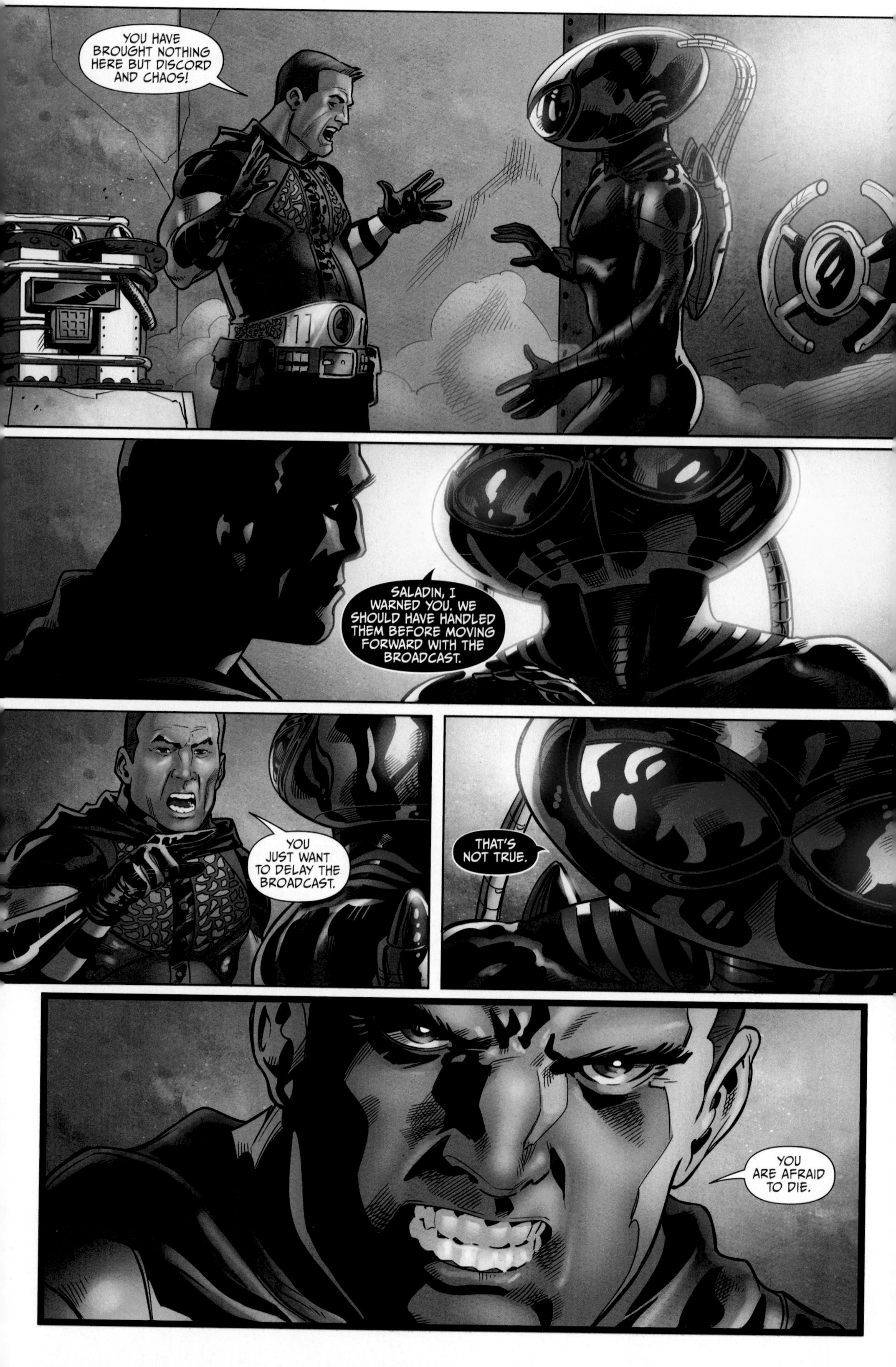
YOU HAVE BROUGHT NOTHING HERE BUT DISCORD AND CHAOS!
SALADIN, I WARNED YOU. WE SHOULD HAVE HANDLED THEM BEFORE MOVING FORWARD WITH THE BROADCAST.
YOU JUST WANT TO DELAY THE BROADCAST.
THAT'S NOT TRUE.
YOU ARE AFRAID TO DIE.

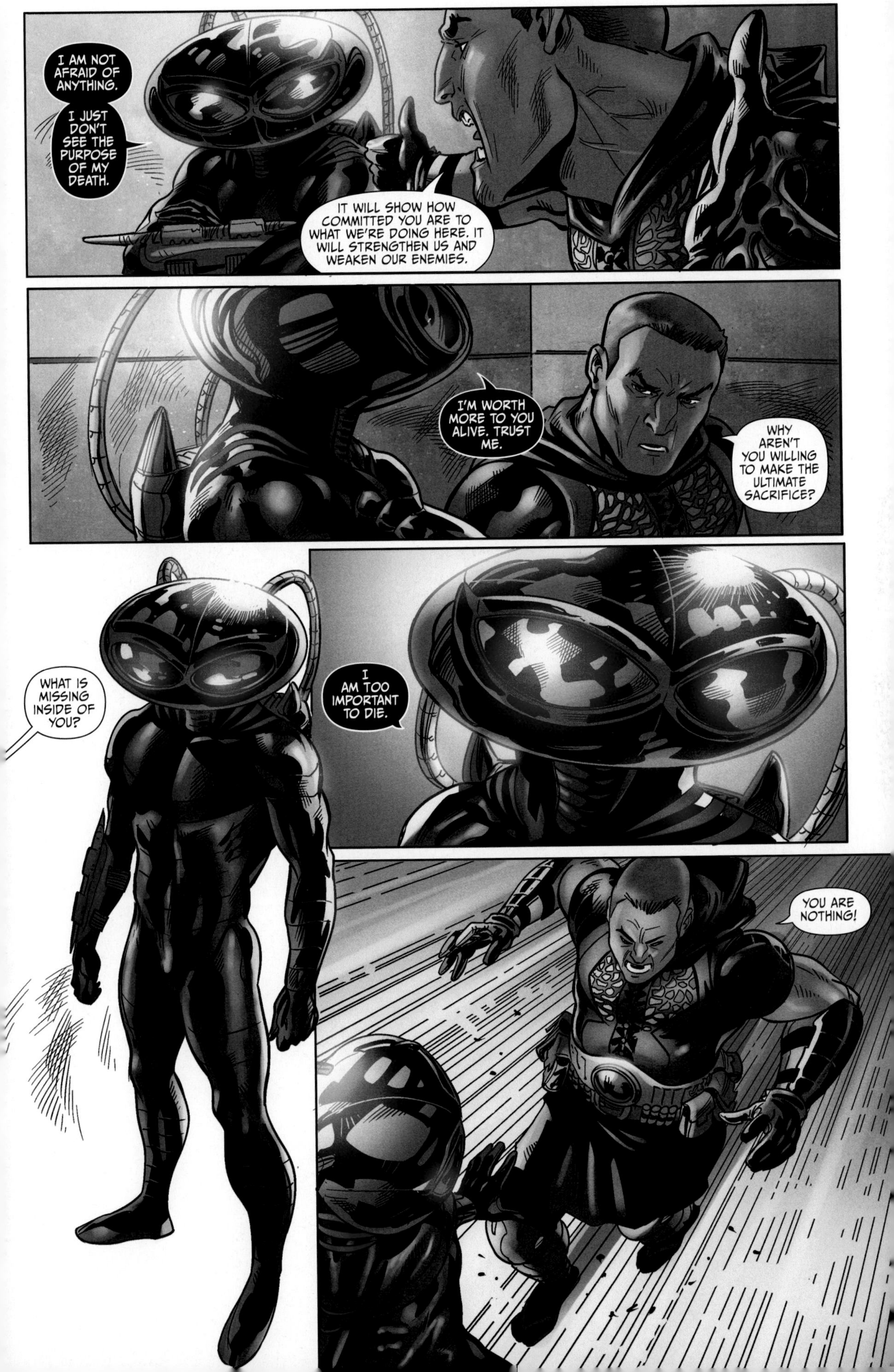
I AM NOT AFRAID OF ANYTHING.
I JUST DON'T SEE THE PURPOSE OF MY DEATH.
IT WILL SHOW HOW COMMITTED YOU ARE TO WHAT WE'RE DOING HERE. IT WILL STRENGTHEN US AND WEAKEN OUR ENEMIES.
I'M WORTH MORE TO YOU ALIVE. TRUST ME.
WHY AREN'T YOU WILLING TO MAKE THE ULTIMATE SACRIFICE?
WHAT IS MISSING INSIDE OF YOU?
I AM TOO IMPORTANT TO DIE.
YOU ARE NOTHING!

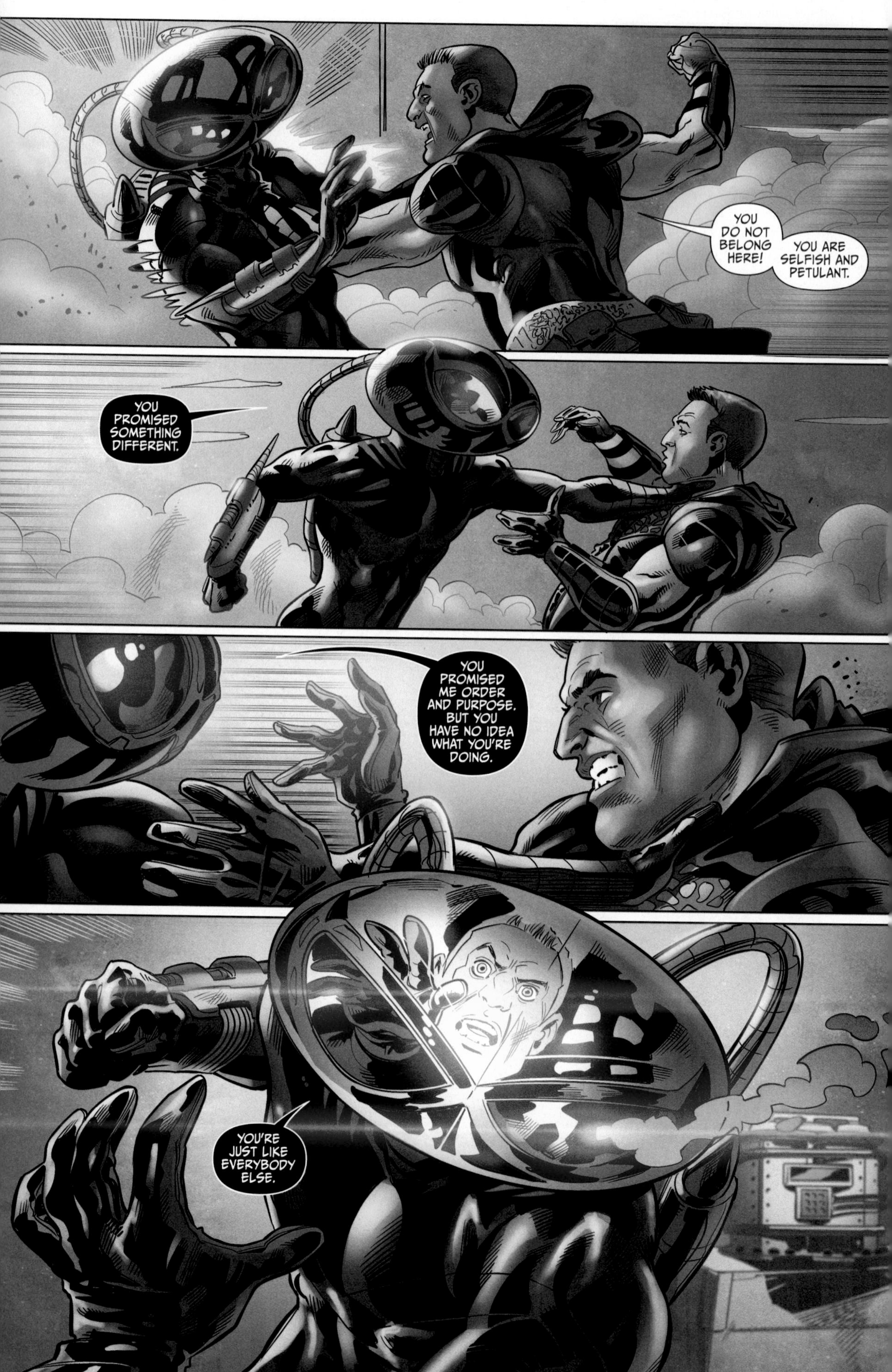
YOU DO NOT BELONG HERE!
YOU ARE SELFISH AND PETULANT.
YOU PROMISED SOMETHING DIFFERENT.
YOU PROMISED ME ORDER AND PURPOSE. BUT YOU HAVE NO IDEA WHAT YOU'RE DOING.
YOU'RE JUST LIKE EVERYBODY ELSE.

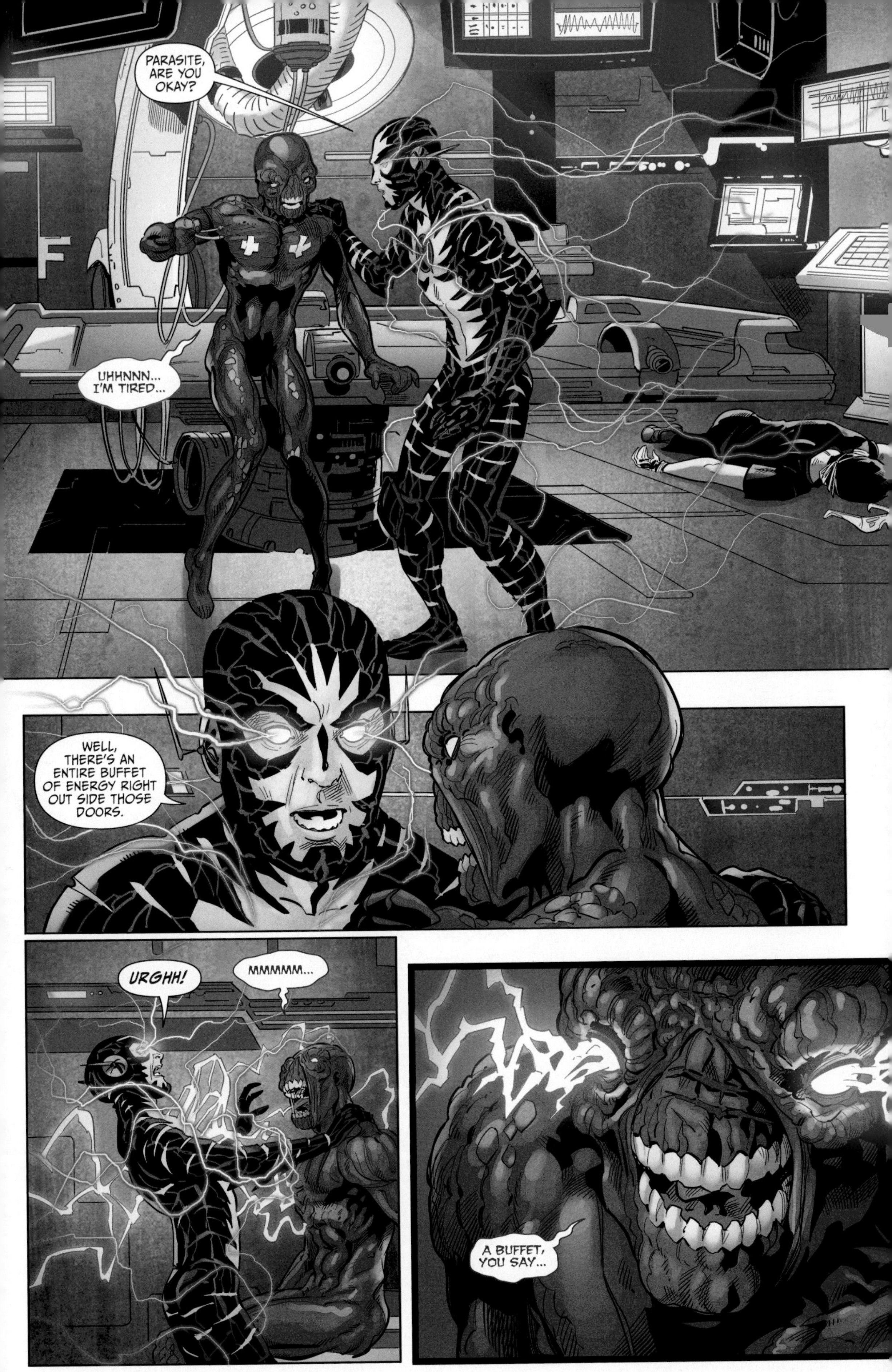
PARASITE, ARE YOU OKAY?
UHHNNN... I'M TIRED...
WELL, THERE'S AN ENTIRE BUFFET OF ENERGY RIGHT OUT SIDE THOSE DOORS.
URGHH!
MMMMMM...
A BUFFET, YOU SAY...

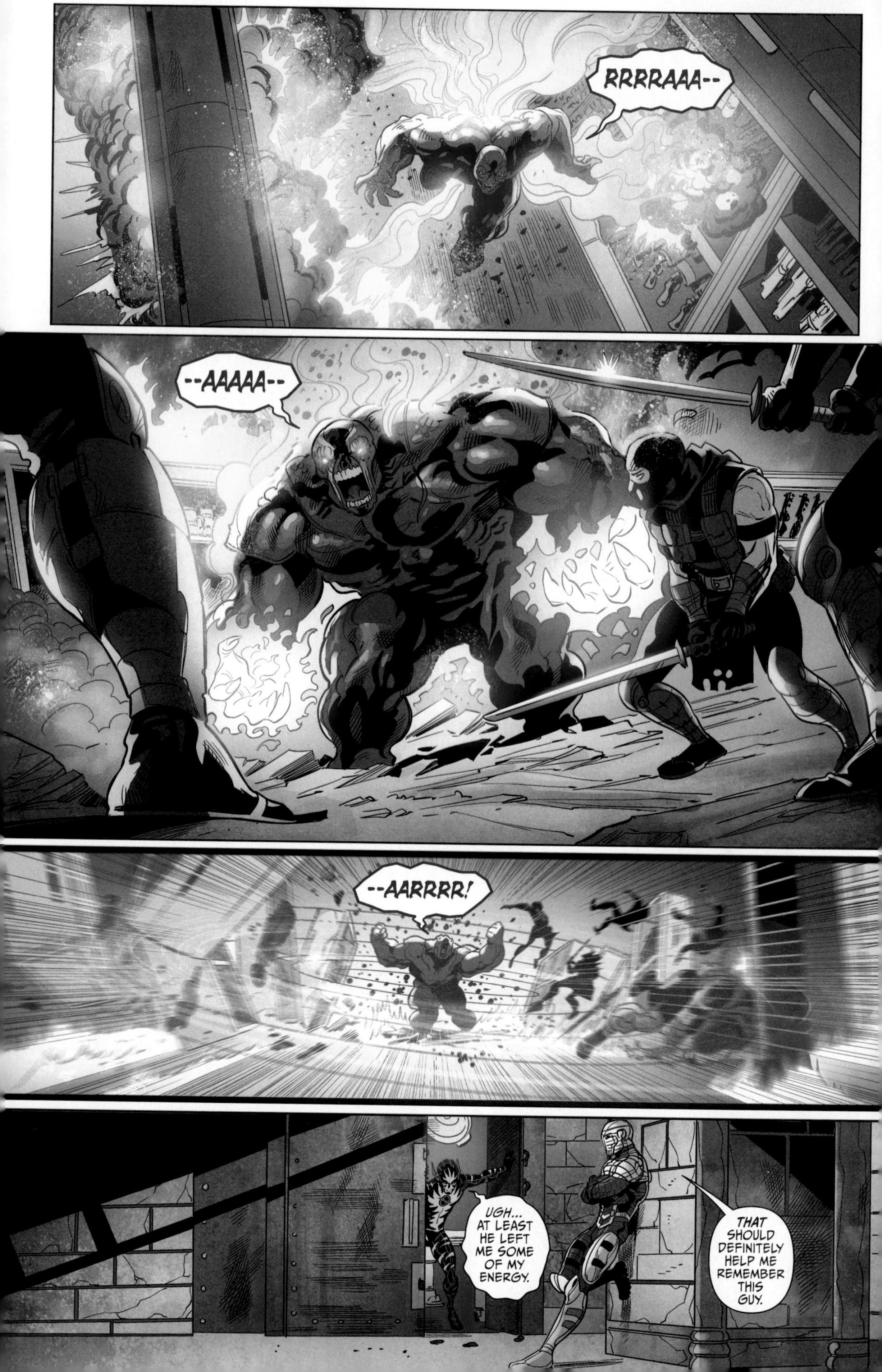
RRRRAAA--
--AAAAA--
--AARRRR!
UGH... AT LEAST HE LEFT ME SOME OF MY ENERGY.
THAT SHOULD DEFINITELY HELP ME REMEMBER THIS GUY.

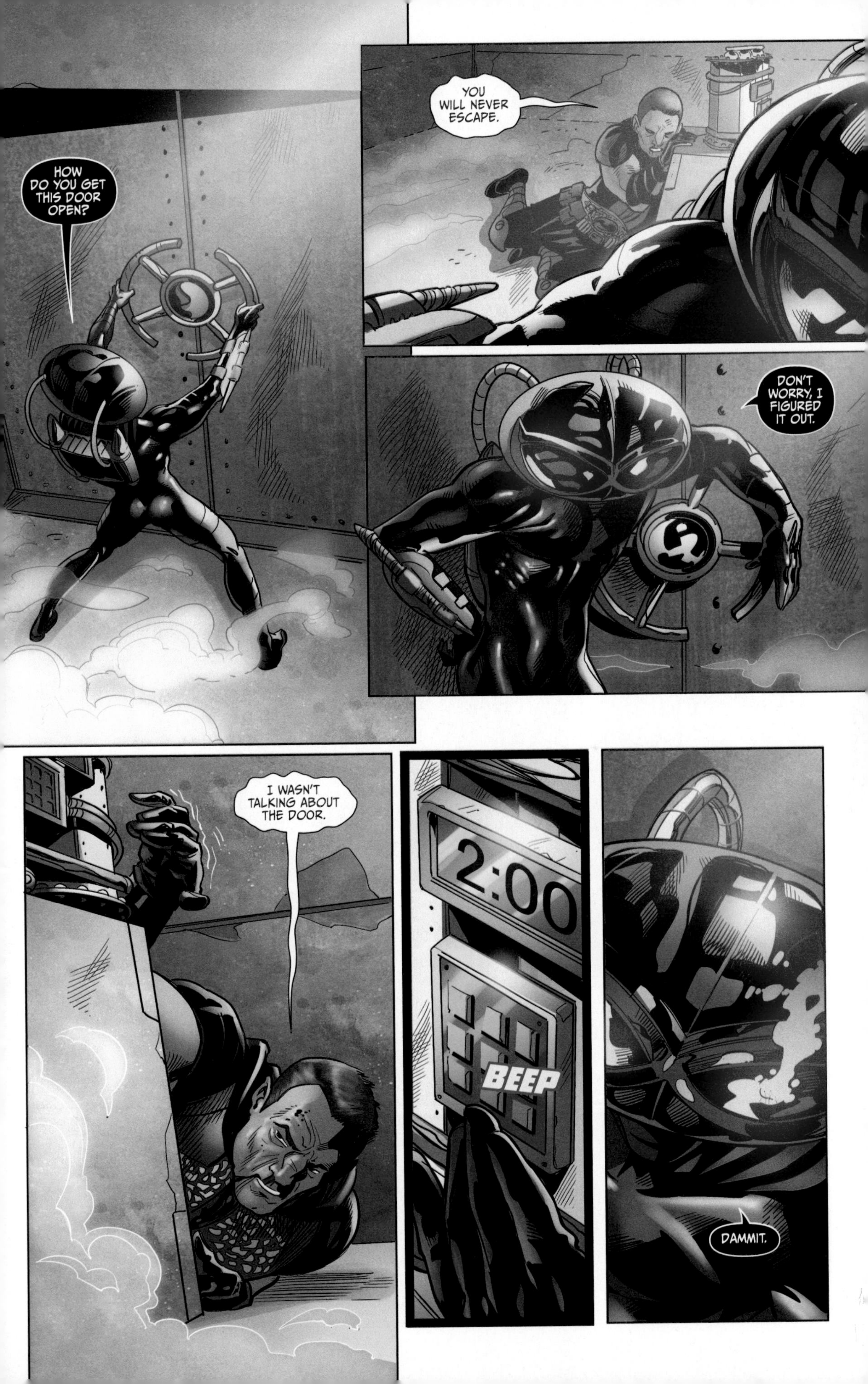
HOW DO YOU GET THIS DOOR OPEN?
YOU WILL NEVER ESCAPE.
DON'T WORRY, I FIGURED IT OUT.
I WASN'T TALKING ABOUT THE DOOR.
2:00
BEEP
DAMMIT.

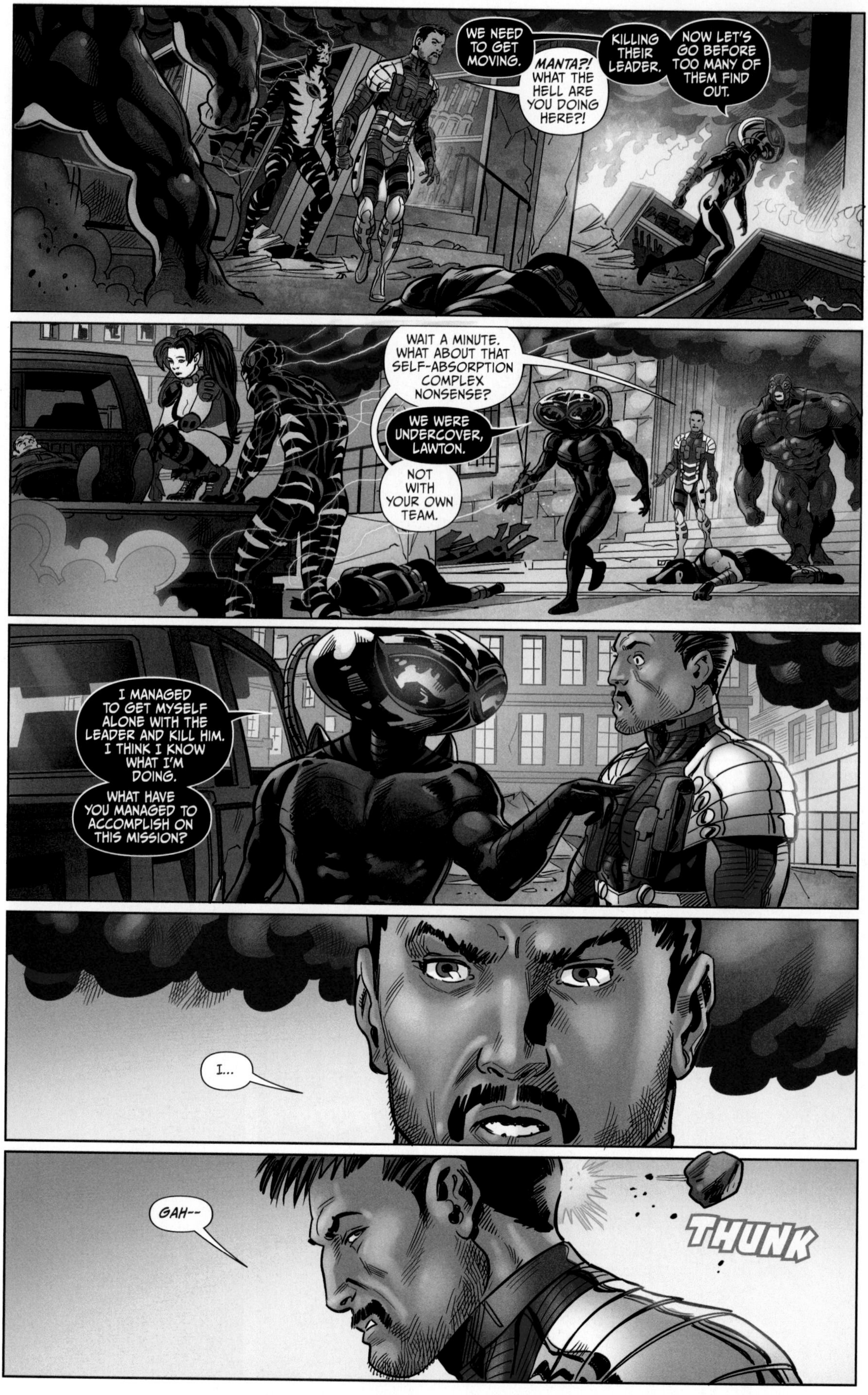
WE NEED TO GET MOVING.
MANTA?! WHAT THE HELL ARE YOU DOING HERE?!
KILLING THEIR LEADER.
NOW LET'S GO BEFORE TOO MANY OF THEM FIND OUT.
WAIT A MINUTE. WHAT ABOUT THAT SELF-ABSORPTION COMPLEX NONSENSE?
WE WERE UNDERCOVER, LAWTON.
NOT WITH YOUR OWN TEAM.
I MANAGED TO GET MYSELF ALONE WITH THE LEADER AND KILL HIM. I THINK I KNOW WHAT I'M DOING.
WHAT HAVE YOU MANAGED TO ACCOMPLISH ON THIS MISSION?
I...
GAH--
THUNK

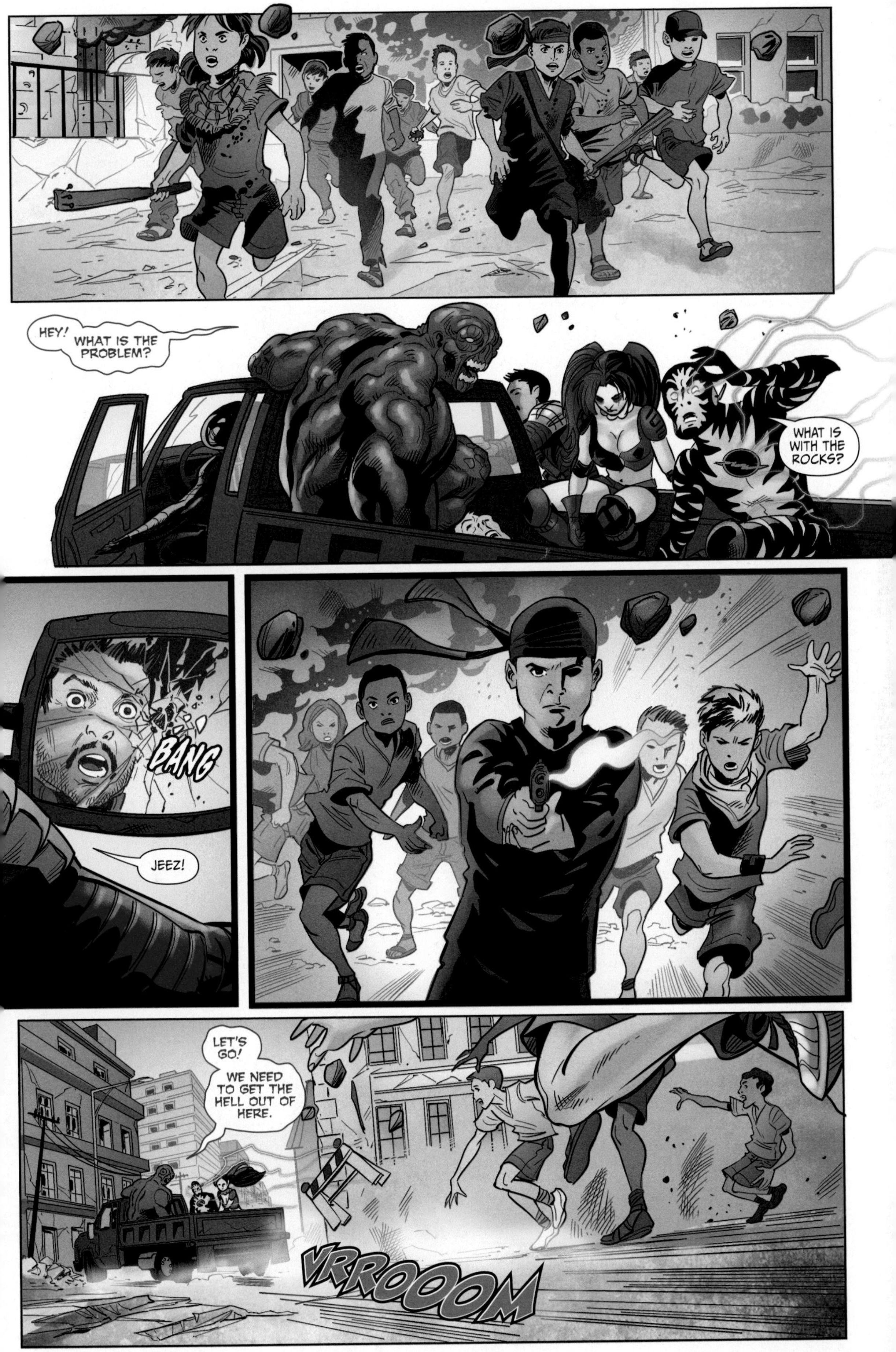
HEY! WHAT IS THE PROBLEM?
WHAT IS WITH THE ROCKS?
BANG
JEEZ!
LET'S GO!
WE NEED TO GET THE HELL OUT OF HERE.
VRROOOM

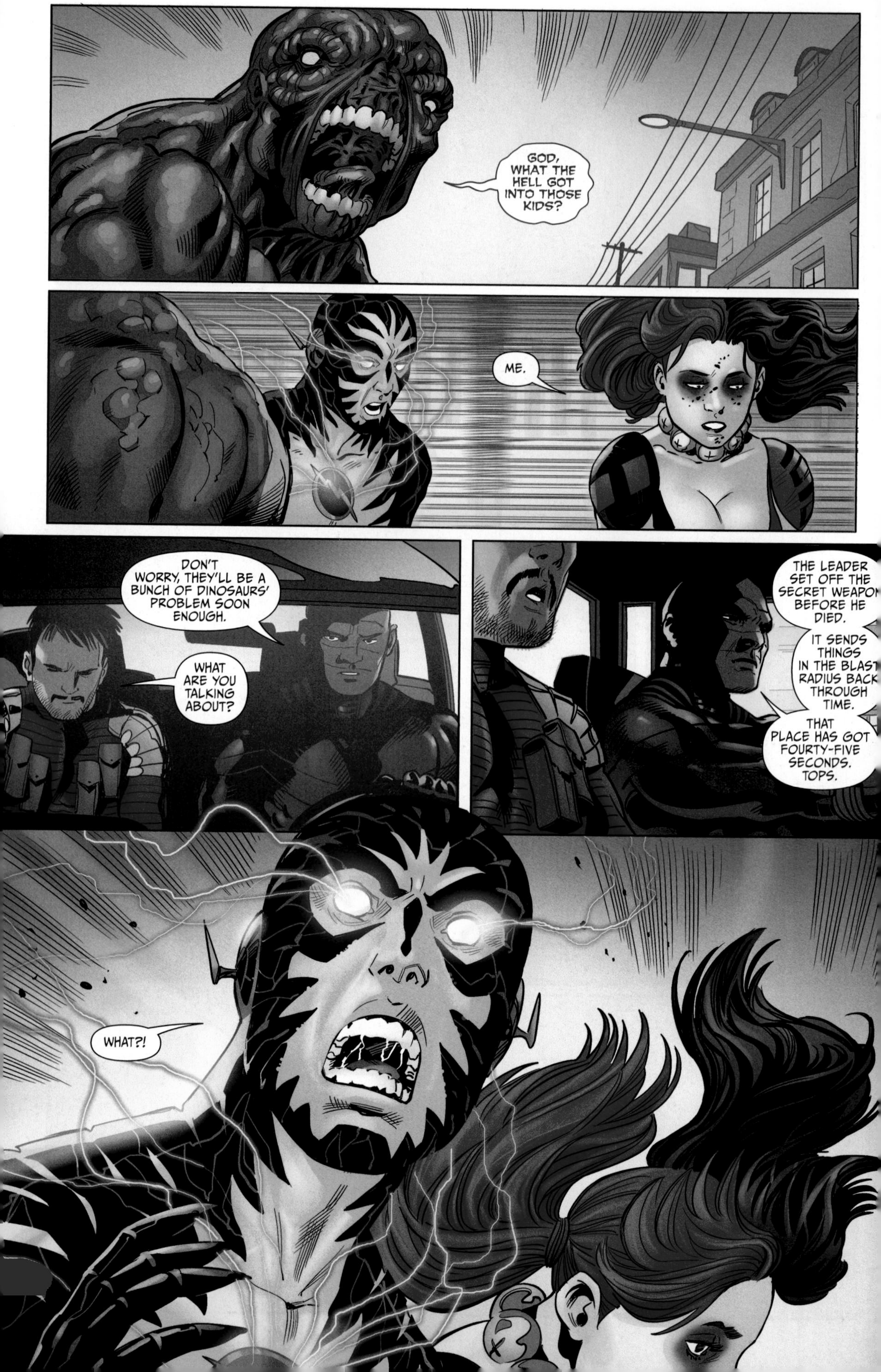
GOD, WHAT THE HELL GOT INTO THOSE KIDS?
ME.
DON'T WORRY, THEY'LL BE A BUNCH OF DINOSAURS' PROBLEM SOON ENOUGH.
WHAT ARE YOU TALKING ABOUT?
THE LEADER SET OFF THE SECRET WEAPON BEFORE HE DIED.
IT SENDS THINGS IN THE BLAST RADIUS BACK THROUGH TIME.
THAT PLACE HAS GOT FOURTY-FIVE SECONDS. TOPS.
WHAT?!

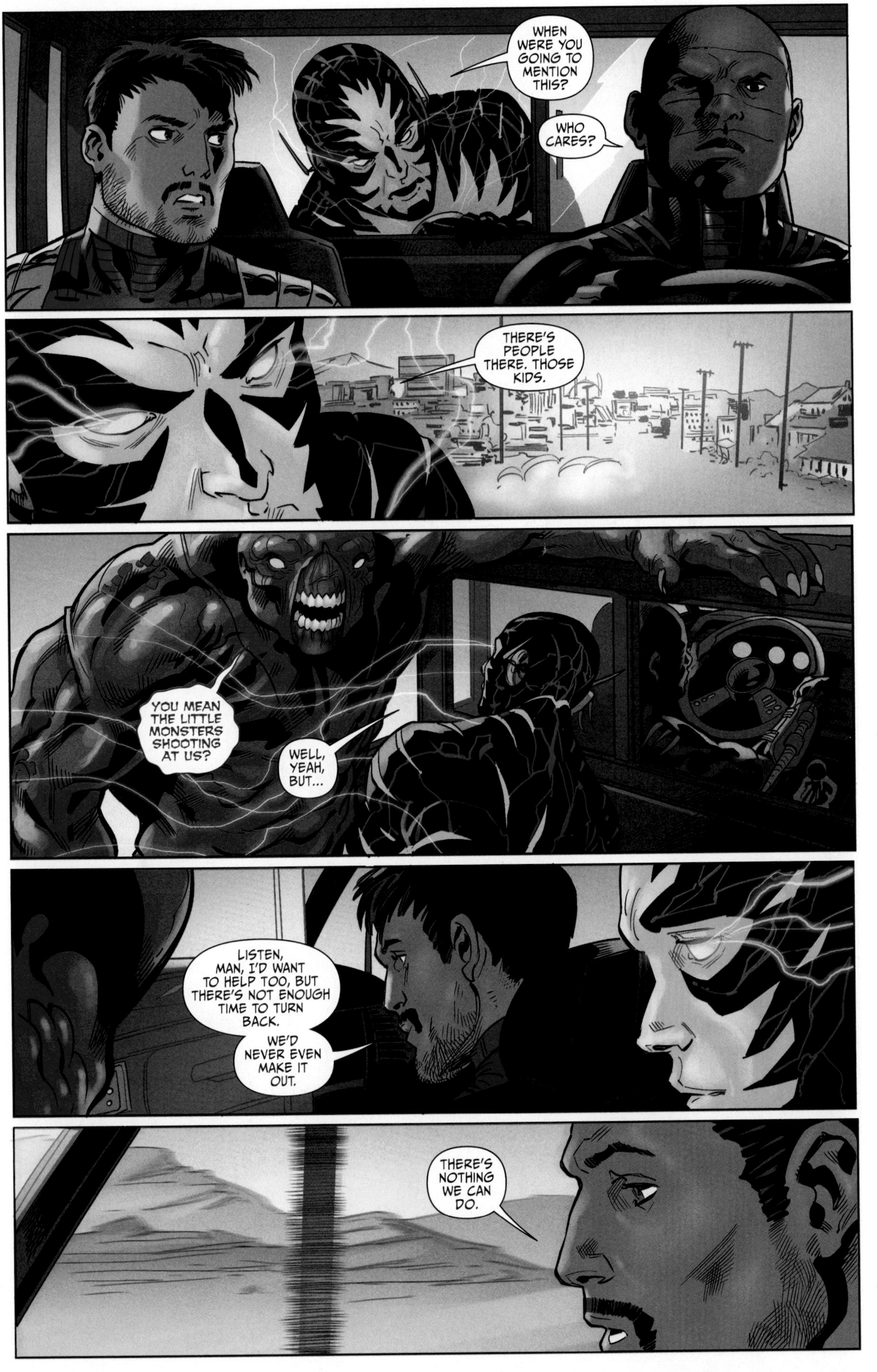
WHEN WERE YOU GOING TO MENTION THIS?
WHO CARES?
THERE'S PEOPLE THERE. THOSE KIDS.
YOU MEAN THE LITTLE MONSTERS SHOOTING AT US?
WELL, YEAH, BUT...
LISTEN, MAN, I'D WANT TO HELP TOO, BUT THERE'S NOT ENOUGH TIME TO TURN BACK.
WE'D NEVER EVEN MAKE IT OUT.
THERE'S NOTHING WE CAN DO.

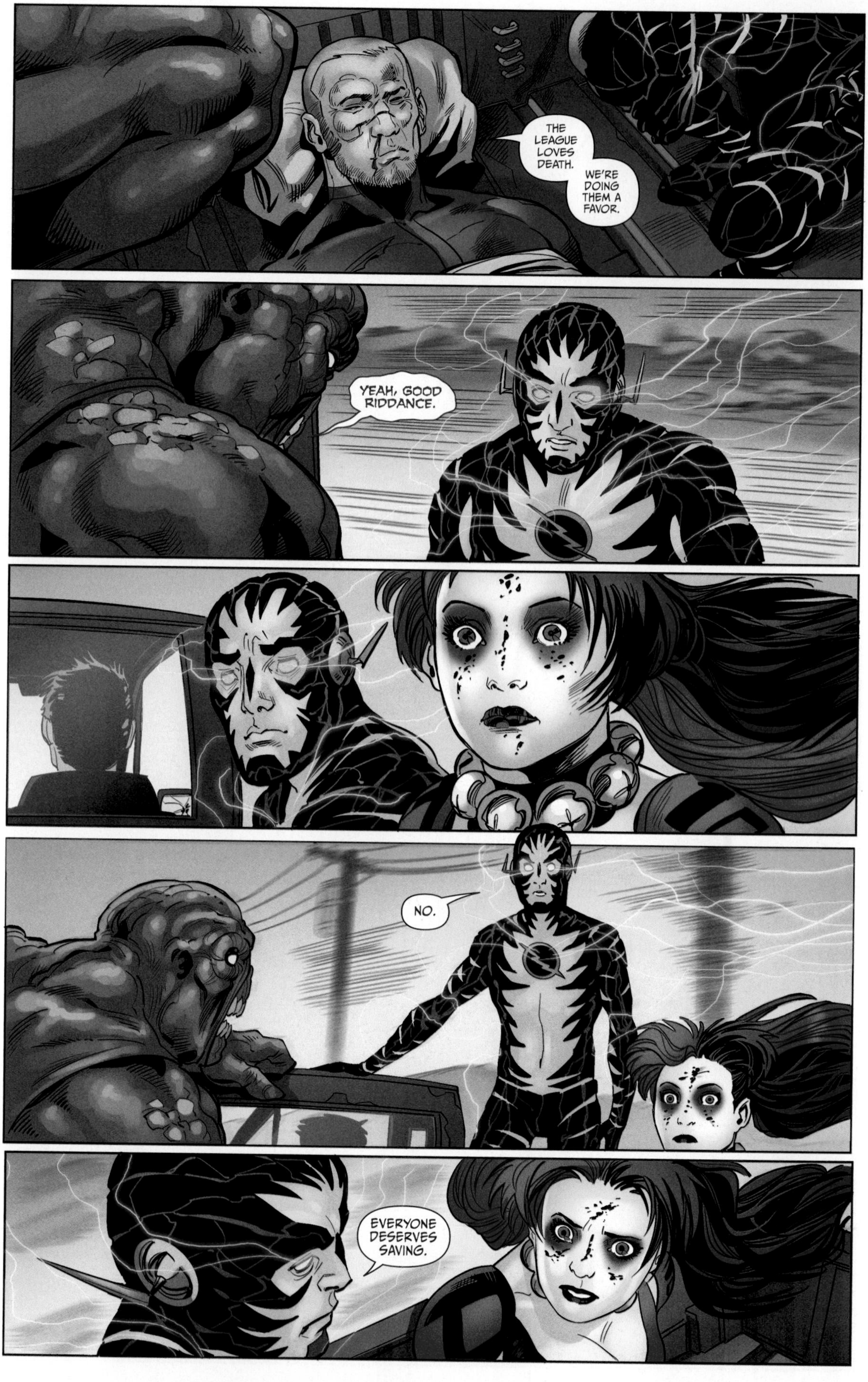
THE LEAGUE LOVES DEATH.
WE'RE DOING THEM A FAVOR.
YEAH, GOOD RIDDANCE.
NO.
EVERYONE DESERVES SAVING.

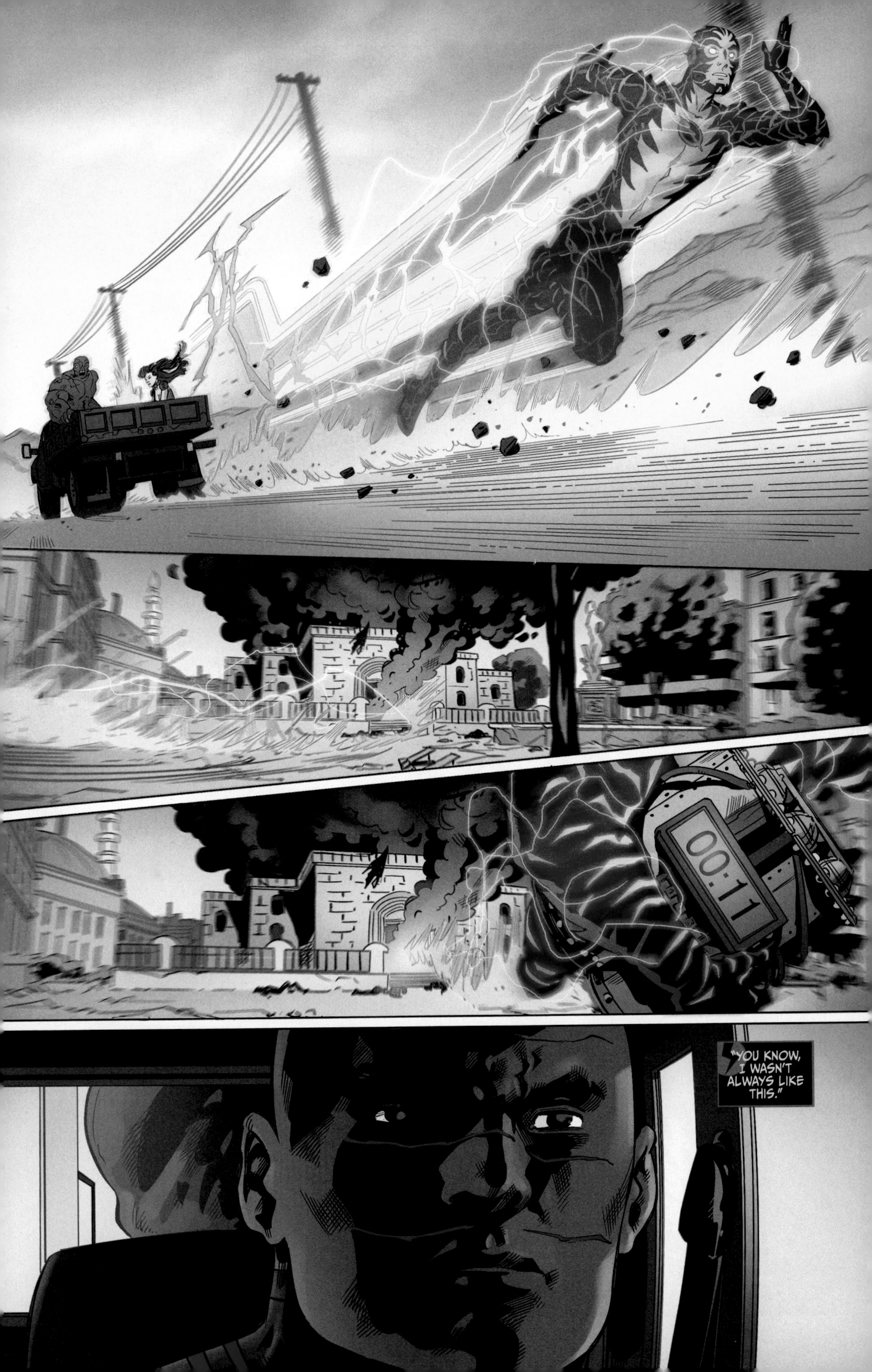
00:11
"YOU KNOW, I WASN'T ALWAYS LIKE THIS."

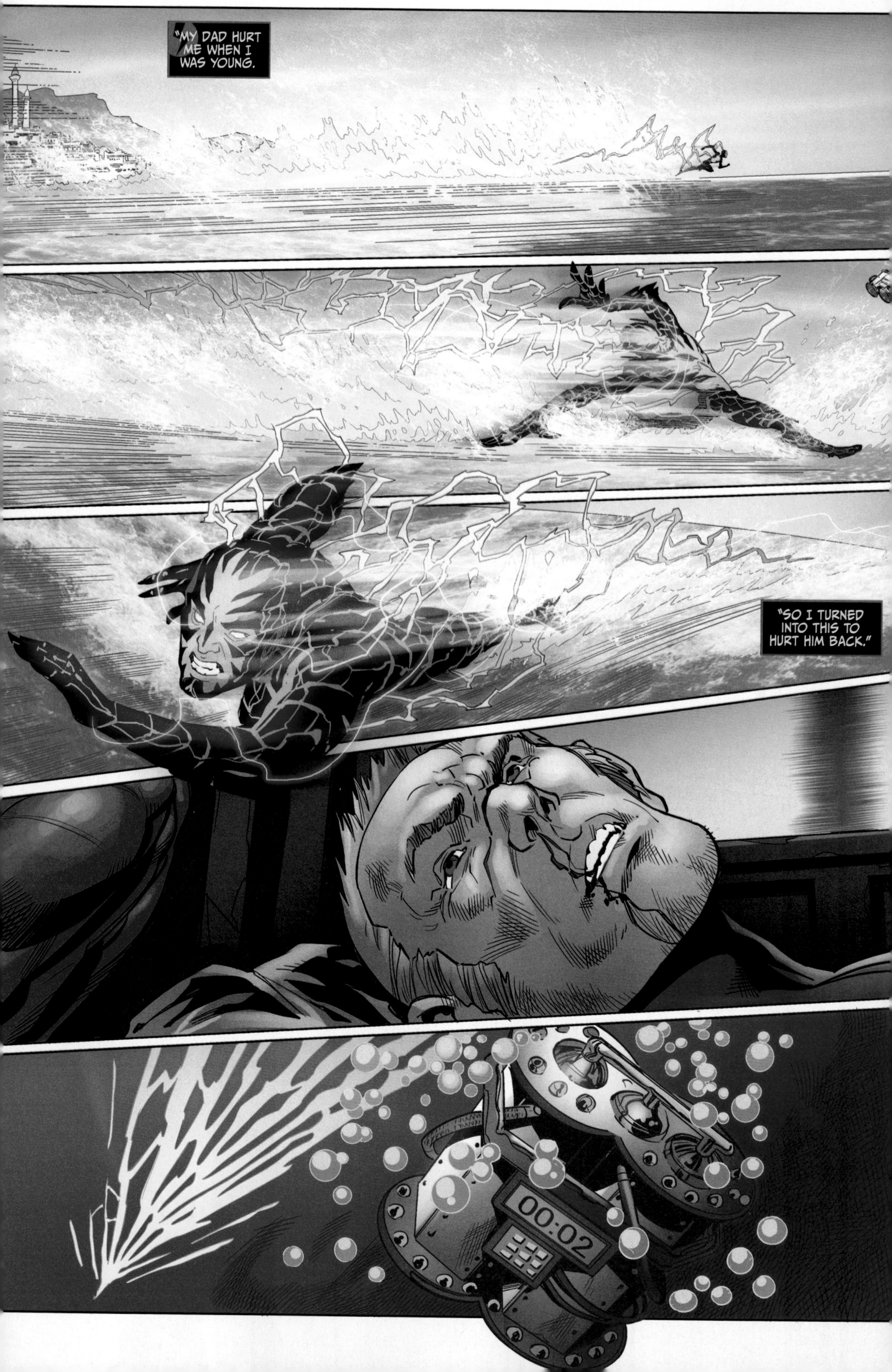
"MY DAD HURT ME WHEN I WAS YOUNG.
"SO I TURNED INTO THIS TO HURT HIM BACK."
00:02

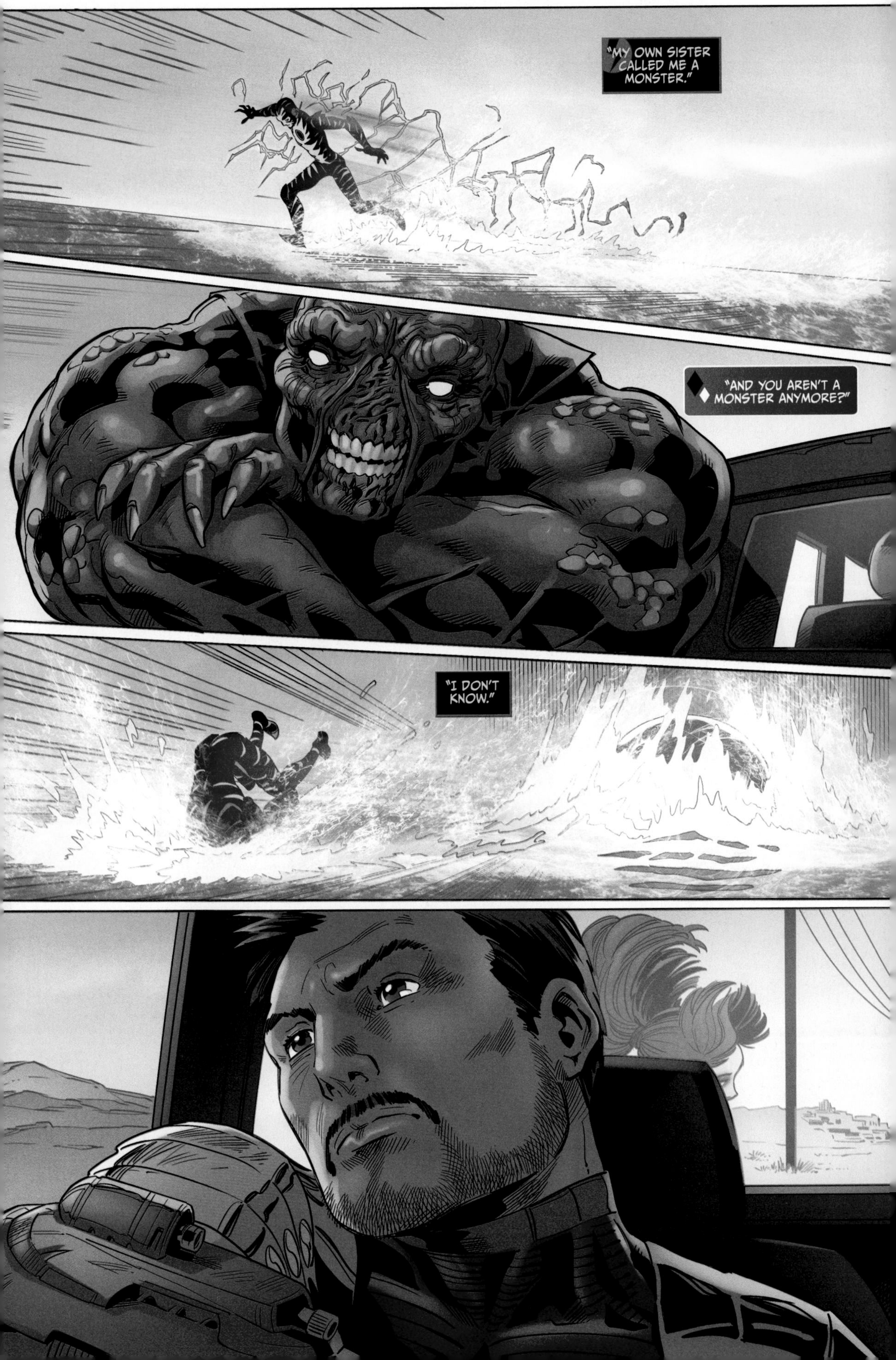
"MY OWN SISTER CALLED ME A MONSTER."
"AND YOU AREN'T A MONSTER ANYMORE?"
"I DON'T KNOW."

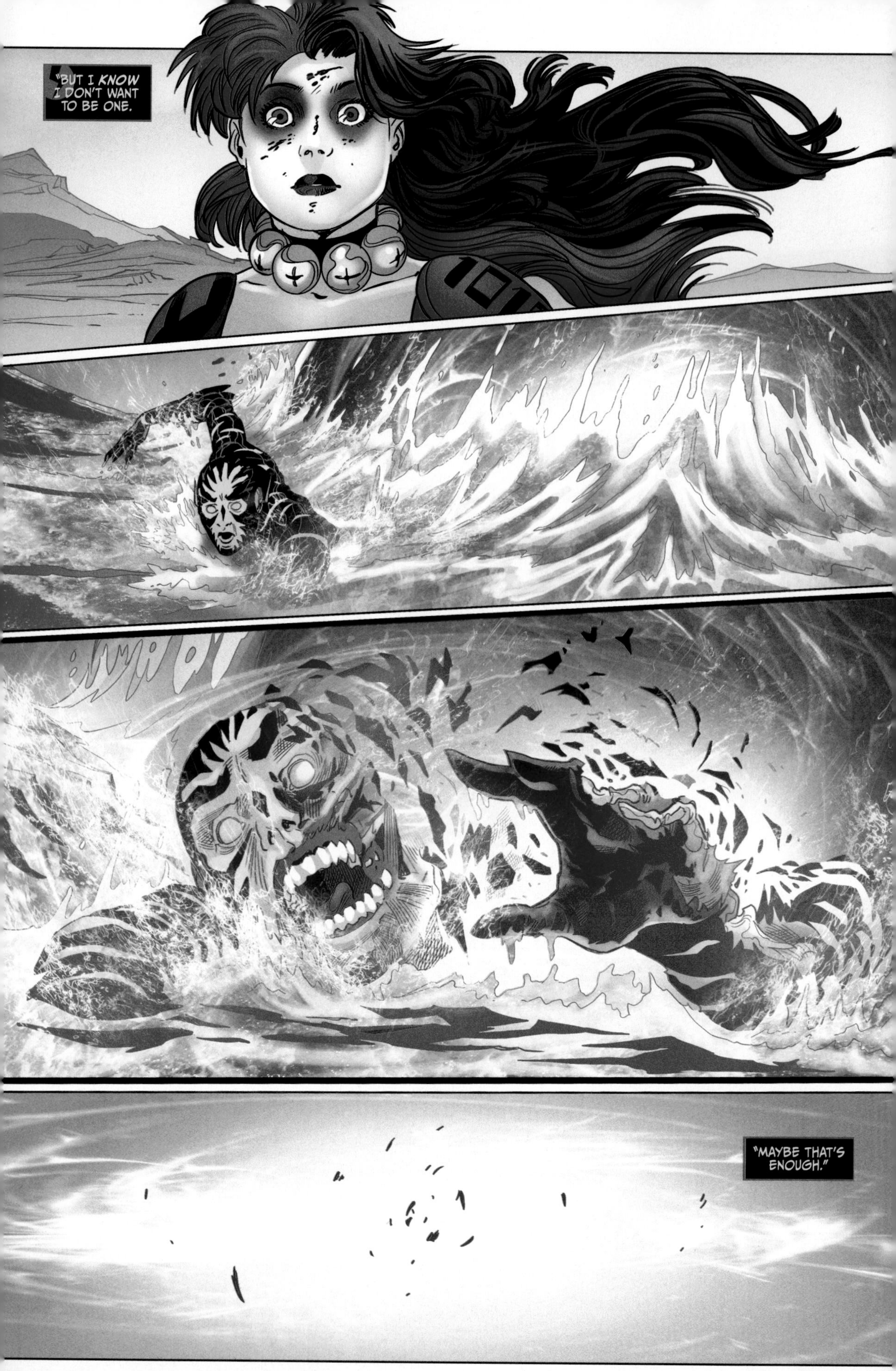
"BUT I KNOW I DON'T WANT TO BE ONE.
"MAYBE THAT'S ENOUGH."

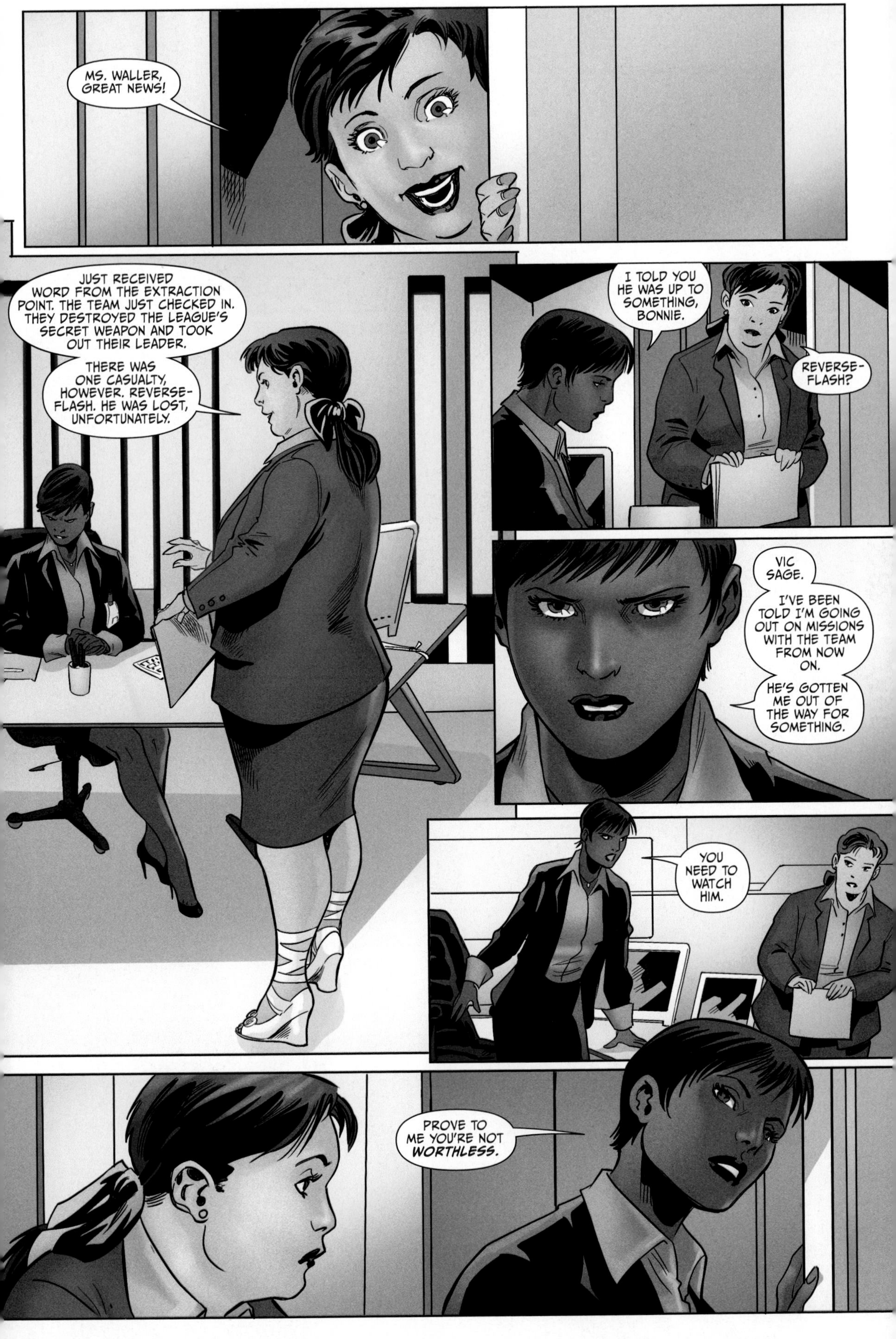
MS. WALLER, GREAT NEWS!
JUST RECEIVED WORD FROM THE EXTRACTION POINT. THE TEAM JUST CHECKED IN. THEY DESTROYED THE LEAGUE'S SECRET WEAPON AND TOOK OUT THEIR LEADER.
THERE WAS ONE CASUALTY, HOWEVER. REVERSE-FLASH. HE WAS LOST, UNFORTUNATELY.
I TOLD YOU HE WAS UP TO SOMETHING, BONNIE.
REVERSE-FLASH?
VIC SAGE.
I'VE BEEN TOLD I'M GOING OUT ON MISSIONS WITH THE TEAM FROM NOW ON.
HE'S GOTTEN ME OUT OF THE WAY FOR SOMETHING.
YOU NEED TO WATCH HIM.
PROVE TO ME YOU'RE NOT *WORTHLESS.*

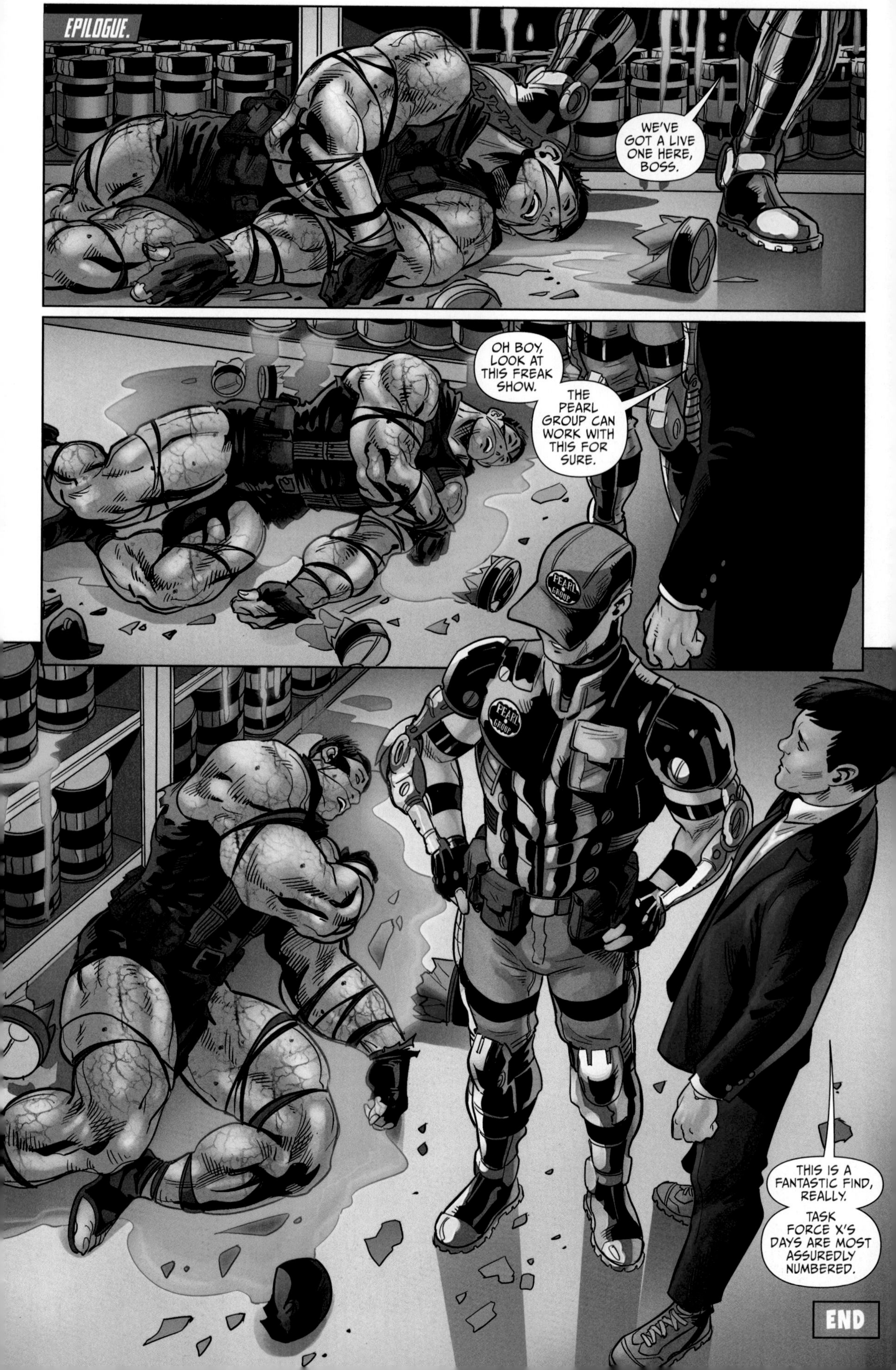
EPILOGUE.
WE'VE GOT A LIVE ONE HERE, BOSS.
OH BOY, LOOK AT THIS FREAK SHOW.
THE PEARL GROUP CAN WORK WITH THIS FOR SURE.
PEARL GROUP
THIS IS A FANTASTIC FIND, REALLY.
TASK FORCE X'S DAYS ARE MOST ASSUREDLY NUMBERED.
END

NEW SUICIDE SQUAD #9 Variant Cover by **JIM LEE** and **SCOTT WILLIAMS** with **ALEX SINCLAIR**

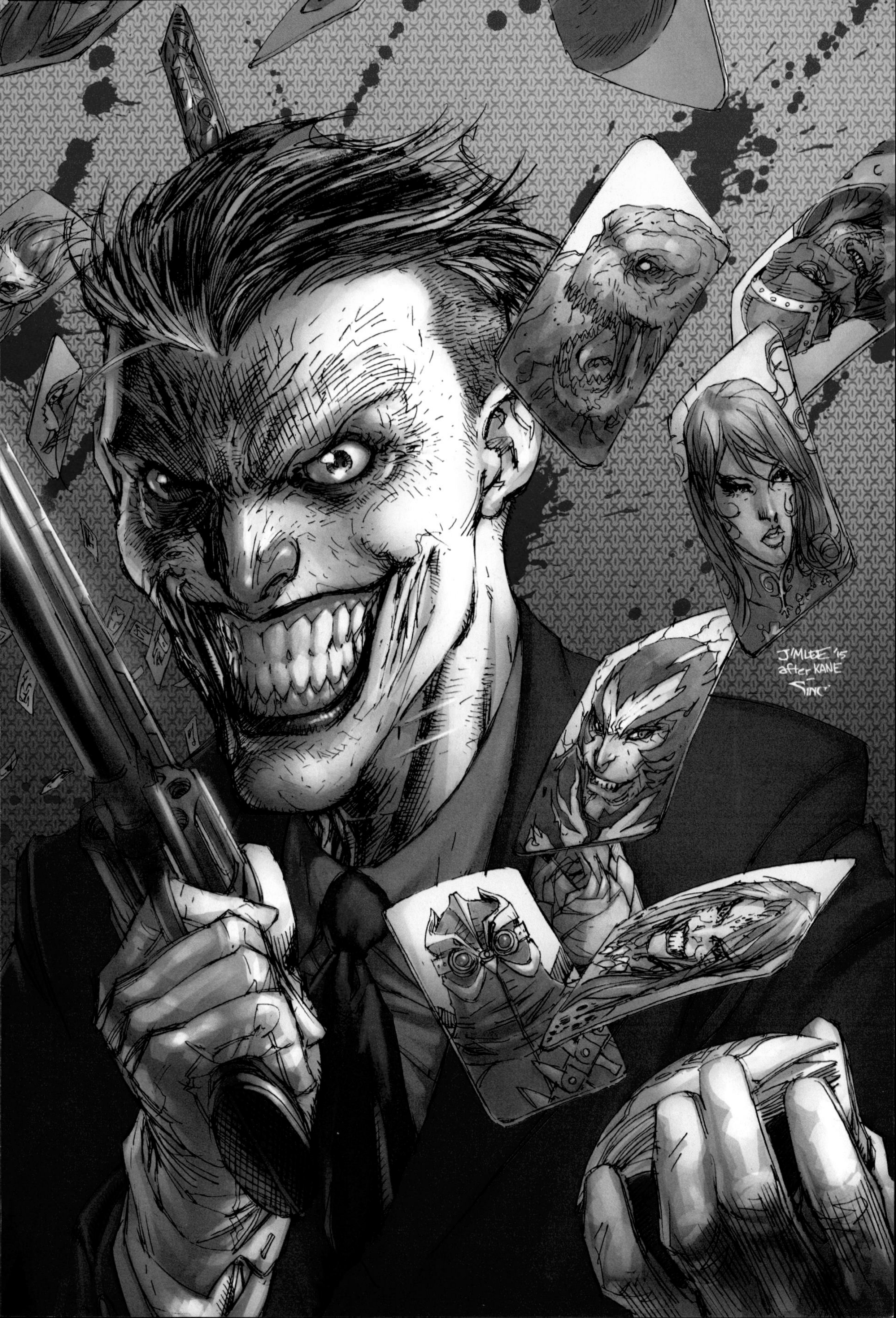
JIMLEE '15
after KANE
SINC

NEW SUICIDE SQUAD #10 Variant Cover by **CRAIG ROUSSEAU**

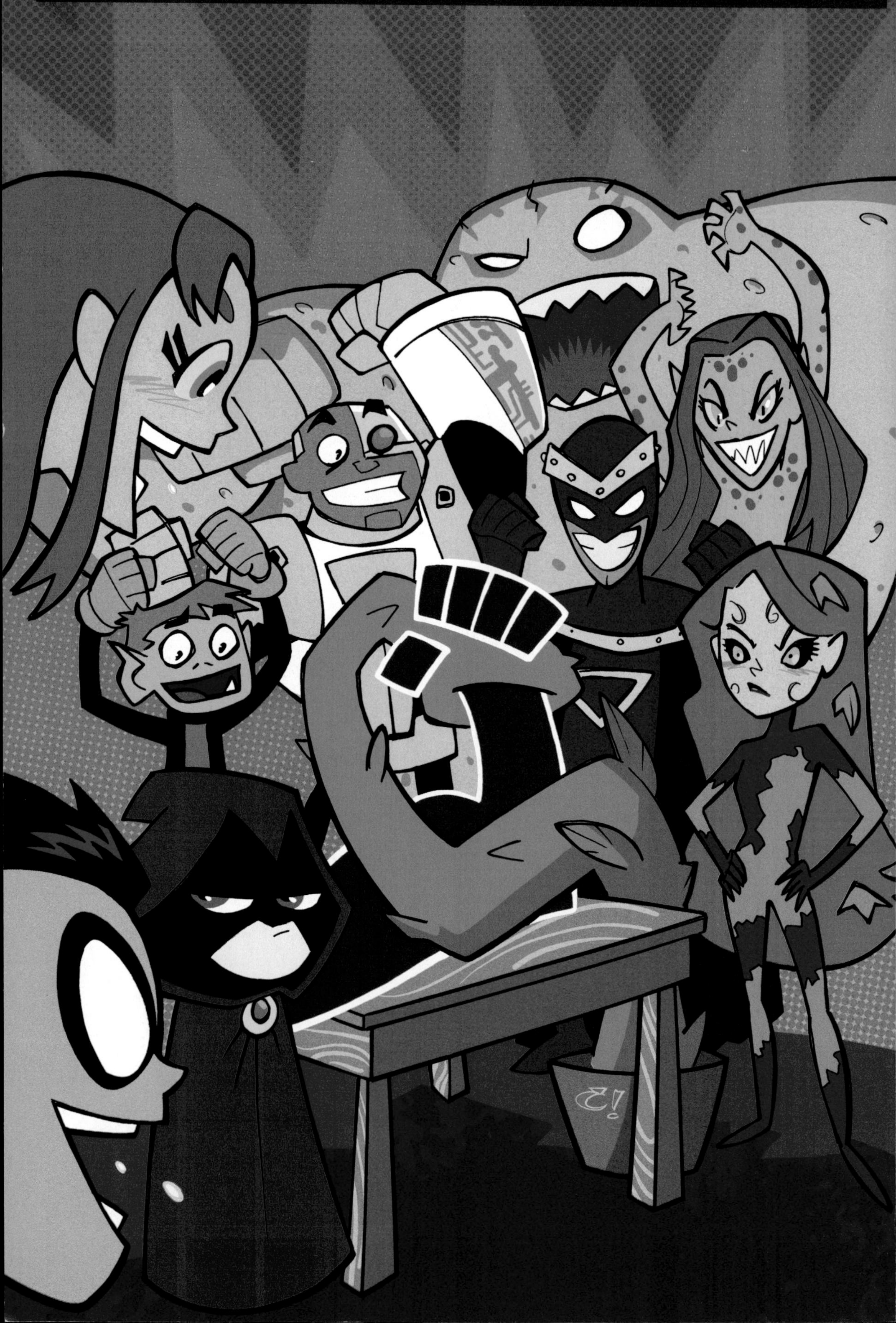

NEW SUICIDE SQUAD #11 Variant Cover by DES TAYLOR

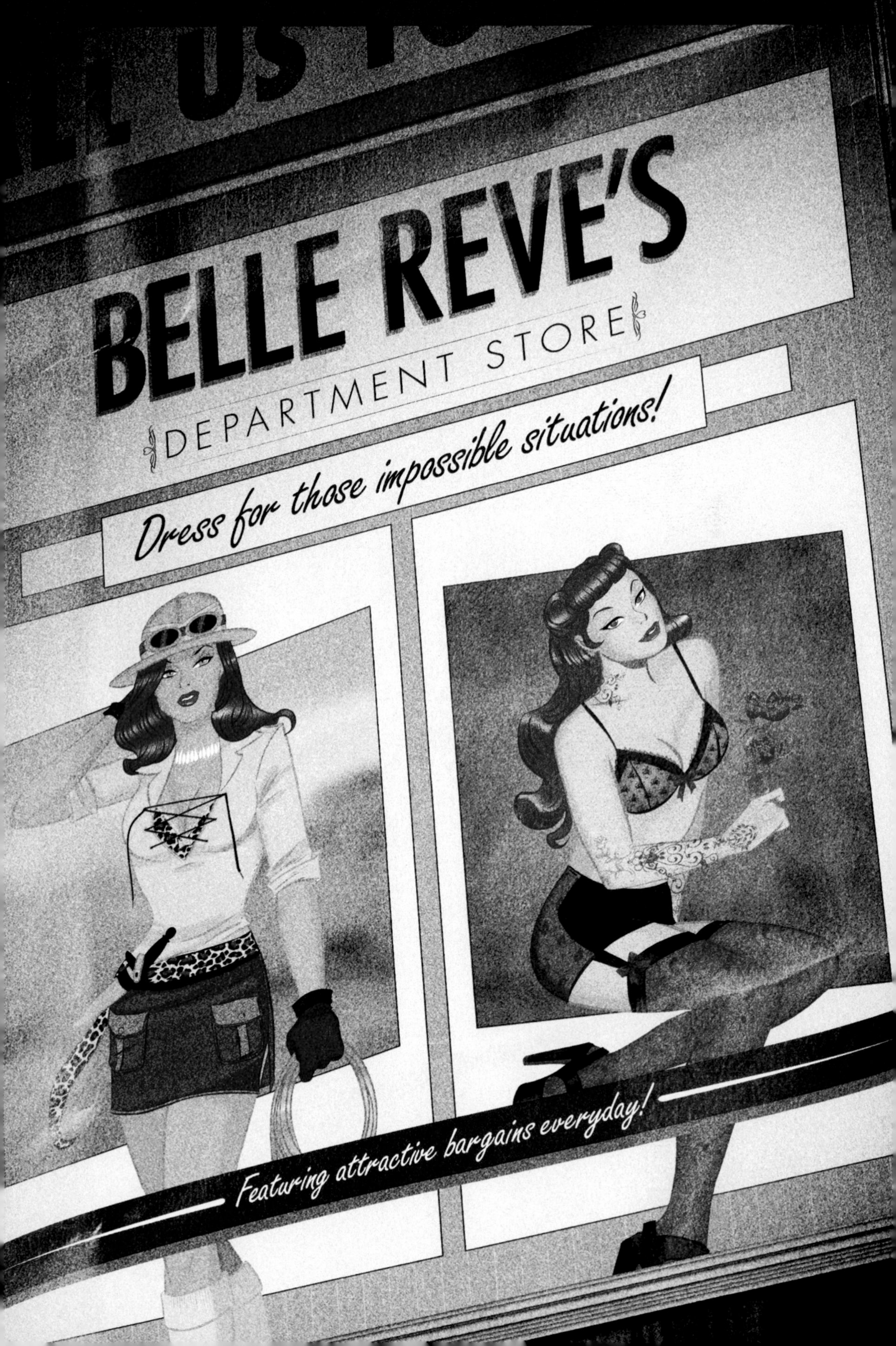
BELLE REVE'S
DEPARTMENT STORE
Dress for those impossible situations!
Featuring attractive bargains everyday!

NEW SUICIDE SQUAD #12 Variant Cover by **RYAN BENJAMIN**

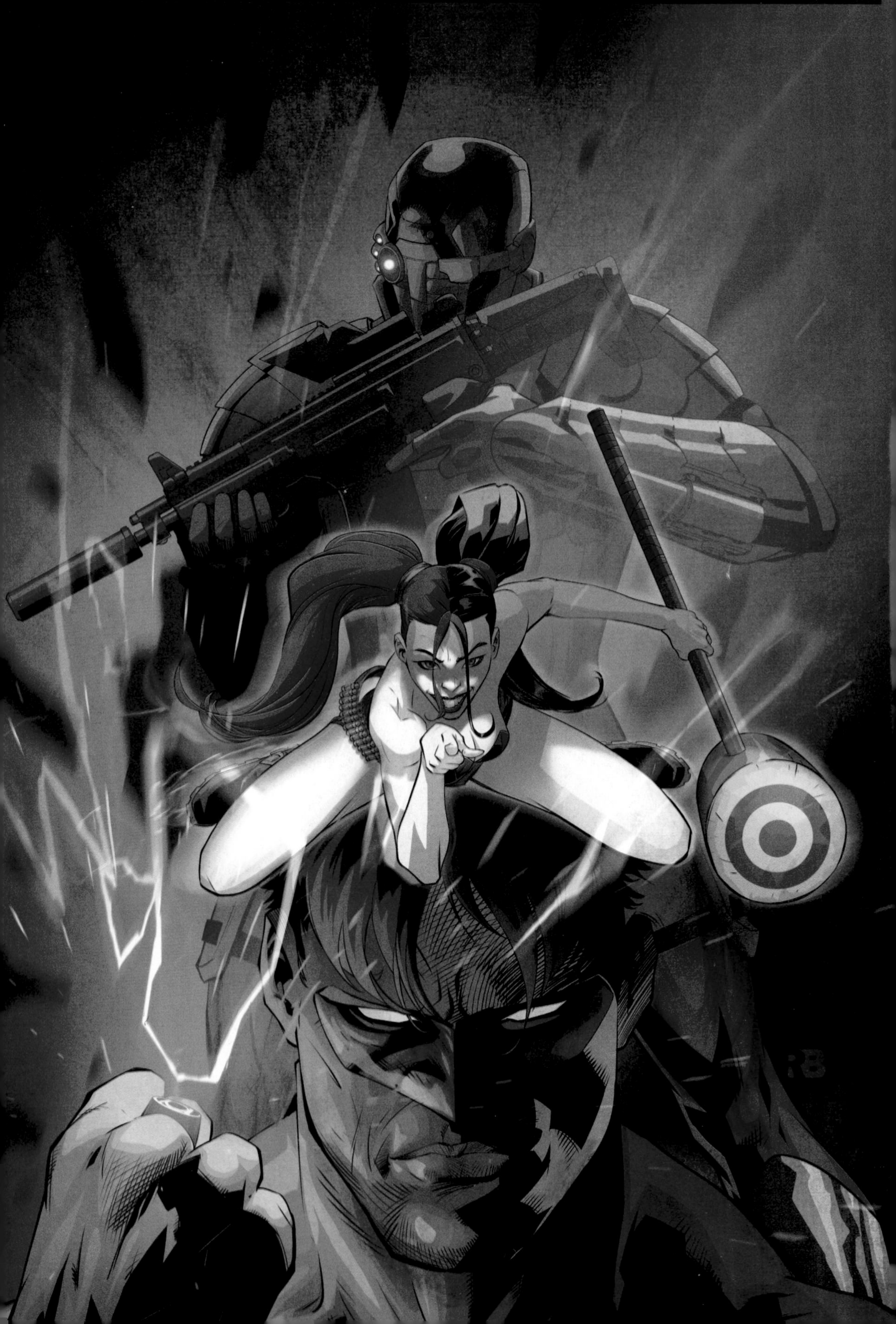
RB